1995

12th Edition · 1995

The Complete & Easy Guide to
SOCIAL SECURITY & MEDICARE

by FAUSTIN F. JEHLE

a publication of *FRASER-VANCE PUBLISHING*
Peterborough, New Hampshire
trade distribution by Williamson Publishing Company
Church Hill Road, PO Box 185 • Charlotte, Vermont 05445

Library of Congress Cataloging-in-Publication Data

Jehle, Faustin F.
    The complete & easy guide to Social Security &
Medicare.
    Includes index.
    1. Social security—United States.
    2. Medicare. I. Title. II. Title: Complete and
easy guide to Social Security and Medicare.

Library of Congress Catalog Card Number 94–61274
ISBN 0–930045–13–0

Fraser-Vance Publishing Company
Peterborough, New Hampshire 03458
First Printing: January 1995

This publication is designed to provide accurate and
authoritative information in regard to the subject
matter covered. It is sold with the understanding that
the publisher is not engaged in rendering legal,
accounting, or other professional service. If legal
advice or other expert assistance is required, the
services of a competent professional person should be
sought. **From a Declaration of Principles jointly
adopted by a Committee of the American Bar
Association and a Committee of Publishers and
Associations**

Printed in the United States of America

To the Reader

The long debate in Congress over health care reform has served to alert more people to the enormous growth of health care costs over the last few years and made us all aware that these spiraling costs affect both the insured and the uninsured.

Year	Total Cost	Cost Per Capita
1960	$ 27 billion	$ 143.00
1970	74 billion	346.00
1980	250 billion	1,064.00
1990	666 billion	2,566.00
1993 (est.)	903 billion	3,380.00
2000 (est.)	1,738 billion	6,148.00

The impact these rapidly rising costs have on Medicare, and the fact that Medicare and Social Security represent such a large part of the so-called entitlements budget has not gone unremarked either.

It seems likely now that incremental reforms for health care will be the eventual outcome rather than a comprehensive new system. Whatever these reforms encompass, a strong public constituency will have to be evident for them if they are to be viable in the partisan climate of the current political scene.

The 1994 legislation which established the Social Security Administration as an independent agency also instituted a new bi-partisan advisory board intended to have a much broader role than that of advisory councils under prior law. The new board will have 7 members; 3 appointed by the President and subject to Senate confirmation and 4 appointed by the Congress. These advisors will meet 4 times a year and will advise the Social Security Commissioner, the Congress, and the President on policies. As with past boards, one of its most important charges is to help ensure the short-term and long-term solvency of the programs' funds.

(This legislation also established some limitations on SSI and Disability payments to drug and alcohol abusers and some other minor adjustments discussed in the appropriate chapters).

As always, we will keep our readers advised of all changes that are available at the time we go to press for this and subsequent editions of the book.

Faustin F. Jehle

Table of Contents

Tables and Charts

Forms

A Note From the Publisher

Social Security and Medicare are social insurance programs that have their roots in other social programs in the United States and in England more than a century ago. History tells us that changes in economic conditions and political circumstances have a major impact on programs such as these. Elected officials and contenders for their seats in legislative bodies in both countries often campaign with promises to increase benefits or defend the status quo for their constituents.

As this 12th edition of *The Complete & Easy Guide to Social Security & Medicare* goes to press, the Congress, the Administration, lobbyists and others outside of the formal institutions of government are struggling as never before with problems of deficits, health care, social insurance and welfare programs, not to mention problems in education, flood relief, unemployment and defense. Entitlement programs, especially Social Security and Medicare, are expensive and there is more pressure than ever before to reduce their costs. Cost cutting can be accomplished only in ways that are painful for beneficiaries and politically hazardous. Reducing or delaying benefits, increasing taxes on retirement benefits, or increasing premiums are the principal alternatives and all of these are happening.

Social Security and Medicare are dynamic programs; changes in regulations, procedures, and laws, as well as the information on which they are based, occur continuously. One of the important advantages of this book is that it is revised every year to keep it up-to-date. Our purpose is to make the subject as clear as possible for the general reader and to help you determine what benefits you are entitled to and how to obtain them. Other books deal in more depth with the complexities of these programs for the professional. More academic works on the subject address social, political, and philosophical issues in greater detail.

As we approach the end of 1995, most of what is in this edition will be correct, but new information becomes available all year long. Please remember that the Social Security Administration is the final and most current authority.

The Social Security Administration gets high marks for the quality of its service, in terms of accuracy, efficiency, sensitivity, and increasing productivity. One important area of recent and continuing improvement is reduction of paperwork. To that end, there is much more emphasis on obtaining necessary information from beneficiaries through interviews and less on the use of forms, most of which are included in our book. We continue to include them because some offices still use them and they do provide insight as to the information that will be required.

We would like to thank all the reviewers who have read and commented on the manuscript for this 12th edition. Thanks as well to the readers of previous editions whose constructive criticism and generous suggestions have helped us make improvements, year after year. To help us continue to improve, we invite you to send comments to us at:

Fraser-Vance Publishing
PO Box 3056
Peterborough, NH 03458-3056

We will gladly forward to the author any comments addressed to him.

1

Introduction and Overview

The Complete & Easy Guide to Social Security & Medicare has been written to help you find out which benefits you are entitled to, how much money you can expect to receive in your particular circumstances, how to maximize that amount, and how to apply for and get your benefits in as simple and painless a way as possible.

HOW TO GET THE MOST OUT OF THIS BOOK

You probably do not need to know about all of the Social Security programs, just the ones that relate to you. For that reason, we have arranged this book so that you don't have to read all of it to find the parts that apply to your particular situation.

The Table of Contents shows the basic divisions of the book, and each chapter starts with a short explanation of what it covers. All major topics appear in **boldface** type, and there are often references to other parts of the book where more information on the subject can be found. Throughout the book, special *NOTES* appear with suggestions and further explanations.

In this chapter you will find a brief background about the history of Social Security, as well as a glimpse of each of the benefits programs covered in the book—Retirement, Disability, Survivors', Supplemental Security Income, and Medicare. Chapters 2,4,5,6, and 7 go into detail about these programs.

Chapter 3 is basically a "how to" chapter, because it explains what documents you will need to present to claim benefits, what to do if you don't have them, what to do about errors in your work record, and how to file your application. You'll also find some timesaving tips to help speed things along when you deal with the Social Security Administration.

Chapter 8 consists of questions compiled from the reader mail we've received over the years. Some of these questions and the answers we've provided may help you or at least prompt you to ask questions of your own. For convenience, Chapter 8 is divided according to topic.

In Chapter 9, you will learn how to appeal a decision

that is not in your favor. We hope you won't have to use the information in this chapter, but it's important to know what to expect—and what to do—if you should have to file an appeal.

Throughout the text, you will see references to Appendixes A, B, and C. These are at the back of the book, after Chapter 9. Appendix A serves as a glossary to explain some of the terms and "alphabet soup" that you are likely to encounter as you deal with the government.

Appendix B, "Sources of Additional Information and Help," supplies addresses and telephone numbers for a variety of state, local, federal, and private resources.

In Appendix C, you will find copies of the forms the Social Security Administration and the Health Care Financing Administration used (and in some cases, still use) to gather information from applicants before the use of on-site computers became commonplace.

Though these forms are for reference only, and cannot be used to apply for benefits, they can be extremely useful to you as a reference. They will enable you to know—in advance—the questions you will be asked and the information you should be ready to provide. That information, most likely, will be keyed directly into a computer, a procedure that is being used in more and more Social Security offices across the country. A careful review of the forms pertinent to your circumstances will help you to be prepared for any questions that might be asked, and may even save you an extra trip to the Social Security office.

Finally, the Index at the end of the book will help you look things up by key word.

Although this book contains the most current information available from the Social Security Administration and the Health Care Financing Administration at the time it went to press, you should be aware that all these programs are administered through a vast body of laws and regulations that are constantly being revised. Each year, we ask a number of experts to review the manuscript to make sure our facts are accurate, but in the end, **it is the Social Security Admin-**

istration that has the last word in administering its programs.

A LITTLE BACKGROUND

Before going into the details about obtaining benefits, we believe it will be helpful for you to know something about the background of Social Security, how the system works, and how it might change in the future.

In 1935, during this country's severest Depression, President Franklin Delano Roosevelt signed the Social Security Act into law, thereby establishing the Old Age, Survivors and Disability Insurance (OASDI) system. The first retirees began collecting benefits in 1940. It took these people, at most, 4½ months to collect in benefits an amount that was equal to what they had paid into the system.

Today, in contrast, a retiree with maximum withholding taxes each year has paid in 214 times what the first retirees paid in 1940, and it takes about 5 years to collect an amount equal to his or her contribution. In recent times, inflation and newly added programs such as Medicare have driven program costs up, even as high unemployment and a change in demographics have dramatically altered the worker-to-beneficiary ratio.

Judging from the mail we get, it is a fairly common belief that Social Security recipients get back the very dollars they paid into the system, but that is not the case. The way it actually works is this: When you were working, the Social Security taxes you paid went to provide benefit checks for the workers who were then retired or disabled, or for their dependents. Now, if you are receiving benefits, current workers are paying into the system for the benefits paid to you.

A problem develops when the number of people working is small in relation to the number of Social Security recipients, a situation that we find ourselves in today, as the overall American population ages. This situation is made worse when inflation causes the price for everything we need, from groceries to medical care, to increase even faster than workers' wages.

Each year, Congress must find ways to finance the increasingly expensive programs that eligible retirees want and need with taxes taken from the salaries of a shrinking work force. Recently, laws have been passed to shift more of the burden to the retirees by taxing some of the benefits they receive. More

changes will surely come in the future, as policy makers continue to adjust the system to be responsive to ever-changing conditions.

Because all of us are the beneficiaries or prospective beneficiaries of these programs, we need to understand how they function and to keep abreast of various changes. Some of the most important changes in the system are summarized at the end of this chapter.

THE FIVE SOCIAL SECURITY PROGRAMS COVERED HERE

Social Security is really a group of insurance programs, for which you earn your eligibility by working and paying into the system. Briefly stated, here are the different programs and what they offer:

Retirement Income

You can begin collecting retirement benefits at age 65 or as early as 62, but electing to receive benefits before you are 65 reduces the amount of your benefit —**permanently.** Your spouse, at age 65, can also collect on your earnings record; she or he is entitled to 50%, or half, of the amount you receive (or a reduced benefit at 62).

Should you die leaving your spouse to care for any or all of your children younger than 16 (or an unmarried child who became totally disabled before age 22), your widow or widower can collect benefits (subject to earnings tests) regardless of age. Benefits can also be paid to your unmarried children under 18, unmarried children under 19 if they are full-time high school students, or your children of any age if they became totally disabled before age 22. See Chapters 2 through 5.

Disability Payments

If, at any age, you become severely disabled, you and certain members of your family may qualify for monthly benefits. The government defines a disability as a clinically determinable physical or psychiatric impairment that will prevent you from doing any substantial work for at least 12 months or a similar impairment that is expected to result in death. See Chapters 5 and 7.

Survivors' Benefits

Payments are made to your family if you are insured "fully" or "currently" and die at any age. Being insured means having worked in a covered occupation for a specified time. See Chapters 2 through 4.

Medicare

Medical insurance for hospital and other medical services is available to you at age 65, whether you retire or not, and regardless of your income or ability to pay. If you receive Social Security disability benefits for 24 months, or if you (or a dependent) have end-stage kidney failure, you also qualify for Medicare. See Chapter 7.

Supplemental Security Income (SSI)

SSI is the only Social Security program that is not based on earnings records. It provides monthly assistance checks for needy people over the age of 65 and the needy blind and disabled of any age. Eligibility and the amount you receive depend on your assets, income, living arrangements, and whether or not your state government supplements the federal payment. See Chapter 6.

WHO ADMINISTERS WHAT

The Retirement, Survivors', and Disability programs are all administered by the Social Security Administration, usually called the SSA, which is a federal agency with its central office located in Baltimore, Maryland. The Health Care Financing Administration (HCFA) is the federal agency that directs the Medicare program. The main office for the HCFA is also in Baltimore. Supplemental Security Income (SSI) is a program for both retirement and Disability and is partially administered by the states as well as the federal government. Effective March 31, 1995, the SSA is an independent agency, but the HCFA remains under the jurisdiction of the U.S. Department of Health and Human Services.

The Social Security Administration processes Medicare applications and claims, but it does not make Medicare policy; rather, the Health Care Financing Administration sets the standards that hospitals, skilled nursing facilities, home health care agencies, and hospices must meet in order to be certified as qualified providers of Medicare services.

FINANCING THE BENEFITS

Money to pay the benefits comes from the payroll taxes you—or you and your employer—pay as FICA (Federal Insurance Contributions Act) or SECA (Self-

Employment Contributions Act) and from Medicare premiums. This money is divided between three trust funds—Old Age, Survivors and Disability Insurance (OASDI), which is managed by the Social Security Administration, and Medicare's Hospital Insurance (HI), managed by the Health Care Financing Administration.

If you have a job, your employer withholds a percentage of your earnings (up to a yearly maximum), adds the employer's contribution of the same percentage of the amount you earned, and pays to the Internal Revenue Service the FICA (payroll tax) on your wages. If you are self-employed, you pay all the tax (as SECA) to the IRS yourself.

1995 PAYROLL TAXES

FICA	Percent of Earnings
Social Security	6.2% of earnings to $61,200
Medicare	1.45% of ALL earnings

Total rate of 7.65% to $61,200, then 1.45% on all further earnings

SECA*	Percent of Earnings
Social Security	12.4% of earnings to $61,200
Medicare	2.9% of ALL earnings

Total rate of 15.3% to $61,200, then 2.9% on all further earnings

* One-half is tax deductible as a business expense.

Most payroll taxes are used immediately to pay current benefits. When payments into the fund exceed what is needed to pay benefits, these surpluses are borrowed by the U.S. Treasury Department for general government spending. As Social Security taxes have increased at a faster rate than income tax increases (Social Security and Medicare tax collections have grown from $100 billion to $200 billion between 1960 and 1992, while income tax revenues have risen from $100 billion to $150 billion), the surplus has gradually grown to about $300 billion, all of which has been borrowed and spent.

This does not mean that Social Security surpluses are lost—the Treasury Department issues IOU's for the money it uses from the funds in the form of special bonds that cannot be sold, promising to replace the cash when it is needed.

Still, the money will have to be paid back if there are to be benefits for people in the future, and the taxpayers are the ones who will have to pay it.

SOUNDNESS OF THE FUNDS

In 1983, when there was a crisis in financing for the Social Security system, steps were taken to ensure the financial soundness of the programs. Some of the assumptions underlying these corrections were that the American economy would continue to grow and be able to provide plenty of employment. That has not been the case in the last few years; in addition there has been another major financial problem: health costs have risen so much and so fast since 1983 that without further changes in policy, experts believe the Health Insurance fund may be exhausted shortly after the year 2000.

By then, people over 65 years of age will represent 13% of the population. By 2030, the percentage will rise to almost 22%. Careful planning and periodic adjustments are required to make sure there will be enough money in the trust funds to provide for this growing segment of the population.

Elected officials have trouble with these problems because in order to get sufficient money to shore up the trust funds, Congress will have to either borrow money or raise taxes, and both actions represent politically unpopular choices. Without additional money, benefits will have to be reduced or taxed more than they are currently, so Congress finds itself between a rock and a hard place.

Continued financing of these programs is, without a doubt, one of the crucial areas of government where creative and courageous solutions are very much needed. If you have any solutions to suggest, your government representatives need to hear about them.

A BRIEF SUMMARY OF MAJOR CHANGES MADE IN THE SOCIAL SECURITY PROGRAMS

Social Security has always been a dynamic program; there have been additions and modifications to its laws and regulations ever since they were first enacted and put into effect. Some of these changes have come about as a result of new legislation by Congress or through decisions made in the law courts, and some have been made within the administrative confines of the programs themselves.

When Social Security began in 1935, it covered a smaller proportion of the work force than it does today. Beginning in 1950, the program was extended to cover more and more categories of workers. For lists of which categories are currently covered and which are not, see the table at the end of this chapter.

MOST RECENT CHANGES IN SOCIAL SECURITY LAW

The most far-reaching alterations to Social Security since the introduction of Medicare came about in 1983 with financing reforms of the programs. Among those measures were the taxation of some benefits and a provision that will gradually increase the age at which people can begin collecting their full benefits. Beginning in the year 2000, the Normal Retirement Age (NRA) will begin to rise gradually, over a 27-year period so that by 2022, the NRA will be age 67 rather than age 65, as it is now.

Other amendments in 1983 extended coverage to a number of new kinds of employment and eliminated some gender-based inequities and distinctions.

In 1988, a Catastrophic Care Coverage bill was passed by Congress and then repealed in a matter of months. The next year, in addition to the legislated efforts to contain Medicare costs, a little-noticed provision was passed that exempts certain qualified elderly poor people from paying the monthly Medicare Part B premium as well as certain deductibles and coinsurance amounts.

Changes made in 1990 through 1993 were also chiefly in the area of Medicare, reducing expenditures and defining new ways of payments for hospitals and physicians, raising the taxable income base to pay for the program, stipulating that the health care provider rather than the patient fill out the paperwork, and prohibiting the sale of more than one Medigap policy to an individual. In mid-1992, Medicare Part B benefits were expanded to include new preventive services. All of these measures are covered in detail in Chapter 7.

Children, age 1 or older, who will be claimed as a dependent on Internal Revenue Service returns must now have a Social Security number. Certain working and nonworking aliens who need to report income to the IRS must also have Social Security numbers.

Several significant improvements in the disabilities claims process have been made. A disabilities specialist now takes the claim and gathers medical evidence. In cases where the claim is going to be denied, a face-to-face pre-denial hearing with a disability examiner in the Disability Determination Service (DDS) is provided. Face-to-face meetings are also held when the claim is reconsidered at the federal level, and reconsiderations at the first level of appeal have been eliminated so that a claimant whose claim is denied can go directly to a hearing by an administrative law judge.

With the passage of the Americans with Disabilities Act, many employers will now be required to do more to accommodate disabled workers. Benefits provided under Social Security and the SSI program, including continued cash benefits and health care coverage, are designed to provide further incentives for people with disabilities who wish to work.

1994 Changes

The Social Security Administration, which has in the past been a part of the Department of Health and Human Services, is now (as of March 31,1995) an independent agency of the federal government. Under the new law, the SSA will continue to administer the OASDI and SSI programs as well as assist in the administration of Medicare.

Effective on signing the law in August 1994, all states can now extend Social Security coverage to police officers and firefighters who are under a retirement system.

Other provisions in the law authorize other governmental agencies' use of Social Security numbers in limited circumstances and for specified purposes. State and local governments and federal district courts may use them in jury selection to eliminate duplicate names and to avoid listing convicted felons as potential jurors. The Department of Labor may use Social Security numbers for claim identification in workers' compensation cases and the Department of Agriculture may disclose them to federal agencies investigating food stamp fraud.

Provisions restricting benefit payments to individuals whose disability results from drug addiction or alcoholism were also included in this new legislation, and are described in Chapters 5 and 6.

Changes to Come

The programs covered in this book will face enormous challenges in the coming years as the numbers of the eligible grow while the numbers of those working to pay the benefits decrease. More changes will have to be made, and the assumption that these will not be popular with voters makes most politicians reluctant in the extreme to propose, much less vote for, such changes.

Probable areas for more financing reforms would seem to be more of the same that we've seen: increased Medicare premiums and taxes on benefits, reduction or elimination of Cost-of-Living Adjustments, and more means testing.

This Year's Figures

Certain figures relating to Social Security change each year, usually at the beginning of the calendar year. Annual changes are made in the Medicare premium and deductible, maximum earnings subject to Social Security taxes, amount of earnings necessary for a quarter of coverage, maximum earnings allowed without reduction of benefits, bend points (to be explained later), the SSI payments standards, and the maximum family benefit. A Cost-of-Living Adjustment (COLA) may or may not be added to benefits, and the tax rates (FICA and SECA) for Social Security and Medicare are set.

As you begin to look for the information that applies to you, please bear in mind that all figures in this book were current for 1995 when we went to press in January.

COVERED AND NONCOVERED EMPLOYMENT

Currently Covered

Regularly employed farm workers

Domestic workers (with some exceptions)

Federal employees (with some restrictions)

Federal civilian employees not under the federal retirement system (hired after 1984)

Ministers and members of religious orders

State or local government employees not under state or local retirement systems

Children age 18 or over in trade or business of a parent

Spouse in trade or business of a spouse

Employees of nonprofit organizations

Self-employed professionals

Members of uniformed forces, active duty and reserve

Citizens employed outside the U.S. by American employers or foreign affiliate of an American employer

Citizens employed within the U.S. by foreign governments or international organizations

Currently Noncovered

Farm workers receiving less than $150 annually for hand-harvest labor, on a piecework basis, commuting daily from a permanent residence and working in agriculture less than 13 weeks during the preceding calendar year

Parents working as a domestic for son or daughter (with some exceptions)

Federal employees hired before 1984

Members of religious orders claiming exemption on the grounds of conscience or religious principles

Some state and local government employees, police officers, and firefighters who are under a retirement system

Children under 18 delivering newspapers to local subscribers

Enrolled students employed by the educational institute which they regularly attend

Railroad employees who are covered by the Railroad Retirement System

Convicted felons working for the institution where they are inmates

2

Retirement and Survivors' Benefits

The Retirement and Survivors' Benefits portion of the Social Security system provides for payment to workers who have, during their working lives, paid taxes on their earnings into the system. It also provides payments to the families of workers when those workers die. You earn your eligibility for Social Security benefits by paying your FICA (Federal Insurance Contributions Act) or SECA (Self-Employment Contributions Act) payroll tax and by earning "quarters of coverage" or "credits," the terms the Social Security Administration uses to convert the combination of time you have worked and the money you have earned into a formula to calculate and determine your eligibility for benefits.

This chapter explains how you earn credits for eligibility, what benefits that eligibility entitles you or your survivors to, and what those benefits are. It also discusses some special conditions, situations, and exceptions that have come into being because of changes in the laws and regulations. If some of the government terminology is unfamiliar, see Appendix A for definitions of terms.

Social Security Credits Needed for Coverage

Social Security eligibility is based on whether or not you have earned enough work credits, or quarters of coverage, to qualify for benefits. These credits have to be earned on a job where you and your employer (or you yourself, if you were self-employed) paid the Social Security payroll tax on your earnings. This is defined by the Social Security Administration as "covered employment." A list of which occupations are considered covered and which are not appears in the table at the end of Chapter 1.

Before 1978, a work credit or quarter of coverage (QC) was earned for any 3-month period of a year, beginning in January, in which a worker received $50 or more in earnings for covered employment. After 1978, the regulations were changed to tie quarters of coverage more directly to money earned. Because of inflation, the earnings amounts pegged to quarters have risen steadily.

The chart that follows shows, for each specified year since the earnings amounts began increasing, the amount of covered earnings necessary to be credited with a quarter of coverage (QC).

1978	$250	1987	$460
1979	$260	1988	$470
1980	$290	1989	$500
1981	$310	1990	$520
1982	$340	1991	$540
1983	$370	1992	$570
1984	$390	1993	$590
1985	$410	1994	$620
1986	$440	1995	$630

You cannot earn more than 4 credits or QC's in any given year, but it is possible to earn all 4 of a year's allowed quarters in less than 52 weeks. For example, say you are paid a total of $2,520 (4 × $630 = QC) in the first 2 weeks of 1995. You will have earned your 4 credits for 1995, even if you don't earn anything more the rest of the year. (What you do earn above this amount, up to the maximum subject to FICA or SECA taxes, will increase your benefit.)

YOUR WORK RECORD

The Social Security Administration maintains a year-by-year record of your covered earnings. It's a good idea to check the SSA's records against your own records from time to time while you are still working to be sure everything has been properly reported. If you've not done so already, order a copy of your record by requesting a Personal Earnings and Benefit Estimate Statement (PEBES). The SSA furnishes this statement free of charge. You can get the form to order your PEBES by calling 1-800-772-1213.

CREDITS NEEDED FOR RETIREMENT BENEFITS

Any worker who has earned 40 credits or quarters of coverage is considered "fully insured." This means you are fully and permanently insured under Social Security for retirement, survivors', and disability benefits. If you were born before 1929, you are fully insured with fewer than 40 credits.

Year of Birth	QC's (Credits) Required
1925	36
1926	37
1927	38
1928	39
1929 and later	40

You are also considered fully insured if you have earned at least 1 quarter of coverage for each year between the year in which you became 21 and the year in which you die or become disabled, provided this is at least 6 quarters.

To receive your retirement benefits, you have to be fully insured. If you don't have enough covered employment credits, but were in active military service before 1957, you can receive special military credits. More information about veterans' benefits is found on pages 14–15.

CREDITS NEEDED FOR SURVIVORS' BENEFITS

Survivors' benefits are paid to your surviving dependents based on your earnings record. Your survivors are eligible for these benefits if you are fully insured, as just described. Even if you should die with fewer credits than are required for retirement benefits, you may be what is called "currently insured."

Currently Insured

You are considered currently insured if you have at least 6 credits or quarters of coverage in the 13-quarter period immediately before you die or become entitled to either disability or retirement insurance benefits.

Your widow or widower may also be entitled to benefits if she or he is caring for entitled children who are under 16 or disabled, or if your surviving spouse is old enough to qualify for widow's or widower's benefits.

SOCIAL SECURITY ELIGIBILITY AND BENEFIT AMOUNTS

If you are eligible for benefits, the amount you (and/or your dependents) receive depends on how much you have earned under covered employment, and at what age you elect to begin drawing benefits. The basic benefit amount from which all benefits on a worker's record are derived is computed from the worker's earnings record by calculating the Average Indexed Monthly Earnings (AIME) and from that, the Primary Insurance Amount (PIA). These calculations are explained and discussed in Chapter 4.

When you get your PEBES, it will tell you in detail, and specific to your earnings, what your current status is and:

• How many credits you have.

• The estimated benefit amounts for your retirement at ages 62, 65, and after 70.

• The figure used for your Primary Insurance Amount (shown as the estimated benefit amount at age 65).

• Your estimated survivors' and disability benefits.

NOTE: All the estimates on your PEBES are based on the earnings the SSA has on record for you from your first covered employment through roughly 18 months prior to your request, plus your earnings for the period the SSA hasn't yet posted and what you told them you expect to earn between the time of the request and the time you plan to begin benefits. The closer you are to being ready to begin collecting benefits, the nearer the estimates will be to the actual figure you will receive. A request for a PEBES is *not* an application for benefits; to receive any benefit, you must apply for it.

Entitlement and Benefits: Retired Worker

If you are a fully insured worker, you are now entitled to collect retirement benefits beginning as early as the first full month in which you are age 62. The amount of your benefit depends on when, between that time and reaching age 70, you elect to begin receiving benefits.

The earliest you can receive your full unreduced benefit (100% of your PIA) is age 65 (unless you are disabled). Your PEBES gives you this figure as an estimate based on the figures you provided and adjusted for anticipated national average wage growth.

Early retirement reduces the basic benefit by a small factor for each month between the time you begin collecting benefits and the time you become 65, or the Normal Retirement Age. Delaying retirement past 65 will increase the benefit, again by a small factor.

The increase in your benefit for late retirement will increase the benefits paid to you and ultimately to your surviving spouse; all other benefits paid on your work record will be calculated on your basic benefit or PIA. If your benefit is reduced because of early retirement, all survivor or other benefits paid based on your work record are also reduced.

The reduction for early retirement is also permanent —your benefits will not be increased when you reach 65.

How these increases and reductions are computed is explained later in this chapter under "Timing Your Retirement" and is also shown in Chapter 4.

Entitlement and Benefits:
Spouse (Husband or Wife)

If you are a fully insured worker, a spousal benefit of 50% (or less) of your basic benefit can be paid on your work record to:

• Your husband or wife at age 62 or older.

• Your husband or wife under age 62, if he or she is taking care of your child who is under age 16 or disabled.

• Your former husband or wife age 62 or older, if you were married at least 10 years.

Up to 100% of your basic benefit can be paid to your widower or widow (or divorced spouse) as a survivor's benefit.

The payment for a spouse is 50% of the worker's basic benefit if the worker retired at age 65 and the spouse is also 65 or older. If the worker retired earlier than age 65, and is getting a reduced benefit, the spouse's benefit is still calculated on the amount of the worker's full unreduced benefit, not the amount the worker is being paid.

If the spouse also chooses to retire before the normal retirement age, then the spousal benefit will be reduced—specifically, $^{25}/_{36}$ of 1% for each month of entitlement before 65.

A spouse's benefit is not reduced for age if he or she is caring for an entitled child of the worker, but that benefit is subject to a family maximum (explained on pages 32–33).

Divorced Spouse (Husband or Wife)

A divorced spouse is entitled to benefits on a former husband's or wife's work record if the marriage lasted at least 10 years. The divorced spouse must be at least 62 and unmarried, and the worker must be 62 or older.

If the former husband and wife have been divorced at least 2 years, the divorced spouse is entitled to benefits even if the insured worker has not yet retired. If the worker was receiving benefits before the divorce, the 2-year rule does not apply.

The benefit payment to a qualified divorced spouse is the same as for a spouse. If the worker on whose record these benefits are based has remarried, the family maximums do not include the divorced spouse.

Dependent Child and Grandchild

Social Security defines a dependent child as one under the age of 18 (or 19 if still in high school full-time), or one with a continuing disability that began before the age of 22. Such a child (grandchild, great-grandchild, a natural child, stepchild, or a child adopted or born out of wedlock) is entitled to benefits on an insured worker's work record.

If a grandchild's or great-grandchild's natural or adoptive parents are deceased or were disabled when the grandparents became entitled to retirement or to disability benefits, or when those grandparents died, each dependent child is entitled to benefits if the grandparents or great-grandparents provided his or her support.

The payment to a child of a retired or disabled worker is 50% of the retired worker's benefit for each child, subject to the family maximum.

The payment to a child of a worker who has died is 75% of that worker's benefit, subject to the family maximum.

If both parents are deceased, a child qualifies for benefits on the work record of either parent, whichever yields the higher benefit. If the child marries, the benefits stop.

The benefit amount for each entitled dependent

grandchild is the same: 50% of the grandparent worker's benefit if the grandparent is living and 75% if the grandparent is deceased, subject to the family maximum. These rules apply for great-grandchildren as well.

A child's earnings can affect his or her benefits, as they are subject to the exempt earnings rule, which is discussed on pages 14 and 26.

Survivors' Benefits (Widow or Widower)

A surviving spouse age 60 or over is entitled to payment if the worker was fully or currently insured at the time of death.

Regardless of age, a widow or widower (or divorced widow or widower) who is caring for an entitled child of the deceased worker gets benefits if the worker was either fully or currently insured and the child is under 16 or disabled. This benefit also applies to a surviving divorced spouse meeting the same conditions, or if the divorced widow or widower is disabled.

The amounts of survivors' benefits vary, depending both on how much the deceased worker was entitled to and what category the survivor or survivors fall into. The payment to a widow or widower at age 65 is 100% of the worker's benefit if, at the time of the worker's death, the worker was receiving (or could have received) unreduced benefits. If the worker was receiving reduced benefits before he or she died, the same reduced benefit would go to the widow or widower. If the surviving spouse elects to take the benefit before she or he reaches 65, the amount is reduced by 0.475% ($^{19}/_{40}$ of 1%) of the benefit amount for each month of entitlement before age 65.

EXAMPLE: If you apply at 60, there are 60 months (12 × 5 years) to reduce. Multiply 60 × 0.475 to get the total percent of reduction. It comes to 28.5%, so the payment would be 71.5% of the benefit.

A widow or widower caring for an entitled child or children under 16 or disabled is also eligible for 75% of the worker's benefit as a parent's benefit.

These benefits are all subject to the family maximum (see pages 32–33).

Divorced Widow or Widower

The rules that apply to surviving spouses also apply to divorced surviving spouses, provided the marriage lasted for 10 years before the divorce and the survivor is not married at the time of applying for benefits.

If more than one divorced spouse, or a divorced spouse and the spouse married to the worker at the time of his or her death, both apply for survivors' benefits on the same worker's record, the benefits paid to a divorced spouse are paid independently of the family maximum and do not affect the benefits paid to other survivors.

Dependent Parents of a Worker Who Dies

Dependent parents (or only one parent), age 62 or over, are eligible for benefits if the worker was fully insured at the time of death. To qualify, dependent parents must show that the worker was providing at least one-half of their support.

To show this, you must prepare a statement listing the amounts paid out over the period of support for food, clothing, shelter, and medical and dental care. Attach canceled checks, receipts, or charge account bills to demonstrate that you (the worker) contributed more than 50% of the cost of these items, and submit them through your local Social Security office.

The payment to one parent is 82.5% of the deceased worker's benefit. If both parents are alive and eligible, the benefit amount is 150% of the basic benefit, adjusted for the family maximum.

NOTE: Benefits paid to a person on another's work record are sometimes called "auxiliary benefits," and the person who receives them is referred to as the worker's "auxiliary."

Lump-Sum Death Benefit

Regardless of a worker's age, if the worker was either fully or currently insured at the time of death, a one-time payment of $255 is payable to the eligible surviving spouse living in the same household at the time of the worker's death.

Children of the worker may receive this benefit only if they are eligible for a benefit on the worker's record and if there is no surviving spouse.

Though intended to help pay for burial expenses, this benefit cannot be paid directly to a funeral home—nor can it be paid to someone (other than the surviving spouse) who has already paid the funeral bill.

A claim for a lump-sum death benefit must be filed with the Social Security office within 2 years of the worker's death.

Special Cases, Conditions, and Choices

TIMING YOUR RETIREMENT

If you have some choice about when to stop working as well as when to start taking benefits, be sure you examine all the options carefully and be aware of the time limitations you have in which to make changes in your status. For example, when you are near retirement from your job, if you can choose the time when you will stop working, remember that you can work until you earn the maximum allowable under that year's earnings limitation, then retire and not lose any of that year's benefits.

In determining when to file for your retirement benefits and under which record to file—should you have that option—the best guidance is to be found in your Personal Earnings and Benefit Estimate Statement. It will give you the information you need to evaluate the effect your individual options have on your particular benefits. Remember, the nearer you are to applying for benefits, the more accurate and more useful to you the estimates in your PEBES will be.

Retiring at the Normal Retirement Age

At present, full retirement benefits under Social Security begin at age 65; this is the age which the SSA considers to be the Normal Retirement Age (NRA).

The NRA is scheduled to increase gradually beginning in the year 2000 until it reaches age 67 in 2027. As the increases in the NRA begin for people reaching age 62 in 2000, those who were born in 1938 or later will be the ones affected. The age increase applies to Social Security only; it does not change the age of eligibility for Medicare.

The projected increase in the NRA will not change the availability of reduced benefits at 62 (or 60 for widows and widowers), but it does, over time, increase the amount the benefit will be reduced, from up to 20% to up to 30% (remaining at 20% for widows and widowers). Again, these changes will be gradual and will apply only to those reaching age 62 in 2000 and thereafter.

NOTE: "Retired" doesn't necessarily mean not working. The SSA uses the term to mean you have begun collecting Social Security retirement benefits.

Choosing Early Retirement

The longer you wait between ages 62 and 65 to begin receiving benefits, the smaller the reduction in your PIA will be, as the table at the end of this chapter shows.

Your basic benefit or Primary Insurance Amount (PIA) will be reduced by 0.555%, or $\frac{5}{9}$ of 1%, for each month in which you take your benefit before you become 65.

EXAMPLE: Aaron begins collecting benefits at age 63, 24 months before entitlement at age 65. Multiply 24×0.555 to get the total percent of reduction; it rounds off to 13.33%. So in this case, his benefit is reduced by 13.33%. The benefit check would be 86.67% of his basic benefit or PIA.

NOTE: To apply for benefits for the month you become 62, you must be 62 for all days of that month.

Once again, if you choose to collect Social Security earlier than age 65, your benefit is permanently reduced (disregarding the annual Cost-of-Living Adjustment) and it will **not** increase to your full PIA at age 65.

The decision to collect your benefits early must be based on your individual situation.

Retiring, Then Changing Your Mind and Going Back to Work Again

You can change your mind about working even if you have already begun collecting benefits. They will continue to be paid. When you go back to work, you must inform the SSA. This is done by submitting an Annual Report of Earnings form, which is shown in Appendix C, or by calling your local SSA office.

If you have told the Social Security Administration that you won't be earning over the limit for the year, but you do, you still receive the benefits. The SSA will simply collect any amount it overpaid by deducting the overpayment from future benefits. You must report your annual earnings to SSA by April 15 of the following year.

Choosing to Work While Collecting Benefits

Earning money while collecting Social Security is a necessity for some, an option for others. Some people continue working just as they always have, past 62 (or 65), and elect to begin receiving their benefits at the same time.

If you have a choice, be aware that it isn't a simple matter of adding your earnings to the amount the government sends you—this can be quite a complicated decision. Working can have an effect on the amount of your benefit (it may raise *or* lower it) and there are other points to consider. Here are 3 critical things to think about:

Taxes: Earnings, whether from an employer or self-employment, are subject to federal income tax and, if applicable, to state and local income taxes. Beginning in 1983, Social Security benefits became subject to federal income tax for the first time in the history of the program. Under that law, up to 50% of the benefits of some high-earners were taxed, about 13% of all beneficiaries. In 1993, another law increased the percentage of those benefits taxable to 85%. The Office of Research and Statistics of the SSA has determined that only 11% of those taxed under the 1983 law had more of their benefits taxed under the new law. Under both the old and the new laws, more than 80% of beneficiaries pay no taxes on any part of the benefits they receive. See Chapter 4.

Exempt Earnings: Before age 70, there is a maximum amount you can earn in a year (depending on your age) without reducing your benefit. If you are age 62 through age 64, the SSA reduces your benefit $1 for every $2 earned above the base amount for the year (see page 27). From age 65 through age 69, each $3 earned above the base amount reduces your benefit by $1. However, if you (as a retired worker or other beneficiary) do work, earn more than the exempt earnings, and therefore receive reduced benefits, you will still have more combined income in benefits and earnings than if you had limited your earnings to the maximum amount. After age 70, the maximum earnings rule no longer applies; all earnings are exempt. You still pay taxes, as explained above, but no matter what you earn, your benefit itself is not reduced.

Recomputation: Another consideration is the possibility of an increased primary benefit through recomputation because of higher earnings. If you have annual earnings in any year between ages 65 and 70 that are as high as or higher than your highest pre–age 65 earnings, these earnings might raise your average earnings enough to result in a higher PIA.

Increasing your basic benefit through higher earnings after age 65 will also raise the benefit paid to anyone else who receives payments based on your work record.

NOTE: You need not ask the SSA to recompute your benefit; if you are working and paying taxes, it will be done automatically.

Filing for Benefits Later Than Age 65

The surest way to increase your primary benefit is by delaying your application for Social Security. The SSA will increase your benefit by a percentage that goes up with each year you delay retirement up to age 70. If you were born in 1924 or before, the rate is 3% a year for each year you wait. For people born in 1925 or 1926, the rate is 3.5%; for those born after 1926, the rate goes up another .5% each 2 years until it reaches 8%.

Unlike the increase in a benefit made by an increase in average earnings, the increase made by delayed retirement applies only to the benefit paid to the worker or that worker's surviving spouse or ex-spouse.

BENEFITS FOR PEOPLE WITH DISABILITIES WHO WORK

Special rules make it possible for people with disabilities receiving Social Security or Supplemental Security Income (SSI) to work and still receive monthly benefits. These work incentive rules are slightly different from those for Social Security and SSI beneficiaries, but the goal for both is the same—to provide encouragement to people who want to work and to continue their benefits until they can work on a regular basis.

Disabled Social Security recipients can work for a 9-month trial period without having their earnings affect their Social Security benefits. Impairment-related work expenses may also be deducted when counting earnings. Chapters 5 and 6 provide more information on disability benefits and SSI.

If you are disabled, eligible for Social Security disability benefits or SSI, and wish to continue work, begin working, or train for a job, ask to discuss your special situation with your local Social Security work incentives expert.

FILING ON THE WORK RECORD OF A SPOUSE

Everyone has the choice as to when to begin collecting benefits; some people can also choose whether to file for benefits on their own work record or that of a husband or wife. You have to have been married at least 1 year (or less in some cases). Even if your spouse is deceased or you have been divorced and your former spouse has remarried, you may be entitled to file on his or her work record and may receive higher benefits if you do. In any case, you need to be aware of all your options.

As a husband or wife, you may receive benefits at any age if you're caring for the child of a qualified retired, disabled, or deceased worker if that child is under age 16 or disabled. If you have no children or they are grown, you'll be eligible for half of your spouse's benefit when you reach age 65 or for a reduced benefit at age 62.

As a widow or widower, you may receive a survivor's benefit at any age if you're caring for a child who is under age 16 or disabled. Otherwise, you may receive benefits as early as age 60 or, if you are disabled, at age 50. Survivors' benefits range from 71.5% of a deceased worker's benefit amount (if they begin at age 60) to 100% (if you wait until age 65).

As a divorced spouse, you're entitled to the same benefits you would have received as a spouse or widowed spouse if your marriage lasted 10 years or more. (Length-of-marriage rules do not apply to survivors with minor children.) You may lose your right to these benefits if you remarry.

For the purpose of exploring the options available to people eligible to collect retirement benefits under more than one work record, let's look at a situation where a person has these choices to make.

Suppose Betty, who divorced Cal after 15 years of marriage, has worked at covered employment off and on for 30 years and is a fully covered wage earner entitled to benefits on her own work record. She then marries Darwin, who is also a fully covered worker. They divorce 11 years later, and then Darwin dies. Now, at 65 years of age, Betty wants to retire. Whose record should she use when she files for benefits?

For the sake of comparison, let's look at the 3 categories that cover Betty's situation: wage earner, unmarried divorced spouse, and widow. Betty is eligible for benefits as any one of the 3, since she was married to each of the men for more than 10 years.

Betty has earned more than enough work credits to qualify on her own work record. She has, however, worked at low-paying jobs, so her average earnings figure is not high, and her PIA is only going to be $460.

Cal, her first husband, is still alive and still working, at age 70. He has always earned a good salary. Betty, as his eligible divorced spouse, is entitled to half his PIA of $1,270, which would give her $635. But the survivor's benefit as a divorced widow is **all** of Darwin's PIA, or $1,150, so this is clearly the best choice.

Even though Betty is entitled to benefits under 3 categories, she can't collect them all. Instead, she is allowed to choose the highest-paying category, or whatever combination of benefits yields her the highest payment.

Suppose Betty is only 60 when she needs to begin collecting benefits. At that age, the only category under which she can file is as Darwin's divorced widow. She's too young to get benefits as either a worker or divorced spouse of a worker.

Different Kinds of Spouses

Besides being a divorced or widowed spouse, there is another circumstance under which someone might qualify for spousal benefits. This is a case in which a person has gone through a marriage ceremony which he or she believed to be legal but later found was not. Such a person, as of 1992, may be what is called a "deemed spouse." As such, he or she is eligible for the same benefits as a legal spouse.

For people who live together without being formally married, the situation may be different. Few states recognize "common law" marriages, and the Social Security Administration usually makes no provision for them when the state does not. If this is your situation, you need to determine what your state law provides for in such cases. Being considered legally married can work either for you or against you. Although you cannot collect benefits as a spouse, if you are collecting 100% of a benefit as a widow or widower, you will not lose that benefit. Also, an unmarried companion's income and assets will not be considered for any benefits for which there is a means test.

THE "NOTCH"

"Notch" is the term used to refer to the difference in benefit amounts paid on similar earnings records to people who, because of when they were born, have had their benefits calculated under different formulas. What happens is that people born before 1917 received a windfall if they continued to work after age 62.

There have been 3 formulas for calculating benefits from work histories: the original one (for people born before 1917), a transitional formula (for those born between 1917 and 1921), and the current formula (for everyone else). The point of all these methods of calculation was, and is, to have an equitable way of determining benefits as a stable percentage of workers' earnings.

But when automatic Cost-of-Living increases were enacted and factored into the formula in 1972, an error was introduced with them in the way inflation was calculated. This error caused people born from 1912 through 1916 to receive benefits that were greater than intended and would have eventually led to the bankruptcy of the system.

In 1977, Congress corrected the error by adopting the new benefit formula which applies to everyone born after 1921.

To ease the transition for those closest to retirement, the 1977 law provided that they (people born from 1917 through 1921) could use either the new formula or a special transition formula created for them to calculate their benefits. They could then take the higher of the 2 benefits. In most cases, for these people, the replacement rates—the percentage of a worker's earnings that Social Security replaces—are higher than for those born later, who can only use the new (current) formula.

There has been much controversy over this difference in benefits, with a number of groups and individuals campaigning to raise the benefits of younger recipients to match those of the "notch babies." Finally, the Senate asked the National Academy of Social Insurance to appoint a panel of experts to study the situation.

Briefly, their findings were that duplicating the formula error for those born later would increase expenditures from the trust funds by $50 billion to $300 billion. The panel concluded that although the present situation regarding the notch is unfortunate, they recommended no further change in the law because of enormous cost, administrative feasibility, and equity considerations.

The American Association of Retired Persons (AARP), though militant in protecting COLA's and fighting increases in Medicare premiums and taxes on benefits, also opposes efforts to change the notch. Their position is that the current benefit formula keeps the ratio of workers' benefits to earning history stable and fair.

Further, the problem is not that those born between 1917 and 1921 get less than they deserve; they receive the proper benefits. Instead, some of those born right before got a larger benefit than they should have. To raise the benefits to match these larger ones would cost around $324 billion—a cost that would bankrupt the system or have to be borne by our children and grandchildren in the form of benefit cuts and higher payroll taxes. That would be a real injustice.

If you would like to go into this question in more detail, the report of the National Academy of Social

Insurance is available as SSA Publication 05-10042, which can be obtained through your Social Security office or ordered from the Government Printing Office in Washington, D.C.

STUDENTS AGE 18 AND OVER

The benefits paid to a child of a retired, disabled, or deceased worker are terminated when the child reaches age 18. Benefits will be paid up to age 19 if the child is a full-time student at an elementary or secondary school in the month he or she reaches the age of 19. The child will remain eligible for benefits only for the semester or quarter during which he or she reaches age 19. If the school does not use the quarter or semester system, the student may be allowed to receive benefits for up to 4 months to complete the course.

Benefits for a child will also stop if the child marries, and children's benefits are subject to the exempt earnings rule (discussed on page 12); benefit checks are reduced by $1 for each $2 earned by the child above the 1995 ceiling of $8,160.

A disabled child of a retired or disabled worker may receive benefits (50% of the worker's PIA) after age 22 if the child's disability began before age 22. The benefits for a disabled child are also subject to the same exempt earnings rule as are those of a disabled wage earner. Benefits are terminated if the child marries.

VETERANS

If you worked irregularly or very little after leaving military service, either because of illness or because of a lack of technical skills, the information below may be important to you, your spouse, and your children. If, on the other hand, you went to work after leaving military service and paid Social Security taxes on the maximum or near maximum earnings, the information below may not apply to your benefit situation.

Entitlement to Credits

Since 1957, serving in the armed forces has been considered covered employment by Social Security, and FICA taxes have been withheld from military pay. If you were in active military service between 1940 and 1956, you are also entitled to 1 quarter (1 credit) of Social Security coverage for each of the calendar quarters you were in active service, provided you did not receive a dishonorable discharge.

For each month you were in active service, $160 of

earnings is credited, even though no Social Security taxes were paid during the period 1940 to 1956. These wage credits are not payable as a separate benefit; rather, they are used, if needed, to establish insured status or to increase your benefit. You must file for benefits before a determination can be made as to whether or not these credits can be applied.

Proof Requirements

In order to claim your credits, you must furnish proof of your age, the time of your active service, and your record of service during that period. Appendix B explains how to request a certified copy of your military record.

Restrictions on Work Credits

Should you get credit toward military retirement benefits for military service in any of the armed forces, the SSA will not give you any work credits toward Social Security benefits covering the same time period, with the following exceptions:

Armed Forces Disability Benefits: If you are receiving military retirement pay from the armed forces because of disability—rather than length of service—you are also entitled to credits for Social Security benefits covering the same time period. This is very important if you are a veteran of Korea or Vietnam, for you may be entitled to Social Security disability benefits *in addition* to your armed forces disability retirement benefits.

Length-of-Service-Retirees: If you are a Length-of-Service retiree from the armed forces and were on active duty after 1950, you can receive credits for Social Security for each quarter during those periods—unless another federal agency is also using this same period of time to compute an annuity.

Widows and Widowers: Under some circumstances, surviving spouses are permitted to waive the right to a civil service survivor's annuity and receive credit (not otherwise possible) for military service prior to 1957 to determine eligibility for, and the amount of, Social Security survivors' benefits.

WOMEN'S SPECIAL ISSUES AND CONCERNS

When Social Security was established in the Depression, far fewer women than men held jobs outside the home. The assumption behind the language and structure of the original Social Security law was that women raised children and kept house and men went out and earned the money to keep it all going. In the last 60 years, this arrangement has undergone a profound change.

Though some minor alterations have been made in the law, such as giving widowers and surviving fathers the same rights as widows and surviving mothers, they are minor in comparison to the changes that have taken place in the past half century in marriage and divorce rates, childbearing patterns, and life expectancy.

The SSA established a task force in 1992 to examine issues affecting the adequacy and equity of benefits for women. Although Social Security has been very effective in improving the economic status of elderly women, there are many other areas where it does not help, such as for the numbers of minority household workers who have no coverage and no protection should they become disabled. And in some cases, there are serious questions about whether the rules for spousal benefits which were made a half century ago still serve us well.

For example, dual earners pay for two, but only collect for one. (While the rules for spousal benefits apply to men as well as women, it is primarily women who have paid taxes for their own work but collect on husbands' higher-earnings work records.) Working wives who qualify for Social Security benefits as spouses may get a benefit that is no higher than they would have received if they had never worked or paid Social Security taxes on their earnings. In some cases, one-earner couples actually get a higher Social Security benefit than two-earner couples with the same total lifetime earnings.

That so many more women go out to work today has not changed many of society's expectations of them. Women leaving the work force to care for small children or elderly parents are unable to earn work credits for any of the quarters they are away, which can substantially lower their average earnings and benefits.

An important mitigating factor for working women is that because of Social Security, those who work in covered employment do have valuable disability and survivor protection for themselves and their families during their working years.

Two things to keep in mind when filing for Social Security—**you may be eligible for benefits under more than one work record and you are always entitled to the highest benefit available.** When you make your application to the SSA, be sure to give them information on all the various work records under which you may be entitled to benefits. They will check each record you claim and pay you the highest benefit, but it is up to you to see that they are aware of all the different work records under which you may be eligible.

NOTE: If you change your name (for marriage, divorce, or any other reason), report the change to Social Security so that your wages will continue to be credited properly to your work record.

If you are in business with your husband, make sure your name is on the business so that you have Social Security credits for your earnings and disability insurance.

BENEFITS AS A PERCENTAGE OF COVERED WORKER'S PIA AT SPECIFIC AGES

Retirement Benefits for	Age	% PIA
Covered Worker		
At normal retirement	65	100.0%
Before normal retirement	64	93.3
	63	86.6
	62	80.0
Disability	any age	100.0
Blindness	55 or over	100.0
Spouse of Retired or Disabled Worker		
At spouse's normal retirement age	65	50.0
	64	45.8
	63	41.7
	62	37.5
Child of Deceased Worker		75.0
Child of Retired or Disabled Worker		50.0
Widow(er) or Divorced Widow(er) of Worker		
At widow(er)'s normal retirement age	65	100.0
Before retirement age	63	88.6
	60	71.5
Disabled Widow(er) or Disabled Divorced Widow(er)	50–60	71.5
Widow(er) (Mother or Father) Caring for Child Under 16 or Disabled		75.0
Dependent Parent of Deceased Worker		
One parent	62	82.0
Two parents (payable to each parent)	62	75.0

Benefits for families are subject to the maximum family benefits rule.

3

Starting Your Claim to Social Security Benefits

One of the first steps to take in starting your claim to Social Security benefits is to be sure you have the most up-to-date version of your Personal Earnings and Benefit Estimate Statement. Use the SSA's toll-free number (1-800-772-1213) to request a copy. As Chapter 2 points out, your PEBES will provide guidance as to what benefits to claim and when to claim them.

If you are past age 62 and thinking about retiring anytime this year, contact a Social Security representative now to discuss your plans. Because Social Security rules permit people to work and receive retirement benefits at the same time, it could be to your advantage to have your benefits begin before your employment ends. In any event, you should contact Social Security 3 months before you want to begin receiving benefits.

Once you have determined which benefit you will be applying for, and when, you must be prepared to prove your eligibility. Besides furnishing your Social Security number, you will need to offer proof of age, marital status, age of spouse if any, and a W-2 form

for your earnings from the prior year. You may need other documents as well, depending on the benefits for which you apply.

This chapter details the kinds of information you will need and how to get what you don't have on hand. It also includes a number of notes like the one below to help you with the process of application. The addresses in Appendix B will tell you where to order documents you may not have.

NOTE: Be sure to double-check all the rules for all other programs (private and public pensions, veterans' benefits) to which you may be entitled. Collecting one benefit may affect your right to collect others. Some pensions may be reduced by an amount equal to the amount of Social Security benefit received. You may find that by careful timing of your claims for various benefits, you can maximize the amounts you are able to collect.

The more information you have, the better able you will be to make the best decision about what benefits to claim and when to claim them.

Legal Documents for Your Claim

The basic facts you have to establish for retirement benefits are your age, your marital status, and your Social Security number.

Age can be proved in a variety of ways. The Social Security Administration will determine your date of birth by the best available evidence, usually a birth certificate recorded before age 5, religious record of birth established before age 5, or certified copies of these documents. If none of these records is available, a variety of sources described on the following pages can be used to establish your date of birth.

Marital status can be proved by a marriage certificate or other evidence, such as affidavits from the per-

son who performed the ceremony or witnesses to the marriage. Age of children can be proved by documents like the ones you would use to establish your own age.

If you are a naturalized citizen born in another country, you will also need immigration and naturalization records.

NOTE: A **certified** copy of a public record is one that bears the official seal of the office issuing it. These are usually made with a pressure clamp seal that makes an impression in the paper itself, and sometimes a stamp or sticker will also be affixed to the document. Documents made this way cannot be duplicated on a copy machine, so if you order a certified copy and get as many copies as you're going to need, you'll save time.

If you need to send for copies of official documents, use Appendix B to find the appropriate office. When you write or call, be sure to furnish all the information needed to locate the file. Usually, you will need to give your full name, mother's maiden name, father's name, and the date and place of your birth.

You can save time by telephoning the state or city office to be sure you are furnishing the correct information and sending the right fee. (These offices frequently change the fees they charge for various documents.) Some states will locate your records, then send them as soon as your payment is received. A few will accept payment by credit card over the telephone and send your documents immediately. Some prefer to send you a special form for your request that you return along with your payment.

BIRTH CERTIFICATES

You can apply for copies of a birth certificate from the office that records vital statistics in the state where you were born. Hospitals also keep birth records, and you can write or call the one in which you were born and request a copy.

NOTE: If you gave an incorrect birth date when you originally applied for a Social Security number, this fact will become apparent when you apply for benefits. If this is the case, be prepared to furnish 2 pieces of evidence to establish your correct date of birth. There is no penalty for having given the wrong date originally.

Other Proofs of Birth

If your birth certificate is not available, the following alternate proofs showing a date of birth may be used, in order of desirability: baptismal record, U.S. passport (or application), school records, draft registration record, census records, voter registration, department of motor vehicle driver registration, personal testimony by affidavits, or family documents.

If you have to rely on a proof of birth other than a birth certificate, your Social Security office will advise you, but you will probably need to present several of the above records in lieu of a birth certificate.

PROOF OF SUPPORT

To claim benefits as the dependent parent of a worker, proof of support has to be established. An affidavit (a sworn statement in writing signed by you in the presence of and notarized by a notary public) stating that you were dependent upon that worker for more than 50% of your support and giving the reason for your dependency will serve as evidence. You may also have to furnish receipts for rent, utilities, groceries, medicine, clothing, and other necessities, along with canceled checks.

MARRIAGE DOCUMENTS

An original marriage license bearing an official seal, or a certified copy, is the best evidence of marriage. Certified copies can be obtained from the records office of the state or, in some cases, the city or town where the marriage took place.

Documents issued by the person who performed the ceremony and signed by witnesses may also be used. Write to the church or synagogue where the marriage was performed.

If the marriage was not a legal one, but one or both of the parties believed it to be, talk to your local Social Security office about how to demonstrate "deemed spouse" status.

ADDITIONAL DOCUMENTS

When applying for Social Security benefits, you may need other documents in addition to proof of age. You will, of course, need your Social Security card or some other record of your Social Security number. You will also need to have a copy of the last income tax filed with W-2 forms or with Schedule C, if you are self-employed. The Personal Earnings and Benefit Estimate Statement will show your Social Security number. Depending on the kind of benefit for which you are applying, you may also need some of these documents:

Marriage certificate, if applying for a wife's, husband's, ex-spouse's, mother's, father's, widow's, or widower's benefits.

Divorce decree, if making a claim on the work record of a divorced spouse to whom you were married for at least 10 years.

Death certificate, if applying for a lump-sum death payment or any other claim on the record of a deceased worker.

Child's birth certificate, of any child for whom you are applying for benefits.

Medical records and income tax forms, for disability claims.

Proof of support, if claiming benefits as the dependent parent of a deceased worker.

NOTE: These must be original documents or certified copies. The SSA will make photocopies of original documents and return them to you, but obviously it would be safer to send certified copies.

Whenever possible, applications for benefits should be made 3 months in advance of eligibility. If you don't have all the documents you need for your claim, begin the application process without them.

Your Work Record

Your work record is crucial to your claim for Social Security benefits for 2 reasons. First, your eligibility for benefits depends on having earned enough work credits (quarters of coverage) to qualify. Second, the amount of your benefit is tied to the amount of money you have earned. When FICA or SECA taxes were paid on your wages, those wages became a part of your work record.

The SSA has always been obliged to tell you, if you asked, what record it has of your Social Security taxed earnings, what you have paid into the system, and how many credits you have earned. In 1988, the SSA introduced a new service that not only provides this information but also estimates what your retirement, disability, and survivors' benefits will be. The estimate is based on what you are able to tell the SSA about your future earnings, and it shows you the amount of your retirement benefits if you retire at 62, 65, or 70. This information is called the Personal Earnings and Benefit Statement, or PEBES.

To order yours, as you should do routinely each 3 years or so, call either your local SSA office or 1-800-772-1213 and ask for a request form, SSA-7004-PC-OP1, reproduced in Appendix C. (Please do not send this form to Fraser-Vance Publishing—we do not have access to your earnings record. Call the SSA for a form and mail it to the address provided.)

NOTE: This estimate comes from, and is calculated by, the Social Security Administration. The service is **free.** You need not and should not pay anyone to get this information for you.

ERRORS IN YOUR WORK RECORD

When you receive your personalized statement, check it carefully. It is important that **all** your covered earnings are on record because your benefit amount is calculated from your highest-earning years.

Because so many records are kept, it is no surprise

that errors, oversights, and omissions do occur. An employer's failure to report earnings, a name change because of marriage, or a jumbled Social Security number could cost you benefit dollars.

If you have a problem or a question about your record, call the number shown on page 5 of your PEBES. The Social Security representative who will talk to you has computer access to your records and can help identify or confirm what the problem is and tell you what to do about it. Often, you can resolve the problem entirely on the telephone.

NOTE: It may be a number of months between the time your earnings are reported (which can be as late as mid-February after the year in which the wages were earned) and their appearance in your record. If that is the problem, the representative can tell you right away.

If you have other earnings that aren't on record, you need to document those earnings to the SSA so you will be credited for them. If you can't figure out what happened and need detailed information about your record, you can ask to be sent a form, Request for Social Security Earnings Information, SSA-7050-F3. (This form does not appear with the other sample forms in Appendix C. You have to make a request, give your name and Social Security number, and it will be sent to you.) If you only need a yearly total or totals, there is no charge. If more detailed information is required, or if you want the information certified, there is a fee. The form explains how to calculate the fee so it can be included with the request. You must return the form in 30 days, along with documentation of your earnings, or ask for an extension.

Recent changes have made it easier to correct your earnings record. There is no longer any time limit for making corrections in cases where not all of your earnings are on Social Security records. It is even possible to correct an earnings record when proof of earnings cannot be obtained. For 1978 or later years, if the SSA has a record of a person's earnings from an employer in the year immediately before or after the year in question, and the individual's claimed wages are consistent with his or her earlier and later wages, and no evidence is available from either the employer or the individual, the SSA will accept the worker's allegation of wages (for one year of wages only).

NOTE: It is easier to correct recent mistakes than older ones, because newer records, both yours and your employer's, are more readily available. That's why it is a good idea, while you are still working, to check your record every few years and to make any necessary corrections as quickly as possible.

Submitting Your Application for Social Security Benefits

The Social Security Administration will not start your benefits automatically; you must file your application. This is usually no more complicated than calling your local office, or the toll-free number (1-800-772-1213).

There are specific forms for each kind of Social Security benefit, and copies of these are reproduced in Appendix C at the back of this book. **These forms are sample forms only—they are not for official use. Do not try to use them to apply for your benefits.** We have included them to help you know ahead of time what questions will be asked. As more and more Social Security offices are being automated, many of them no longer use these written forms. Instead, an interviewer asks you the necessary questions, and your answers are entered into the computer. Sometimes this is even done over the telephone.

Dealing With Your Local Social Security Office

Despite reductions in staff as well as the increasing numbers eligible for benefits, the people who work for the SSA try very hard to do a good job, and you help them—and yourself—by beginning your relationship well prepared. We suggest the following strategies for your dealings with your Social Security office:

Apply: The Social Security Administration will not search you out to pay you a benefit, or investigate to see how many different benefits you may have coming to you. You must apply, and you should apply for every different benefit to which you think you may be entitled. If you are eligible for benefits under the work record of a spouse, or former spouse(s), as well as your own, have the information necessary (Social Security number and documentation of your relationship) for those work records too. The SSA can then check the benefit amounts from these different eligibilities. You are entitled to the highest one.

Call Ahead: Local or area Social Security offices are listed in the telephone directory's white pages under

"Social Security" or "SSA," and in the directory's Government and Municipal Guide under "U.S. Government." Try to avoid the busiest times for local offices, which are usually between 10 AM and 3 PM each business day, the first half of the week, and the first half of every month.

You may find that your application interview can be conducted over the telephone, so check the forms to see what information you will need to have at hand if you do use the telephone to apply. However, if you have a problem, it is better to conduct your business in writing so you will have a record. If you plan to go into the office, find out the best time to do so, and verify which documents you will need to have with you.

Learn the Language: Use this book to familiarize yourself with the government terminology, words, acronyms, and sets of initials that apply to your claim. Check to see what names have been given to the forms for your claim.

Make a List: Write down all the things you want to ask so you can accomplish as much as possible in one call or visit. Make a note of the name of the person who handles your call, try to find out which service worker you will be assigned to, and note that person's name as well as anything else you may need to remember.

Be Prepared: If you do have to make a visit to your local office, take a box lunch, a book, or some pleasing pastime. You may have to take a number and wait to see a representative, though this is much less common than it once was.

When to Make Your Application

You can file to have your retirement benefits begin any month after the month in which you attain the age of 62. The SSA will automatically adjust the amount of your benefit for the number of months before or after you attain the age of 65.

The earliest you should file your claim is 3 months in advance of the time you want the payments to begin. Early filing gives the SSA time to process your application and will minimize the delay in getting the first check. Benefits may be paid retroactively for no more than 6 months after you attain the age of 65. Retroactive claims for reduced benefits (benefits for months before age 65) will not be approved.

If you are late in making your application, you could lose out on some benefits. If you haven't received all the documents you need, don't wait to get them before filing. Get the process started.

If you are trying to decide whether or not to retire early, work until 65, or work after you reach 65, study the estimates on your PEBES and taking your own figures, use them with the formulas shown in Chapter 4. If you are over 60, you can also go into your local office and discuss your options with an SSA representative.

Organizing Your Records

Set up a file for your dealings with the Social Security Administration. As mentioned before, keep a record of the name of the representative or service worker assigned to you, and keep all the papers relating to separate claims together. Make a note of the dates and names of people with whom you speak, write down what they tell you, and keep those notes in your file. Organize your papers so that you have a record of everything and can find specific information quickly and easily. The better organized you are, the less trouble you are likely to have.

Be sure to put your claim number (usually your Social Security number plus a letter) on **everything** you submit to the Social Security office. And just in case something gets lost or mislaid at the SSA office, **always** make a copy of each item for your own files.

Sort your files according to specific claims or keep everything in chronological order, to help you find things more quickly. You will have an even greater need for a good system for your Medicare files. Give some thought in the beginning to what sort of system will work best for you, and stick with it.

Address your correspondence to the service person in your local office who has been assigned to you. If you can, it is better to hand-deliver important papers to the office, rather than mailing them; it's faster and reduces the chance of their getting lost.

If you always file written claims and ask to receive decisions on those claims in writing, you will have the papers necessary to appeal a decision should you need to do so.

NOTE: Because disability and survivors' benefits applications also take some time to process, it would be a good idea to get these applications and have them in your files along with some of the documents that will be needed to support them. That way, they will be available when and if there is a need for them.

Using the Telephone

You can save yourself time and aggravation by making use of your telephone for some dealings with the Social Security Administration. Besides your local office, which is open on weekdays during business hours, you can call the toll-free SSA number weekdays, 7 AM to 7 PM. The number is 1-800-772-1213. You will get a recording, but if you are calling from a touch-tone telephone, you can report a new address or a missing check, get a PEBES request form or proof of your benefit payments, and you can even ask that an SSA representative return your call during business hours. You will be asked a series of questions which you answer by pressing different numbers on your telephone number pad. It is also possible to speak to a representative at this number. The best times to use the 800 number are early in the morning or late in the afternoon, Wednesday through Friday, after the first week of the month. When the 800 number was instituted, many Social Security offices did away with local service by phone, but that has now been reinstated.

Using the telephone is fine for getting answers to routine questions, but if your needs are more complicated, it bears repeating that it's better to do it in writing, so that you will have a record on file.

Also, if you think you may be eligible for some additional benefit but aren't too sure, you might inquire on the telephone or in person at the local office. In this instance, however, it's definitely better to apply in writing—even if you have been told you aren't eligible. (A written application will get more attention than an oral question, and may work to your advantage.) If it turns out you are eligible after all, the date of the application will be used to calculate the benefits due.

Getting Your Check

The SSA will notify you by letter that your claim has been approved or denied, how much your benefit will be, and when to expect your first check. This takes about 6 to 10 weeks for retirement, 3 to 6 months—or possibly longer—for disability. You will have 60 days to appeal if your claim is denied—or if you think the benefit amount is wrong. Chapter 9 explains how to go about making an appeal.

Save the letter you receive, because if you ever need to appeal or correct any mistakes that have been made, you will need to show the date and content of the decision in question.

Checks are mailed by the U.S. Treasury Department shortly after the end of the month for which payments are being made.

Benefits paid to a married couple are usually combined into one check, made out to them jointly. This is more convenient for most people and saves the government money. Separate checks will be sent if either spouse requests it. Family payments also are usually issued on one check unless otherwise requested.

DIRECT DEPOSIT

The most efficient way to receive your benefit is by direct deposit. The funds are sent to your bank by wire transfer. Not only does it save the SSA in administrative costs, it's more convenient for you. Beneficiaries who receive their checks by mail are *16 times* more likely to report lost, delayed, or stolen benefits than people who have signed up for direct deposit. With direct deposit, you don't have to worry about making a special trip and then standing in line at the bank to make your deposit, or having your check sit in your mailbox if you should be away from home for a while. If you did not sign up for direct deposit when you began getting your benefits, you can do so now.

To authorize direct deposit, call the SSA's toll-free number (1-800-772-1213) and give the representative your Social Security and your bank account numbers, or fill out Form SF-1199 at your local Social Security office, or at your bank. Be sure to ask at the bank if there is any extra charge for this service. Ask also how long it will take them to process the transfer, so you will know when your funds are available.

The Social Security Administration encourages more people to use this method of receiving benefits. Besides being safer and more convenient for benefit recipients, it saves time and money for the SSA, which must continually strive to serve more people with fewer resources and which depends on technology to improve its productivity.

CHECKS OUTSIDE THE UNITED STATES

As a U.S. citizen, you can travel or live in most foreign countries without affecting your eligibility for Social Security benefits. However, some noncitizens who leave the United States for more than 6 months will not be able to receive benefits. And whether you're a citizen or not, no Social Security checks are sent to Cambodia, Cuba, North Korea, the former republics of the U.S.S.R., or Vietnam. The rules for who may receive benefits depend on whether you are eligible under your own work record or someone else's, what kind of benefits you are getting, which country you are living in, and a number of other factors. If you plan to live abroad and want to receive Social Security benefits, ask the SSA for the free pamphlet *Your Social Security Checks While You Are Outside the United States.*

Many foreign countries tax U.S. Social Security benefits; the embassy of the country in question will be able to give you information on that.

NOTE: Whether your benefits will continue or stop, you must notify Social Security when you plan to be outside the United States for more than 30 days. You can do this by calling the toll-free number.

BASIC REDUCTION FORMULAS

Retirement Benefit

A retirement benefit is reduced by $5/9$ of 1% (or .00555) for each month of entitlement before age 65.

Spouse's Benefit

A wife's or husband's benefit is reduced by $25/36$ of 1% (or .00694) for each month of entitlement before age 65.

Widow's or Widower's Benefit

A surviving spouse's benefit is reduced by $19/40$ of 1% (or .475) for each month of entitlement between ages 60 and 65. Surviving spouse's benefits payable before age 60 based on disability are not further reduced for months before age 60.

How to Use the Formulas

Multiply the decimal percentage applicable by the number of months before the month of your 65th birthday. The percentage that results will be subtracted from your PIA.

EARLY RETIREMENT BENEFIT REDUCTION

Retirement at Age	% of PIA Due	Reduces Benefit to		
		If $500	If $700	If $1,000
62	80.0%	$400	$560	$ 800
63	86.6	433	607	867
64	93.3	467	653	933
65	100.0	500	700	1,000

These percentages apply only to workers. Different percentages apply to spouses.

EXAMPLE: A claim filed at age 63, 24 months before age 65 = a reduction of .00555 × 24 = 13.32% from 100%, or 86.6% of the benefit due at age 65.

4

Your Income and Retirement Benefits

In this chapter we will discuss the source of the money that is used to pay Social Security benefits, the relationship between the money you earn and the amount of your benefit, working and collecting retirement benefits, and the effect of other kinds of income on what you receive from Social Security. We will also cover federal income taxes on your benefit, how the benefits are computed, and how you receive your checks.

WHERE THE MONEY COMES FROM

In 1995, over 132 million workers are earning wages in employment covered by the Social Security program, and it is the FICA (Federal Insurance Contributions Act) taxes from these workers' earnings that are being used to pay this year's Social Security benefits.

If you are working at a job covered by Social Security, you must pay the FICA tax on the money you earn (up to the year's ceiling), regardless of your age and even if you have already started drawing Social Security benefits. If you are self-employed and earn more than $400 a year, you must report earnings and pay self-employment tax (called SECA, for Self-Employment Insurance Contributions Act) when you file your income tax returns.

Employee/Employer and Self-Employment Tax Rates

The 1995 FICA rate is 7.65% of earnings up to a maximum of $61,200. The employer and the employee must each contribute this amount of the worker's wage, for a total of 15.3%, to the trust funds described in Chapter 1. *All* earnings beyond $61,200 are taxed an additional 1.45% for Medicare alone. Again, the employer and the employee each contributes this amount based on the worker's earnings. The employer is allowed an income tax deduction for employee FICA payments made to the trust funds.

A self-employed person pays twice what the employed worker pays: 15.3% on earnings up to $61,200, and an additional 2.9% of all earnings above that. A worker paying SECA is allowed an income tax deduction of one-half the SECA tax from his or her adjusted gross income, just as the employer deducts the FICA paid on employee wages. See IRS Publication 505 for more information on self-employment taxes.

Until 1994, FICA and SECA (also called payroll taxes) taxed only a portion of a worker's wage. Beyond a certain maximum amount, the tax no longer had to be paid. Still, as shown in the table of Annual Earnings Taxed at the end of this chapter, this maximum amount began moving gradually upward after 1950, and sharply upward since the early 1970s. By 1993, the vast majority of us paid Social Security taxes on all the money we earned. Now, *everyone* pays some tax on all his or her earnings.

The tax rate for FICA and SECA has risen as well; the amount taken from most people's earnings for Social Security and Medicare is larger than what they pay in other federal taxes.

Your Income

As you have seen in Chapter 3, the money you earn for your work is counted toward your benefits. If you are employed by someone other than yourself, your employer or employers report your wages, deduct your Social Security taxes, and file a W-2 or 1099 form with the Internal Revenue Service. You get a copy of the form from each employer early in the year following the year in which you worked. If you are self-employed, you pay your own Social Security taxes when you make out your quarterly estimated tax payments and file them with the IRS.

ITEMS COUNTED AS EARNED INCOME

When you begin collecting Social Security benefits, you must report your income to the SSA, because some kinds of continued income can affect the amount of your primary benefit.

Not all kinds of after-retirement income are included in the calculations that determine how much your Social Security benefit will be—only that considered to be "earned income." Earned income includes wages, tips, bonuses, commissions and fees, vacation pay, severance, and sick pay. The information sheet that is a part of the reporting form (reproduced in Appendix C) explains these categories, tells you which situations to contact the SSA about before you file, and lists income sources that do not have to be reported because they are *not* considered earned income and will not affect the amount of your retirement benefits.

Generally, the income you don't have to report includes your Social Security, veterans', civil service, and public assistance benefits; pensions not reported on your W-2; interest and dividends, such as those from IRA and Keogh accounts; annuities; capital gains; gifts and inheritances; rental income; jury duty pay; royalties from pre-retirement patents or copyrights; retirement payments from a partnership; and income from a limited partnership.

If you are already receiving Social Security retirement benefits, income sources such as those immediately above do not affect your benefits.

WHO REPORTS INCOME

You must report your income annually to the SSA if:

• You are receiving Social Security benefits (other than disability benefits) and you had not reached the age of 70 by the first month of entitlement in the year for which you have earnings to report.

• You are turning 65 and your annual earned income for last year and the current year is above the annual limit for exempt earnings for age 65 and over for those years. (You report for 2 years because of the way the SSA calculates first-year benefits.)

OR

• You are under 65, are collecting benefits, and your annual earned income for last year and the current year is above the annual limit for exempt earnings for those under 65 for those years.

You report income to the Social Security Adminis-

tration on Form SSA-777-BK, Annual Report of Earnings, a copy of which is reproduced in Appendix C.

You are not required to report your income to the SSA if:

• You are receiving Social Security benefits but no other money that meets the SSA definition of earned income.

• You became 70 more than a year ago. After you become 70, everything you earn is exempt, but you have to file a report for the year in which you turn 70, reporting for that year only the earnings for the months before the month in which you reached 70.

• You are not receiving Social Security benefits.

WHY THE SSA NEEDS THE ANNUAL REPORT OF EARNINGS

Even though you have filed your federal tax return with the Internal Revenue Service, which shares its information and matches records with the SSA, if you are in the "must report" group above, you are still required to tell the SSA what you earned last year and what you expect to earn in the current year.

On the basis of this report, the SSA confirms that it paid you the correct amount in the previous year and determines what to pay you in the current year. If you were underpaid, you will be sent a check. If you were overpaid, you'll get a letter explaining what the SSA will do to recover the overpayment and what to do if you think you were sent the correct amount in the first place.

If you cannot file this report for any reason, or if you will be unable to make the deadline, write to the SSA and explain your predicament. You will be granted an automatic extension for 30 days. If you have any further questions, you can call the Social Security Administration at 1-800-772-1213, or the Internal Revenue Information for Retired Persons at 1-800-829-3676.

If you do not file this report by the deadline or if you do not ask for an extension, the SSA can stop your benefit checks and may even charge you a penalty. It can also, if necessary, deduct overpayment of benefits from future benefit checks and recover overpayments from any income tax refund you may have coming to you.

The SSA will send you Form SSA-777-BK, Social Security Administration Annual Report of Earnings, at the beginning of each year so you can report your earnings from the year before. You can get a copy from your Social Security office should you need to report a change. The form is short, clear, and self-explanatory. An addressed envelope comes with it for its return.

DELAYED RETIREMENT CREDIT

People who continue working between age 65 and age 70 without collecting Social Security benefits will receive Delayed Retirement Credit (DRC). This is additional credit toward your Social Security benefits when you do retire, and it will be added automatically when your wages after age 65 and up to age 70 are reported. There is no DRC given for working past age 70.

The DRC increases your primary benefit (PIA) by a percentage factor for each of the years between ages 65 and 70 that you do not receive your benefit. The percentage factor will rise gradually (.5% every other year) from 3% for those born in the years 1917 through 1924, to 8% for workers born after 1942. A worker born before 1925, for instance, would have an increase of 3% for each year retirement is delayed; someone born in 1925 or 1926 would have an increase of 3.5%; someone born in 1927 or 1928 would have 4%; and so on. See the end of this chapter for a table of these percentages by age.

EXAMPLE: Edward, who was 65 in 1992, was entitled to a monthly benefit of $700. As noted above, the DRC rate for people born in 1927 is 4%. For each year Edward delays his retirement, up to age 70, his monthly benefit will be increased by that rate, compounded. In 1993 his benefit rose to $728. In 1994 it would increase to $757, and so on. This example of compounding does not include either the affect on Edward's monthly benefit of Cost-of-Living Adjustments or increases that may come because he is earning at a higher rate.

NOTE: The DRC increases affect only the benefits paid to workers or to their surviving spouses. It is not applied to benefits paid to other family members. However, any **earnings** after age 65 until age 70 that result in an increase to a worker's benefit will increase the benefit paid to anyone else drawing on that worker's record.

DETERMINING YOUR AGE FOR REPORTING PURPOSES

You are considered by the SSA to be 65 in the year your 65th birthday occurs or if your birthday is on January 1 of the next year. Thus, everyone born in 1930 through January 1, 1931 is considered to be 65 in 1995.

For people turning 70, the same January 1 through January 1 rule applies, but because the month in which you become 70 is also important, there is a rule for that, too. You are considered to be 70 in the month before your actual birthday.

CIRCUMSTANCES THAT AFFECT BENEFITS

If you are receiving Social Security benefits, you should be aware that a number of circumstances can cause your benefit checks to increase, decrease, or stop. Individual situations vary to such an extent it would be impossible to cover every combination, but the list below will give you a general idea of the events that trigger a change in a benefit amount.

Changes in Status

The Social Security Administration requires all beneficiaries—you or your dependents—to report the following status changes:

• When a person getting benefits is working and has, or expects to have, earnings in excess of the exempt amount.

• When a person who is entitled to benefits (a child's, divorced spouse's, widow's, widower's, parent's benefit) has married.

• When a person under age 62 getting a mother's or father's benefit no longer has in her or his care a child under age 18 or a disabled child.

• When a person getting disability benefits has gone back to work, or his or her condition has improved so that he or she is able to work.

• When a child 18 or over getting benefits as a student is no longer attending school full-time.

• When a person getting benefits has died.

Penalties

Failure to report promptly any of these events or additions to income may result in penalties. "Promptly" means within 3 months and 15 days (usually April 15) of the year following the close of a calendar year.

Reports should be made by calling the toll-free number (1-800-772-1213) or at your local Social Security office. Penalties can be serious and may be the equivalent of the monthly benefit rate for the first default in reporting, 2 times the monthly rate for the second default, and 3 times the monthly benefit rate for the third default.

Earnings Limits

Social Security recipients **under** age 70 receive full benefits as long as their earnings are below the limits for the year. This is sometimes called the "retirement earnings test," or "excess earnings above the exempt amount." Familiarity with this provision is critical if you are going to continue working after age 65 and are trying to decide whether or not to delay collecting your benefits.

Over 70: If you are over 70 years of age for the entire year, you can earn income of any amount without affecting your benefits.

Turning 70: If you are 70 for only part of a year, you only need to report income earned before the month of your birthday. If you were born the first day of a month, the SSA considers you to have become 70 in the month before your birthday. Anything earned in or after the month when you reach 70 need not be reported.

NOTE: For self-employed earnings, divide your net annual earnings amount by 12 for an average monthly figure, and report only the months prior to the month in which you became 70.

Under 70: If you are under 70 years of age and your earned income does not exceed the annual limits, you will continue to receive your full monthly benefit check.

Here are the 1992–1995 figures.

EXEMPT EARNINGS 1992–1995

Year	Under 65	Ages 65–70
1992	$7,440	$10,200
1993	7,680	10,560
1994	8,040	11,160
1995	8,160	11,280

$1 is withheld from your benefit for each $3 you earn over the exempt amount while you are age 65 to age 69. Under age 65, $1 is withheld for each $2 in earnings above the limit.

EXAMPLE: Florence's W-2 form for 1993 shows earned income of $15,588, of which $10,560 is exempt. Her excess earnings are $5,028 ($15,588 − $10,560 =

$5,028). Since she is 65, the reduction in her benefit is obtained by dividing her excess earnings by 3: $5,028 ÷ 3 = $1,676; her benefit checks in 1994 will be reduced until $1,676 has been withheld. If Florence were under 65, the reduction in her benefit would be obtained by dividing her excess earnings by 2 instead of 3.

Beginning in the year 2000, the age at which the withholding rate of $1 for each $3 of excess earnings applies will increase as the retirement age increases.

Irregular and Varying Earnings

If you are self-employed, there may be a gap between the time you perform services and the time you are paid for them. Also, if you are sporadically employed, your earnings may vary widely from month to month. In these circumstances, your earnings for the entire year are averaged, and the average monthly earnings figure is used to determine the effect on your benefits.

Special Treatment of First-Year Earnings

During the first year of retirement, earnings receive special treatment by the SSA. Instead of using an average monthly figure, the SSA calculates first-year retirement benefits on a month-to-month basis. Furthermore, you will receive the full amount of your retirement benefit, without reduction, **for any month** in 1995 in which you (a) earn less than the maximum monthly amount allowable for your age ($8,160 divided by 12 or $680 for people 62 through 64, $11,280 divided by 12 or $940 for people 65 through 69), or (b) do not perform "substantial services" in your business, regardless of how much you earn during the year.

For example, say you begin to collect benefits at age 65 in March 1995 and then earn $15,000—$5,000 per month in April, May, and June—but nothing more for the rest of this year. Because your earnings in April, May, and June are well over the $940 monthly limit, you will not receive any benefits for those months. However, your overall annual earnings of $15,000 will not affect your benefits for the remaining 6 months in the year: you will receive full monthly benefits from July through December.

NOTE: Substantial services are defined as being more than 45 hours of work in your trade or business during any month—but as few as 15 hours can be deemed substantial if they involve management of a sizable business or are spent in a highly skilled occupation. This decision is made by your local Social Security office.

Cost-of-Living Adjustments

Your Social Security benefits are adjusted annually for inflation by the addition of a percentage amount known as a Cost-of-Living Adjustment (COLA). Although Congress is required by law to grant a COLA each year, it can reduce the percentage. In 1983, it "postponed" the COLA until January 1984.

The percentage amount for a COLA is usually calculated on the difference between the Consumer Price Index in the third quarter of the current year and the third quarter of the prior year.

The COLA percentage in effect when you first become entitled to your benefit at age 62 and for each year thereafter determines the percentage of your PIA to be added to your monthly benefit. For example, assume your PIA is $600 and that you became 62 in 1990. The COLA for 1990 (4.7%) would increase your $600 benefit by $28 ($600 × .047 = $28.20) to $628. (SSA rounds down to the next whole dollar.) The 1991 COLA (5.4%) would increase your benefit by $33 ($628 × .054 = $33.91) to $661. The 1992 COLA (3.7%) would increase it by $24 to $685, the 1993 COLA (3%) would increase it by $20 to $705, and, finally, the 1994 COLA (2.6%) would increase your benefit in 1994 by $18 to $723.

December Social Security checks are received in January, and reflect the COLA increase. For the specific COLA percentages since 1975, see the table at the end of this chapter.

Government Pension Offset

Some dependents of retired federal, state, and local government workers are subject to having their payments from those pensions reduced by the amount of Social Security benefits they receive.

These offsets apply to the **dependents'** payments under these government pensions; there are no offsets for the worker's own pension. The offset does not apply to the vast majority of pensions currently collected by the dependents and survivors of government workers.

The complicated law is explained in a fact sheet, *Government Pension Offset*, 05-10007, available from the SSA or the Government Printing Office.

Social Security Integration/Permitted Disparity

Federal pension and tax laws permit companies to reduce pension expense by including the amount of your Social Security benefit when calculating your pension. This practice is called "Social Security Integration" or "Permitted Disparity." Current law limits the reduction to no more than 50% for pension credits earned after December 31, 1988, but credits earned before that date can be reduced by as much as 100%. This means the pension check you are counting on could be a great deal smaller than what you expected.

For this reason, as well as others, it's best to have a clear understanding of your company's pension plan. If you do not understand the material (Summary Plan Description) you were given for your company's pension plan, insist that someone in the company's human resources office explain to you the relationship between your pension payments and Social Security.

Benefits and Taxes

In January, the Social Security Administration mails a Social Security Benefit Statement to all beneficiaries, telling them the total amount of Social Security benefits they received in the year just passed. These statements are used in determining if any of the benefits are subject to federal income tax.

The majority of people receiving these statements (Form SSA-1099) will not owe any taxes on their benefits because their total income is less than the taxable ceiling.

NOTE: If you receive Social Security benefits and continue to work, you must report your earnings to *2* agencies—the Social Security Administration and the Internal Revenue Service.

Some people assume that filing an income tax return takes care of the Social Security earnings report requirement, too. Although the IRS shares tax return information with the SSA, the tax return does not provide all the information the SSA requires.

COMPUTING FEDERAL INCOME TAXES

Social Security benefits received in 1994 become taxable when your Adjusted Gross Income (line 31 of federal income tax Form 1040) added to tax-free interest income (the sum of these two figures is your MAGI, or Modified Adjusted Gross Income), plus 50% of your Social Security benefits for the year (MAGI plus 50% of Social Security benefits is referred to as "Provisional Income") exceed the base amount of $25,000 for a single person and $32,000 for a couple filing jointly.

You **do not** have to pay federal income taxes on your 1994 Social Security benefits if your MAGI plus 50% of your Social Security benefits does not exceed the 1994 base amounts (to repeat, $25,000 for a single person and $32,000 for a couple filing jointly).

Under the 1993 Omnibus Budget Reconciliation Act, the rules have changed for determining tax on this Provisional Income higher than these base amounts. Under the old law, if Provisional Income exceeded these bases, the portion of benefits included in taxable income was equal to half the excess of Provisional Income up to a maximum of 50% of the benefits. The new law adds a new upper tier to Provisional Income —$44,000 for couples and $34,000 for singles, above which the taxable benefit will be the lesser of: (1) 85% of benefits, or (2) the sum of (a) what the taxable benefit would have been under the old law, but not more than $6,000 for couples or $4,500 for singles, and (b) 85% of the excess of Provisional Income over the upper-tier threshold.

For taxpayers with Provisional Incomes between the base threshold ($32,000 for couples, $25,000 for singles) and the new upper-tier threshold ($44,000 for couples, $34,000 for singles), the determination of benefits subject to tax is not changed by the new rules.

EXAMPLE: The Gladstones' total income is $50,000:

$15,000	Combined Social Security benefits
24,000	Taxable company pension
6,000	Taxable investment income from stocks
5,000	Income from tax-free municipal bonds
$50,000	Total

They would report $30,000 as adjusted gross income on line 31 of Form 1040 ($24,000 taxable pension plus $6,000 taxable investment income). Their MAGI (Modified Adjusted Gross Income) is $35,000 ($30,000 Adjusted Gross Income plus $5,000 in income from tax-free municipal bonds). They must pay tax on the *lesser* of either 50% of their total Social Security benefits ($7,500), *or* 50% of the difference between their Provisional Income (MAGI of $35,000 plus $7,500, half their Social Security, totaling $42,500), and their base amount of $32,000. Since 50% of the $10,500 difference ($5,250) is less than 50% of the Social Security benefits ($7,500), the $5,450 is the amount subject to tax.

For taxpayers with Provisional Incomes above the upper-tier threshold ($44,000 for couples, $34,000 for singles) the tax will apply to the lesser of 85% of such excess plus $6,000 for couples, or plus $4,500 for singles; or, 85% of total Social Security benefits received ($6,000 for couples and $4,500 for singles being 50% of the difference between the lower- and upper-tier thresholds.)

Assume that the Goldstein's income was the same as in the foregoing example except that the income from tax-free municipals was $11,800 instead of $5,000:

$41,800	MAGI of $24,000 pension, $6,000 stocks and $11,800 municipals
7,500	50% of $15,000 Social Security
$49,300	Total
$ 5,300	Excess of total over $44,000
4,505	85% of this excess
6,000	Statutory amount for couple
10,505	Sum of above 2 lines
12,750	85% of $15,000 Social Security

The taxable amount would be $10,505, the lesser of the last 2 lines.

Internal Revenue Service Worksheet, Notice 703, is part of the benefit statement sent by the Social Security Administration in January. It gives a step-by-step explanation of how to determine if any of your benefits are taxable.

If you complete the worksheet and still have questions, call the IRS toll-free at 1-800-829-1040. At that number, you can also request *Social Security Benefits and Equivalent Railroad Retirement Benefits* (IRS Publication 915), which contains tax information about Social Security.

Retroactive Income and Taxes

If, for some reason, you were not paid some income due you at a given time and it is eventually paid in a lump sum, that amount could put your total income over the base amount (defined above) for the year. In such a case, you can choose to treat the retroactive income as either wholly payable in the year in which you receive it (and pay taxes on it) or count it for the year in which it should have been paid.

For example, suppose you receive a lump-sum payment in 1995 for earned income that should have been paid in 1993 and 1994. This money is enough to put your retirement benefits over the base amount for 1995 and enough to cause you to have to pay taxes on some of your Social Security benefits. By attributing the amounts to the 2 other years in which they should have been paid, you may not have to pay any taxes on your benefits. (You will have to file amended tax returns for those years, though.)

Tax Credit for Elderly or Disabled People

If you are age 65 or over, you are eligible for a credit equal to 15% of the base amount applicable to your filing situation. The base amount is $5,000 if single, or married and filing a joint return with only one spouse eligible; $7,500 if married and filing a joint return with both spouses eligible; or $3,750 if married and filing separate returns.

This credit is also available if you are *under* 65 and retired with a permanent and total disability and have disability income from a public or private employer on account of that disability. In this case, the credit is

limited to the amount of the disability income. See IRS Schedule R (IRC 22).

NOTE: Should you become disabled after starting your retirement benefits but before reaching age 65, notify your Social Security office. By doing so, you may increase the amount of your lifetime benefits.

Workers' Compensation Benefits

For tax purposes, Workers' Compensation benefits are defined as Social Security benefits to the extent that they cause a reduction in Social Security and Railroad Retirement Tier 1 disability benefits. This provision is intended to assure that these social insurance benefits, which are paid *instead* of Social Security payments, are treated similarly for purposes of taxation.

Nonresident Aliens

Under the Internal Revenue Code, nonresident aliens who have income from U.S. investments have 30% of that income withheld at the source for U.S. taxes, including FICA, unless a tax treaty provides otherwise. If and when a nonresident alien qualifies for Social Security benefits, the IRS will withhold 30% from half the benefit for U.S. taxes. See IRS Publication 519.

How Benefits Are Computed

OLD VS. NEW METHODS

Until recently, there were several different methods used to compute primary benefits, depending on the year in which the beneficiary was born. Recent law has streamlined the computation process and eliminated some inequities that were the result of prior changes. Under this new law, those who have become entitled to benefits since 1990 have the benefit they are entitled to receive (their Primary Insurance Amount, or PIA) calculated by one simplified, standard formula.

The easiest way to get an idea of what your benefits will be is to order your Personal Earnings and Benefit Estimate Statement from the SSA. To order your statement, call 1-800-772-1213 and ask to have a copy of the request form sent to you.

If you were born in 1930 or before and if you have a good record of your earnings subject to FICA since

1950, you can also calculate an estimate for yourself. The later you were born after 1930, the more difficult it will be to estimate your benefit as you will have to estimate earnings, FICA contributions, and other factors beyond 1994 needed for the computation. While this calculation is not simple, with the information which follows, plus care and patience, you should be able to determine approximately what your benefits should be and understand how the SSA arrives at the figure it will give you. Doing your own calculation can also help you to understand how such options as early or delayed retirement will affect your benefit.

If you do your own calculation and find that there is a major discrepancy between what you believe your benefits should be and the figure you obtain from the SSA, check each year of your reported earnings. **Be sure that all your covered wages for prior years appear on your statement.** If all your covered wages were not reported, the record can be corrected. (For how to do this, see Chapter 3.) If you still do not agree with the benefit figure you obtain from the SSA, you are entitled to request a review and reconsideration. But you must request the reconsideration within 60 days after the initial decision. (See Chapter 9 for a full description of the appeals process.)

How to Compute Your AIME/PIA

All the 1995 figures in this section were the latest available when we went to press, but both the SSA and other government agencies release new figures throughout the year every year. You may wish to contact your Social Security office to confirm that the government figures you are using are the current ones. They have a sheet they can send you, called *Social Security Update*.

Step 1: Your Primary Insurance Amount (PIA) is computed under a "wage indexing method" applied to earnings over a fixed number of years after 1950, referred to as the "computation years," the number of years of highest earnings on which benefit computation is based. For people born in 1929 and later, the number of computation years will be 35. People born in 1928 will have 34; those born in 1927 have 33; those born in 1926 have 32; and so on. (The applicable number of computation years is determined by subtracting 1951 from the year in which the beneficiary reaches age 62—or dies—and subtracting 5 from this number. For example, if the beneficiary became 62 in 1989, the number of computation years is 33 (1989 − 1951 − 5 = 33).

Step 2: When you turn to the worksheet at the end of this chapter, you will see that the italic figures in Columns B, C, E, and F provide an example to show how the worksheet would be completed by someone who reached 62 in 1989.

Column A lists the maximum earnings taxed for each year from 1951 to the latest available figure. In Column B, list **your** earnings for each of these years. If your earnings exceeded the maximum taxed figure in any year, enter only the maximum taxed figure. If your earnings were less than the maximum taxed figure, enter the actual figure.

Step 3: On the left-hand side of Column C, enter the National Average Earnings (NAE) figure from Column D of the Worksheet for the year you reach 60. For our example of the person who reached 62 in 1989, note that we have entered the National Average Earnings figure of $18,426 for the length of Column C through 1987.

Step 4: Divide the figure you have entered in Column C by the National Average Earnings figure for each year from Column D. Enter your result on the blank side of Column E. (Your quotients are likely to differ from our example.)

Step 5: In Step 1, you determined your number of computation years. In our example of a person who became 62 in 1989, this number is 33. This person's benefit will be based on the 33 years of highest earnings from 1951 to the year of retirement.

For your computation of your benefit, multiply the earnings figures in Column B by the quotient opposite it in Column E for each year from 1951 until the year in which you reach(ed) age 62. The results are your indexed earnings. Enter these figures in Column F. (In the example, for 1959: $4,800 × 4.8 = $23,040; and so on.) For years in which you reach(ed) the ages 63 and 64, enter actual or estimated actual figures, again up to the maximums in Column A.

Step 6: Check off the highest indexed earnings in Column F for the number of computation years determined in Step 1 and find the sum of these figures. In our example (right side of Column F) there are figures for 41 years. We have eliminated the indexed earnings figures for the 8 lowest years (the crossed-out numbers), leaving the 33 highest earnings years. The sum of these is $1,075,840.)

Step 7: Convert your number of computation years to number of months (35 years = 420 months. Or in the case of our example, 33 years = 396 months).

Step 8: Divide the sum of your indexed earnings (Step 6) by the number of computation months (Step 7). The result is your Average Indexed Monthly Earnings (AIME). (Our example: $1,075,840 ÷ 396 = $2,716.)

Step 9: Now, following the Dollar Bend Points table at the end of this chapter, multiply your AIME figure by the percentages applicable to the year you reach(ed) 62. Add the results to determine your Primary Insurance Amount (PIA). In our example we apply the bend points for 1989 to our AIME of $2,716 (SSA rounds each step down to the dime).

first $339 × 90% = $305.10
next 1,705 × 32% = 545.60
($2,044 − 339 = $1,705)
last 672 × 15% = 100.80
($2,716 − 2,044 = $672)
total $951.50

The PIA in this example is $951. (The SSA rounds the total down to the dollar.)

Step 10: Your monthly retirement benefit is determined by applying Cost-of-Living Allowances (COLA's) to your PIA. You are entitled to COLA's beginning with your first year of eligibility (the year you become 62 or disabled or die—this last for determination of survivors' benefits). A table of COLA's appears at the end of this chapter. To determine the monthly retirement benefit at age 65 in our example of a person who became 62 in 1989 and for whom we determined above that the PIA is $951, application of COLA's works as follows:

APPLICATION OF COLA'S

Age	Year	PIA Adjusted		COLA %	COLA $	Adjusted Benefit
62	1989	$ 951	×	4.0	$38	$ 989
63	1990	989	×	4.7	46	1,035
64	1991	1,035	×	5.4	55	1,090

Using this estimating procedure, $1,090 is our estimated monthly benefit for our example of a person who became 65 in 1992. (This compares with the SSA actual figure of $1,088. The $2 difference may be attributed to rounding of decimals or other minor adjustments.) It is our estimate of the amount our beneficiary would have received monthly in 1992, had he elected to start doing so the month after reaching 65. The 1992 COLA of 3.7% would have been applied to this figure as of the first of the new year and the estimated monthly benefit payments in 1993 would then have increased to $1,130.

Estimating the Effect of Delayed Retirement

Credit for delayed retirement was explained earlier in this chapter. If, in the case of our example who became 65 in 1992, payment of benefit had been delayed until the month after the 66th birthday, the $1,130 benefit determined above would have been in-

creased by the 3.0% 1993 COLA to $1,163 and by an additional 4% or $46 for one year of delayed retirement to $1,170. In fact, if earnings subject to FICA in this worker's 66th year were high enough to replace the indexed earnings for one of the earlier computation years, there would be an additional upward adjustment, as well as the application of the COLA, in the following year. Should he continue to work to age 70 with higher earnings subject to FICA taxes than those of earlier computation years, he would have the benefit of 4 additional years of growth compounded by 4% per year plus the continuing advantage of replacing lower indexed earnings years in determination of PIA, plus COLA's. For many in this situation, it is clear that waiting to take benefits would be advantageous.

With some Social Security benefits now subject to federal income tax, a growing awareness that Social Security benefits alone will not meet retirement income needs for most people, and more people living longer, many who are able to do so will elect to continue working, paying more into the system, and delay drawing benefits.

SOME OTHER FACTORS AFFECTING YOUR BENEFIT

Spouse's Benefit

If your spouse is drawing a benefit based on your work record rather than his or her own, the benefit for him or her at normal retirement age is 50% of your benefit. If your spouse starts to receive benefits before 65, the rate is permanently reduced, just as yours is for early retirement, but the rate of reduction is greater (.555% per month before 65 for a worker, .694% per month before 65 for the worker's spouse).

Your spouse's benefit is added to whatever benefit you are receiving and is usually paid in a single check. If you prefer, you may request separate checks.

Maximum Family Benefit (MFB)

The Social Security Administration places a limit on the amount of benefit it will pay for any given earnings range to a retired worker and his or her dependents, or to the survivors of a covered worker entitled to retirement benefits. The MFB also applies for benefits paid on the work record of a disabled worker.

If the total benefits due the worker and all the worker's dependents exceed the amount of the MFB, the worker's benefit is paid in full but the other benefits paid on that work record are reduced proportionately to the MFB.

Family members' benefits are calculated as a percentage of the worker's Primary Insurance Amount (not necessarily the benefit). Maximum Family Benefit amounts are derived by a sliding percentage of the PIA. The formulas for these calculations appear in table form at the end of this chapter.

Because the Maximum Family Benefit is determined in each case by the amount of the individual worker's PIA, age, and date of retirement, MFB amounts will vary from family to family. Generally, they are equal to 150% to 180% of the PIA. The MFB for your family will appear on page 4 of your Personal Earnings and Benefit Estimate Statement.

NOTE: The benefits paid to divorced spouses, or divorced widowed spouses, are not counted as part of the family benefit and so they are not reduced to meet the MFB on that worker's record.

Benefit Amounts

To illustrate the range of benefit amounts, a covered worker who was always a low earner (45% of average national earnings) and who claimed benefits at age 65 in 1995 receives a monthly retirement benefit of $520 ($416 at age 62). The average retirement benefit paid out in 1994 was $643. The maximum monthly benefit for a high earner (all earnings at or above the maximum subject to FICA) who becomes 65 in 1995, and waits to collect until then, is $1,199.

Your Social Security Check

Social Security checks are issued by the Treasury Department of the United States. A lightweight, multicolored paper check features a picture of the Statue of Liberty, and has been designed to be easy for financial institutions to process and difficult to alter or counterfeit.

The Social Security Administration requires about 2 months to process your application and issue your first check, so bear this in mind when you plan to begin receiving your benefits and apply about 3 months in advance. Checks are generally mailed out so they will be received by the third day of the month for the preceding month's benefit. Checks to U.S. residents in foreign countries are mailed from the U.S. Treasury, or from overseas U.S. diplomatic or consular offices.

You should be aware of the following rules and procedures concerning payment of your benefit(s).

Separate Checks

A husband and wife who are living together usually receive a single check made out to both of them. Separate checks will be sent only if requested. Benefits for a minor child are combined into the one check unless the child lives in a different household. If so, separate checks are issued to each family group.

Overpayments/Mispayments

Overpayments will be withheld from the next check or checks. Payments sent to any person not entitled to

them should be returned to the Regional Disbursement Center, U.S. Treasury Department, or to your local Social Security office. If such a check is cashed, the money must be returned. Beware of anyone coming to your door trying to collect cash for "Social Security overpayments." That isn't the way it's done.

Seizure

Social Security checks cannot be assigned for payment to someone else and are not subject to levy, garnishment, or attachment—except to collect federal taxes or by court order for child support or alimony.

Delivery to a Representative

If you fill out a special form at your Social Security office, your checks, made out in your name, will be mailed to anyone you designate. You still have to endorse and cash or deposit them. Social Security will not make your checks payable to anyone else unless you are unable to handle your own financial affairs. In that case, a "representative payee" is designated and required to report regularly to the SSA on how your money is being spent. New regulations were passed in 1990 to improve protection for beneficiaries with representative payees.

All the foregoing policies also apply to direct deposit (wire transfer) of benefits.

ANNUAL EARNINGS TAXED FOR SOCIAL SECURITY AND MEDICARE

Years	Maximum Annual Earnings Taxed	% Rate for Employee & Employer	Annual Maximum Tax Paid by Employee Self-employed†	Rate for Self-employed	Annual Maximum Tax Paid by Self-employed	% of Workers Paying Maximum Tax	% of Covered Earnings Taxable†
1993	$57,600*	7.65%	$5,528.70**	15.30%	$11,057.40**		
1992	55,500*	7.65	5,328.90**	15.30	10,658.80**		
1991	53,400*	7.65	5,123.30**	15.30	10,246.60**		
1990	51,300	7.65	3,924.45	15.30	7,848.90		
1989	48,000	7.51	3,604.80	13.02	6,249.60	6%	87%
1988	45,000	7.51	3,379.50	13.02	5,859.00		
1987	43,800	7.15	3,131.70	12.30	5,387.40		
1986	42,000	7.15	3,003.00	12.30	5,166.00		
1985	39,600	7.05	2,791.80	11.80	4,672.80	6	89
1980	25,900	6.13	1,587.67	8.10	2,097.90		
1975	14,100	5.85	824.85	7.90	1,113.90	15	84
1970	7,800	4.80	374.40	6.90	538.20		
1965	4,800	3.625	174.00	5.40	259.20	36	71
1960	4,800	3.00	144.00	4.50	216.00		
1955	4,200	2.00	84.00	3.00	126.00	26	80
1950	3,000	1.50	45.00	***			
1937–1949	3,000	1.00	30.00	***		3–14	92–88

† +1.45% for wages up to $125,000 in 1991; $130,200 in 1992; $135,000 in 1993.

* Figure includes above.

** Self-employed not covered by Social Security until 1951.

*** Figures from U.S. Department of Health and Human Services, Office of Research & Statistics, 1990 Report.

† 1994 and 1995 figures not included, as there is no cap on wages taxed for Medicare.

COST-OF-LIVING ADJUSTMENTS

Year	COLA
1975	8.0%
1976	6.4
1977	5.9
1978	6.5
1979	9.9
1980	14.3
1981	11.2
1982	7.4
1983	postponed
1984	3.5
1985	3.5
1986	3.1
1987	1.3
1988	4.2
1989	4.0
1990	4.7
1991	5.4
1992	3.7
1993	3.0
1994	2.6
1995	2.6

Each year's COLA is based on either the increase in the Consumer Price Index or the increase in average wages, whichever is lower. Payments are included in the December checks received in January of each year.

DOLLAR BEND POINTS

Year	A	B
1979	$180	$1,085
1980	194	1,171
1981	211	1,274
1982	230	1,388
1983	254	1,528
1984	267	1,612
1985	280	1,691
1986	297	1,790
1987	310	1,866
1988	319	1,922
1989	339	2,044
1990	356	2,145
1991	370	2,230
1992	387	2,333
1993	401	2,420
1994	422	2,545
1995	426	2,567

Percentages applicable to dollar bend points:
90% of amount in Column A
32% of excess up to amount in Column B
15% of excess over amount in B

MONTHLY AND YEARLY PERCENTAGES FOR DELAYED RETIREMENT CREDITS BY AGE

Attain Age 65	Monthly Percentage	Yearly Percentage
Before 1982	$1/12$ of 1%	1.0%
1982–1989	$1/4$ of 1	3.0
1990–1991	$7/24$ of 1	3.5
1992–1993	$1/3$ of 1	4.0
1994–1995	$3/8$ of 1	4.5
1996–1997	$5/12$ of 1	5.0
1998–1999	$11/24$ of 1	5.5
2000–2001	$1/2$ of 1	6.0
2002–2003	$13/24$ of 1	6.5
2004–2005	$7/12$ of 1	7.0
2006–2007	$5/8$ of 1	7.5
2008 or after	$2/3$ of 1	8.0

FAMILY MAXIMUM FORMULAS

If the PIA is:	The Family Maximum will be:
1995 Eligibility Year	
Up through $544	150% of PIA
$544.01 to $785	$816.00 plus 272% of excess over $544
$785.01 to $1,024	$1,471.52 plus 134% of excess over $785
$1,024.01 or higher	$1,791.78 plus 175% of excess over $1,024
1994 Eligibility Year	
Up through $539	150% of PIA
$539.01 to $779	$808.50 plus 272% of the excess PIA over $539
$779.01 to $1,016	$1,461.30 plus 134% of the excess PIA over $779
$1,016.01 or higher	$1,778.89 plus 175% of the excess PIA over $1,016
1993 Eligibility Year	
Up through $513	150% of PIA
$513.01 to $740	$769.50 plus 272% of the excess PIA over $513
$740.01 to $966	$1,386.94 plus 134% of the excess PIA over $740
$966.01 or higher	$1,689.78 plus 175% of the excess PIA over $966
1992 Eligibility Year	
Up through $495	150% of PIA
$495.01 to $714	$742.50 plus 272% of the excess PIA over $495
$714,01 to $931	$1,338.18 plus 134% of the excess PIA over $714
$931.01 or higher	$1,628.96 plus 175% of the excess PIA over $931
1991 Eligibility Year	
Up through $473	150% of PIA
$473.01 to $682	$709.50 plus 272% of the excess PIA over $473
$682.01 to $890	$1,277.98 plus 134% of the excess PIA over $682
$890.01 or higher	$1,556.70 plus 175% of the excess PIA over $890

*COLA's are then added for the eligibility year and the years thereafter.
For disability benefits, the family maximum is limited to the lesser of (a) 85% of
the AIME or 100% of the PIA if larger or (b) 150% of the PIA. If benefit payments
are reduced because of the family maximum, the worker's benefit is not reduced.
The PIA is subtracted from the applicable family maximum and what is left is
divided equally among the other beneficiaries, except in the case of a divorced
spouse, whose benefits are paid outside the family maximum.*

WORKSHEET

Year of Work	A Maximum Earnings Taxed	B Earnings Yearly		C NAE Factor		D National Average Earnings	E Indexing Quotient		F Indexed Earnings	
		Yours	Example	Y	E		Y	E	Y	E
1951	$ 3,600	_____	$ 3,600	_____	$18,426	$ 2,799	_____	6.6	_____	$ 23,760
1952	3,600	_____	3,600	_____	18,426	2,973	_____	6.2	_____	23,320
1953	3,600	_____	3,600	_____	18,426	3,139	_____	5.9	_____	21,240
1954	3,600	_____	3,600	_____	18,426	3,155	_____	5.8	_____	20,880
1955	4,200	_____	4,200	_____	18,426	3,301	_____	5.6	_____	23,520
1956	4,200	_____	4,200	_____	18,426	3,532	_____	5.2	_____	21,840
1957	4,200	_____	4,200	_____	18,426	3,641	_____	5.1	_____	21,420
1958	4,200	_____	4,200	_____	18,426	3,673	_____	5.0	_____	21,000
1959	4,800	_____	4,800	_____	18,426	3,855	_____	4.8	_____	23,040
1960	4,800	_____	4,800	_____	18,426	4,007	_____	4.6	_____	22,080
1961	4,800	_____	4,800	_____	18,426	4,086	_____	4.5	_____	21,600
1962	4,800	_____	4,800	_____	18,426	4,291	_____	4.3	_____	20,640
1963	4,800	_____	4,800	_____	18,426	4,396	_____	4.2	_____	20,160
1964	4,800	_____	4,800	_____	18,426	4,576	_____	4.0	_____	19,200
1965	4,800	_____	4,800	_____	18,426	4,658	_____	4.0	_____	19,200
1966	6,600	_____	6,600	_____	18,426	4,938	_____	3.7	_____	24,420
1967	6,600	_____	6,600	_____	18,426	5,213	_____	3.5	_____	23,100
1968	7,800	_____	7,800	_____	18,426	5,571	_____	3.3	_____	25,740
1969	7,800	_____	7,800	_____	18,426	5,893	_____	3.1	_____	24,180
1970	7,800	_____	7,800	_____	18,426	6,186	_____	3.0	_____	23,400
1971	7,800	_____	7,800	_____	18,426	6,497	_____	2.8	_____	21,840
1972	9,000	_____	9,000	_____	18,426	7,133	_____	2.6	_____	23,400
1973	10,800	_____	10,800	_____	18,426	7,580	_____	2.4	_____	25,920
1974	13,200	_____	13,200	_____	18,426	8,030	_____	2.3	_____	30,360
1975	14,100	_____	14,100	_____	18,426	8,630	_____	2.1	_____	29,610
1976	15,300	_____	15,300	_____	18,426	9,226	_____	2.0	_____	30,600
1977	16,500	_____	16,500	_____	18,426	9,779	_____	1.9	_____	31,350
1978	17,700	_____	17,700	_____	18,426	10,556	_____	1.8	_____	31,860
1979	22,900	_____	22,900	_____	18,426	11,479	_____	1.6	_____	36,640
1980	25,900	_____	25,900	_____	18,426	12,513	_____	1.5	_____	38,850
1981	29,700	_____	29,700	_____	18,426	13,773	_____	1.3	_____	38,610
1982	32,400	_____	32,400	_____	18,426	14,531	_____	1.3	_____	42,120
1983	35,700	_____	35,700	_____	18,426	15,239	_____	1.2	_____	42,840
1984	37,800	_____	37,800	_____	18,426	16,135	_____	1.1	_____	41,580
1985	39,600	_____	39,600	_____	18,426	16,832	_____	1.1	_____	43,560
1986	42,000	_____	42,000	_____	18,426	17,321	_____	1.1	_____	46,200
1987	43,800	_____	43,800	_____	18,426	18,426	_____	1.0	_____	43,800
1988	45,000	_____	45,000	_____	_____	19,334	_____	_____	_____	45,000
1989	48,000	_____	48,000	_____	_____	20,099	_____	_____	_____	48,000
1990	51,300	_____	51,300	_____	_____	21,027	_____	_____	_____	51,300
1991	53,400*	_____	53,400	_____	_____	21,811	_____	_____	_____	53,400
1992	55,500*	_____	55,500	_____	_____	22,935	_____	_____	_____	_____
1993	57,600*	_____	57,600	_____	_____	23,132	_____	_____	_____	_____
1994	60,600*	_____	60,600	_____	_____	N.A.	_____	_____	_____	_____
1995	61,200*	_____	61,200	_____	_____	N.A.	_____	_____	_____	_____
	TOTAL								_____	$1,075,840

Maximum earnings taxed 1937–1950, $3,000 per year.

* The higher maximum earnings taxed figure for Medicare for these years is not used for PIA calculations.

** Lower earning years crossed out.

5

The Disability Program

What Disability Insurance Is and Whom It Covers

In 1956, Congress expanded the Social Security Act to include a disability program offering insurance to workers who become seriously ill or have a disabling accident and are unable thereby to work for an extended period of time.

In order to receive Disability Insurance (DI) payments, a worker (or that worker's dependent or dependents) must meet the program's qualifications for both eligibility and disability.

In this chapter we will discuss these qualifications, how the disability benefits are computed, situations that affect the amount of the benefit, and how to apply.

Defining Disability

The SSA defines a disabling condition as one in which the worker is so severely impaired, physically or mentally, that he or she is not able to perform substantial gainful activity or work. The impairment must be expected to last at least 12 months—or to result in death—and the determination must be based on medical evidence.

These determinations are made on a case-by-case basis, taking into consideration the particular facts of each situation. The opinion of the attending physician (or physicians) is an important factor, but clinical and laboratory findings and other evidence of the severity and probable duration of the disability are also taken into account.

Initial disability determinations are usually made in your state by a government agency known as the Disability Determination Service (DDS), but the Social Security Administration makes the final decision regarding eligibility.

There is a 5-step evaluation process which applies to all applicants for disability benefits. This evaluation asks:

• Is the claimant doing "substantial" work? (The SSA defines "substantial gainful activity" as the performance of significant mental or physical activities—or both—that are productive in nature. Work need not be full-time to be "substantial"; payment for part-time

work, when it is greater than the monthly exempt earnings amount for Social Security retirement beneficiaries, is considered substantial. Earning $500 or more monthly is considered substantial. A "gainful" activity is something that is usually done in exchange for payment or wages, though it is not necessary that there be a profit or a wage in order for the activity to be considered gainful.)

• Does the claimant have a severe impairment?

• Does the impairment(s) meet or equal the level of severity described in a published "Listing of Impairments" maintained by Social Security?

• Is the claimant able to do past relevant work?

• Is the claimant able to do any other work?

WHO IS ELIGIBLE FOR DISABILITY BENEFITS

You do not have to be 65, or even 62, to collect disability benefits; a covered worker who is disabled at any age is eligible, and a disabled widowed spouse is also eligible to collect these benefits on a covered worker's work record after the spouse reaches age 50.

Young people who become disabled before age 22 can begin collecting disability benefits at age 18, but for a child of any age to collect DI, the claim must be made on either the child's own work record or the work record of a retired, disabled, or deceased covered worker.

Covered Workers

You need a certain number of Social Security credits or QC's (as discussed in Chapter 2) to qualify for disability benefits, and some of these quarters must have been earned in recent years. The number of quarters depends on the age at which you, as a worker, become disabled, and the SSA has defined 3 age-group categories.

Under 24: If you are under 24 at the time you become disabled, you need credit for 1½ years of work

(6 quarters) out of the 3-year period preceding the date of your disablement.

Between 24 and 31: If your disability starts between the ages of 24 and 31, you need credit for having worked half of the time between age 21 and the time you become disabled. For example, to qualify at age 29, you would need credits for 4 out of 8 years, or 16 QC's.

Age 31 and Older: In this age group, you need the number of work credits shown in the next chart. Also, you must have earned at least 20 of the credits in the 10 years immediately before you become disabled.

Born after 1929, disabled at age	Born before 1930, disabled before age 62	Quarters of credit (& years) needed
42 or younger		20 (5 years)
44		22 (5½)
46		24 (6 years)
48		26 (6½)
50		28 (7 years)
52	1981	30 (7½)
53	1982	31 (7¾)
54	1983	32 (8 years)
55	1984	33 (8¼)
56	1985	34 (8½)
58	1987	36 (9 years)
60	1989	38 (9½)
62 or older	1991 or later	40 (10 years)

If you are blind, credit may have been earned at any time; you need no recent credit.

Widows and Widowers

A disabled widowed spouse, age 50 to 59, of a qualified worker is eligible for disability benefits on the basis of the deceased worker's earnings record. This spouse's benefit is 71.5% of the worker's Primary Insurance Amount, and the benefit will not stop because of remarriage. However, a widow or widower must become disabled within 7 years of the death of the worker to be eligible.

Over age 60, disabled widowed spouses are entitled to the same benefits as widowed spouses.

NOTE: The same rules that define disability for a worker are now applied to widows and widowers. This is a change: in the past, widows' claims were evaluated solely on a medical basis; no consideration was given to vocational factors. Now, the same 5-step evaluation process outlined earlier in this chapter applies to all applicants for disability benefits. With so many women in the work force today, it is appropriate that their work profile (age, education, and work history) be considered when they apply for disabled-widow benefits.

If you have been denied benefits as a disabled widowed spouse in the past because of the earlier, more stringent rules, you may wish to find out if you now qualify for benefits.

Divorced disabled surviving spouses may qualify for disability benefits on the work record of their former marriage partners. A divorced disabled spouse (like a divorced widowed spouse caring for a qualified minor or disabled child of the worker) is not subject to the rule which says the marriage to the worker on whose record the claim is made must have lasted for at least 10 years.

Disabled Children

If a child of a retired, disabled, or deceased covered worker is, or becomes, severely handicapped—physically or mentally—at any age prior to age 22, payments may start at any age provided the disability continues up to the date of the application for the benefit. They may continue until the marriage or death of the child or the end of the disability. (This provision should not be confused with the benefit payable to a dependent, unmarried **nondisabled** child. Those benefits terminate at age 18, or at 19 if a full-time student. They would also end if the covered worker under whose record the benefit is being paid becomes unentitled to receive payments.)

There is no age limit on filing an application for benefits as long as the disability began before age 22. The definition of disability for children has recently been changed. Children were once evaluated basically by the same rules as adults, including even vocational factors. Under the new guidelines, a child's ability to function in everyday activities (communicating, walking, dressing) is compared to similar abilities in other children of the same age.

Still covered are cerebral palsy, epilepsy, narcolepsy, catalepsy, and schizophrenic disorders. Newly covered are alcohol and drug addiction, hyperactivity, autism, anorexia, anxiety, mental and personality disorders, and tic disorders such as Tourette's syndrome.

Further, if a child's disability does not meet the exact provisions, the child will be given an individual functional assessment.

The evidence required to prove disability must

firmly establish that the child has a severe disability, that the disability began before age 22 and still continues, and that it is expected to last, or has lasted, at least 12 months—or that it is expected to result in death.

NOTE: If you have a child who has been receiving **dependent's** benefits which will stop at age 18 or 19, and who at that time may be eligible for DI, contact your Social Security office 6 months before the child's 18th (or 19th) birthday to replace his or her benefits as a dependent with disability benefits.

Benefit payments for a disabled **adult** child can be made only when a covered parent retires, becomes disabled, or dies.

Special Rules for Specific Disabilities

Blindness: There are special provisions for blind persons applying for disability benefits. A blind person could receive benefits under either the Social Security Disability program or under the Supplemental Security Income (SSI) program or both. Also, while the medical criteria are the same for both programs, the nonmedical criteria are not.

Social Security defines "blindness" as vision no better than 20/200 with corrective lenses, or a limited visual field of 20 degrees or less. If, under this definition, you are blind, you do not have to meet the requirement for recent work.

What you do need is credit for 2½ years of work earned at any time before the application for disability benefits is made. This compares with credit for 5 years of work in the 10 years preceding application for other disabled workers. Even if you do not meet this definition, you may still qualify if your disability prevents you from doing substantial work which, in 1994, means earnings of $850 or more per month for blind disabled workers. Benefits will be withheld for any month in which you earn this amount or more. This compares with $500 per month for other disabled workers. If you qualify for SSI benefits, you are not subject to this provision.

NOTE: If you do continue to work and earn more than the maximum amount allowed—but significantly less than you did before becoming legally blind—you should still apply for disability benefits. Even though you won't receive the benefits, your application allows the SSA to put a "disability freeze" on your earnings record. This means that these years of lower earnings will not be used to determine your average earnings for your Primary Insurance Amount and will not lower your primary benefit.

The legally blind are eligible for Medicare beginning at age 55.

To help keep blind persons informed about Social Security programs, the agency and the Library of Congress have produced a braille publication and a 3-hour audio-cassette entitled *Social Security Programs and Benefits.* The audio-cassettes are available through 160 libraries in the Library of Congress network. The braille publication is available only through braille lending libraries affiliated with the Library of Congress.

(AIDS) Acquired Immune Deficiency Syndrome: Anyone with a documented diagnosis of AIDS who is unable to work because of physical or mental impairment caused by the virus, and who meets the requirements of Social Security coverage described above, will qualify for Disability Insurance benefits.

In January 1992, a new definition of AIDS—and an expanded list of the AIDS-related, life-threatening diseases by which it manifests itself—became effective. This new definition and list from the federal Centers for Disease Control are used by a number of public and private agencies to determine who qualifies for various benefits, such as subsidized housing, nutrition allowances, and disability payments.

The new definition includes any person infected with HIV (Human Immunodeficiency Virus) who has a count of 200 or fewer CD-4, or T-cells, per cubic centimeter of blood. A healthy person has a blood count of about 1,000 T-cells per cubic centimeter.

If you qualify for disability benefits because of HIV, the waiting period for payments to begin is 5 months from the onset of the disability. However, there is no waiting period for Supplemental Security Income (see the next chapter), for which you may also qualify. And if you qualify for Medicaid, you can collect those benefits as well as DI to help cover the cost of treatment.

These programs can provide a lifeline of support to those with HIV infection. The SSA provides confidential interviews for people in this situation; there is also a booklet, *A Guide to Social Security and SSI Disability Benefits for People with HIV Infection,* available free from the SSA.

Kidney Disease: In addition to DI, which you qualify for regardless of age if you have kidney disease, you are eligible for Medicare Parts A and B. If you need maintenance dialysis or kidney transplant surgery because of permanent kidney failure, you are eligible for these Medicare benefits provided you are presently receiving Social Security benefits, have worked long enough to be covered, or you are the spouse or dependent child of someone insured for, or already receiving Social Security benefits.

You do not have to be unable to work to qualify for Medicare, but you do need to have permanent kidney failure and require dialysis or a kidney transplant. Medicare also covers the costs of care of a donor.

Drug Addiction and Alcoholism: People whose disability stems from substance abuse must meet the same medical and nonmedical requirements as anyone else applying for disability benefits. In these cases, the SSA appoints a representative payee (for either DI or SSI payments) to assure that the benefits will be used for necessities rather than to perpetuate the substance abuse. The beneficiary must agree to undergo treatment and compliance is monitored; if the treatment program is not followed, payments are suspended. After 12 months of suspension, the benefits are terminated. There is a new 36 month limit on DI and SSI benefits to substance abusers, with the benefit period for disability insurance payments beginning the first month treatment is available. The 36 month limit does not affect people whose disability is independent of their substance abuse—for example, a qualified blind person who is also an alcoholic would continue to receive benefits.

Computing Disability Benefits

BASIS OF COMPUTATION

Disability benefits are generally based on your AIME (Average Indexed Monthly Earnings), as explained in Chapter 4.

If you are age 65 or over when you become disabled, you will receive the full retirement benefits to which you are entitled instead of disability benefits. But if you are under 65, your benefits may be reduced by Workers' Compensation or by any other disability payments you get from federal, state, or local programs.

A disabled widowed spouse over 60 receives the same survivors' benefit as a widowed spouse (based on 100% of the worker's primary benefit).

A disabled widowed spouse aged 60 to 64 claiming a benefit will have her (or his) payment reduced by .475% for each month before age 65. A disabled widowed spouse between ages 50 and 60 has her (or his) benefit reduced to 71.5% of the deceased worker's PIA. (A disabled widowed spouse under 50 is too young for a widow's benefit—unless she or he is caring for a qualified minor child—but could still be eligible for her or his own disability benefit.) The same benefits apply to divorced widowed spouses, provided they were married to the worker for at least 10 years.

If you become disabled, your dependent family members are eligible for benefits of the same percentage of your PIA that they would be entitled to when you retire. The same rules apply (see Chapter 2). The maximum family benefit, however, is lower for DI than it is for retirement and survivors' benefits. As a general rule, the maximum for DI is 150% of the worker's PIA, but it can be as low as 100%.

The earnings limitation ($500 per month for 1994) also applies to each of the family members receiving earnings on your work record.

ELIGIBILITY FOR OTHER PAYMENTS

If you are a Social Security disability beneficiary, you should know that benefits from some other sources may affect your disability check. To newly entitled disability beneficiaries, it often comes as a surprise that they won't be receiving full Social Security disability benefits.

Another Social Security Check: Disability benefits are not payable if you receive other Social Security benefits. If you are entitled to more than one monthly benefit, the amount you receive usually will be equal to the larger of the 2 amounts.

If a spouse has been receiving a retirement or disability payment which is larger than the spouse's benefit rate, he or she will receive only 1—the retirement *or* the disability benefit.

A reduction method for disability was instituted to avoid windfall benefits to some workers. Before the reduction became effective, some Social Security beneficiaries received more in combined public disability payments than they had been earning when they were working.

NOTE: If you apply for or receive workers' compensation and/or public disability benefits in addition to Social Security benefits, you must report that information to the SSA. Also report if your public disability payments change or stop.

Other Disability Checks: If you are a disabled

worker under 65 and also receive disability payments from federal, state, or local government programs (for example, Workers' Compensation), combined payments to you and your family are limited. Payments cannot exceed 80% of your average current earnings before you became disabled. And **all** earnings covered by Social Security, including amounts above the maximum taxable by Social Security, may be considered when figuring average earnings.

WORKING WHILE COLLECTING BENEFITS

The SSA has a work incentive program which recognizes that returning to work may be a gradual and difficult process, and the program offers various kinds of help to people so they can once again become self-supporting.

Every applicant for Social Security disability benefits is considered for referral to a state rehabilitation agency. A person is referred if it appears that he or she is likely to benefit from such services. Factors such as age, education, work experience, and medical diagnosis are taken into consideration, but personal motivation—the desire to work—is often a key to success. A federal-state task force is developing recommendations to improve the selection and referral process to better identify individuals with the greatest rehabilitation and employment potential and to seek ways to encourage more beneficiaries to enter or return to the work force.

More than 200,000 beneficiaries are referred to state vocational rehabilitation agencies for services each year. Regulations currently being proposed will expand the use of private and other public vocational rehabilitation providers to make available more rehabilitation opportunities for Social Security beneficiaries to receive the help they need to go to work.

Further, the SSA is working to increase public awareness of the availability of rehabilitation services. Improvements in medical technology, new legal protection for people with disabilities in the workplace, and a growing need for skilled labor have helped expand job opportunities.

If this program is of interest to you, you can obtain additional information from your local Social Security office's work incentives expert.

Listed below are some of the rules that apply if you want to earn money and still be eligible for Disability Insurance benefits, Supplemental Security Income (SSI) benefits, and Medicaid or Medicare.

Trial Work Period: If you are disabled, you can work for any 9 months (not necessarily consecutive months) during a 5-year period as a trial work period, and your earnings from that work will not affect your benefit during that time.

Extended Period of Eligibility: For 3 years after a successful trial work period, you may receive your disability check for any month during which your earnings are not at the substantial gainful activity level (in 1994, $500 a month for the disabled, $850 a month for the blind).

Continuation of Medicare: If disability payments stop because you are earning above the limit—even though you are still disabled—Medicare can continue its coverage for up to 39 months after the trial work period.

Impairment-Related Work Expenses: Certain expenses for things you may need because of your impairment in order to work may be deducted when counting earnings to determine the above limit.

Recovery During Vocational Rehabilitation: If you recover while participating in a vocational rehabilitation program and are likely to become self-supporting, your benefits may continue until the program ends.

Special Rules for the Blind: In addition to a higher limit on earnings, other special rules apply for the blind. Ask at the Social Security office for details.

CONTINUING DISABILITY REVIEWS (CDR'S)

The Social Security Administration is required by law to periodically review the status of Social Security disability beneficiaries to determine if they continue to be disabled. The time between reviews depends on the beneficiary's age and the nature and/or severity of the medical condition on which the benefits are based, including the chances of medical improvement.

Based on these factors, disability beneficiaries are placed in 1 of 3 medical reexamination categories. They establish when the review should take place. The categories are:

• Medical improvement expected—beneficiary's status generally scheduled for review within 6–18 months of the most recent medical decision.

• Medical improvement possible—beneficiary's status scheduled for review every 3 years.

• Medical improvement not expected—beneficiary's status scheduled for review every 7 years.

No matter which category a person is placed in, the SSA historically has required that the CDR include a full medical review. This procedure involves a labor-intensive process that includes an in-depth field office interview, evaluation of the medical evidence of record by a state Disability Determination Service (DDS) examiner, and a possible consultative medical exam to obtain any additional information needed to assess the possibility of medical improvement of the beneficiary's present condition.

A full medical CDR process requires an in-person appearance by the beneficiary. It places a considerable burden on both the disabled beneficiary and the SSA in order to determine the beneficiary's continuing eligibility.

The number of people applying for disability benefits has grown rapidly over the last few years, and the resources needed to conduct CDR's have been diverted to handle the increased initial claims workloads. In late 1993, more than 1 million beneficiaries were awaiting CDR's and approximately 400,000 additional Social Security disability beneficiaries were due to have a review each year.

To cope with all this, the SSA's Office of Disability has developed and tested an alternative mailer process: a questionnaire covering key information about a beneficiary's medical condition and his or her attempts, if any, to return to work.

The new CDR mailer process will enable Social Security to identify beneficiaries whose disabilities have not improved in a more efficient, compassionate, and cost-effective manner. If a review of the questionnaire and other information in SSA records offers no indication of medical improvement, the beneficiary will be spared the need for an extensive review of his or her case.

The CDR mailer consists of 7 questions for the beneficiary to answer and a letter explaining the process.

(The SSA staff in local offices are prepared to assist people with the mailer if help is needed.) The beneficiary mails the completed questionnaire to the SSA's disability processing center in Baltimore for technical review.

Based on the information the beneficiary supplies, 1 of 2 actions will occur: the full medical CDR under the current process will be conducted at this time; or the beneficiary's file will be moved into a category to be checked again in the future.

When your case comes up for CDR, you must be notified and informed that you have the right to submit medical or other evidence for consideration. If the SSA decides that your disability benefits should be terminated, it must give you a written notice that explains your right to appeal.

APPEALS OF DECISIONS

More than 250 million people will file for Social Security, Supplemental Security Income (SSI), or disability benefits this year. That means the SSA will be making 250 million decisions about people's eligibility for benefits, and a good many of those decisions will be to deny benefits.

If you are already receiving disability benefits, they could be reduced or eliminated after review. If you receive a decision you disagree with, what can you do?

The answer is to file an appeal. Every decision Social Security makes is subject to review, and the government provides for a series of appeals to make sure you have every opportunity to present your case. See Chapter 9 for a discussion of disability appeals.

Your Application for Disability Benefits

Determining eligibility for DI benefits requires all the same information necessary for an application for retirement benefits (detailed in Chapter 3), plus a great deal more, and the wait can be a very lengthy one. You can help expedite the process if you have the following information available when you file:

Social Security Number

• For you, your spouse, and any dependents applying for benefits. You also will need proof of age.

• Any number(s) on which you or your dependents receive (or received) Social Security checks.

Impairment Information

• What it is and when it started.

• How it keeps you from working.

• How it affects your daily activities.

Treatment Information

• The names, addresses (including Zip Code), and telephone numbers of all doctors, hospitals, or other medical facilities where you have been treated or tested.

• Any medical reports in your possession.

• Dates of medical visits and types of treatments or tests.

• Hospital or clinic account number, Department of Veterans Affairs claim number, or Medicaid number.

• Claim number for any other disability benefits you receive or have applied for.

• Any medication you are taking: names, dosage, and frequency.

• Any restrictions a physician has placed on your activities.

Work History

• Date you stopped working.

• If you are working now, date you returned to work, employer, and information about your current job.

• Summary of where you worked during the past 15 years and the kind of work you did.

• A copy of your latest W-2 Form (Wage and Tax Statement) or, if self-employed, your federal tax return for the past year.

Take all this documentation to your local Social Security office, where you will make your formal application which includes: Disability Report, Authorization to Release Medical Information to the Social Security Administration, and Application for Disability Insurance Benefits. Samples of these forms are shown in Appendix C. You will be seen by a disabilities specialist.

If your disability prevents you from filing your claim at your local office, you may be able to file it over the telephone and by mail. You can have a Social Security caseworker come to where you are to complete your application. If you are unable to file it yourself, your application can be made by your spouse, a relative, or a friend.

The information you provide is sent to your state Disability Determination Service (DDS) for evaluation and a decision. The DDS may request more information, or it may require you to have further examinations and tests done. If so, the DDS must pay for them.

Finally, if you have recently become disabled and you think your disability is likely to prevent you from working for a year, don't wait until you have all the documents you need. There is a 5-month waiting period before you become eligible to receive monthly benefits; establishing entitlement to Disability Insurance payments is a much more time-consuming and complicated procedure than it is for any other Social Security program. Simply processing a claim can take 3 to 6 months, so file for your benefits immediately.

PLANNING FOR YOUR FUTURE

In the last few years, the SSA has introduced a pilot program called PASS (Plan for Achieving Self-Support) to encourage and help people receiving disability and Supplemental Security Income benefits to return to the work force and become independent. Though only a few thousand people have so far taken advantage of this program, the SSA hopes more people will hear of it and apply.

This program is a departure from Social Security's traditional beneficiary service role in that it provides ongoing guidance to the individual in accessing a wide range of services in the private as well as the public sector that furnish rehabilitation, employment, and support services. The services may include education or training, job placement, and job coaching after employment.

Using a PASS plan, you can begin to prepare for a better future while still receiving benefits. To participate in this new program, you must submit a written plan that must be approved by the SSA. All the directions for making up your plan can be found in the booklet *Working While Disabled—A Guide to Plan for Achieving Self-Support,* available from your local SSA office or by calling 1-800-772-1213. The booklet gives a step-by-step explanation of how to set up a PASS. It also tells who can have a plan, how having a plan while receiving benefits affects those benefits, and what happens while a PASS is in effect. To illustrate these points, it provides a sample plan and examples drawing on the experiences of people who have successfully used the program to enter or reenter the work force.

NOTE: See the chart at the end of this chapter for the differences between the Disability and SSI programs for people working while collecting benefits.

For more information about the Social Security Disability program, call Social Security's toll-free number, 1-800-772-1213, any day between 7 AM and 7 PM and ask for the *Disability* booklet.

BENEFITS FOR PEOPLE WITH DISABILITIES WHO WORK

Special rules make it possible for people with disabilities receiving Social Security or Supplemental Security Income (SSI) to work and still receive monthly cash payments and Medicare or Medicaid. Social Security calls these rules "work incentives." The rules are different for Social Security and SSI beneficiaries. Following are the rules that apply under each program.

Social Security

Trial Work Period: For 9 months (not necessarily consecutive), a disabled or blind Social Security beneficiary's earnings will not affect his or her Social Security benefit.

Extended Period of Eligibility: For 3 years after a successful trial work period, a disabled or blind Social Security beneficiary may receive a disability check for any month during which his or her earnings are not at the substantial gainful activity level (in 1994, $500 a month for disabled, $850 a month for blind).

Continuation of Medicare: If Social Security disability payments stop because a person is earning at the substantial gainful activity level but the person is still disabled, Medicare can continue for up to 39 months after the trial work period.

Impairment-Related Work Expenses: Certain expenses for things a disabled person needs because of his or her impairment in order to work may be deducted when counting earnings to determine if the person is performing substantial gainful activity.

Recovery During Vocational Rehabilitation: If a person recovers while participating in a vocational rehabilitation program that is likely to lead to becoming self-supporting, benefits may continue until the program ends.

Special Rules for Blind Persons: Several special rules apply to blind beneficiaries who work. For example, they can earn up to $850 before their benefits are affected. Ask at the Social Security office for details on work incentives for blind beneficiaries.

Supplemental Security Income (SSI)

Continuation of SSI: Disabled or blind SSI recipients who work may continue to receive payments until countable income exceeds SSI limits.

Continuation of Medicaid Eligibility: Medicaid may continue for disabled or blind SSI recipients who earn over the SSI limits if the person cannot afford similar medical care and depends on Medicaid in order to work.

Plan for Achieving Self-Support (PASS): A disabled or blind SSI recipient may set aside income and resources for up to 48 months toward an approved plan for achieving self-support.

Impairment-Related Work Expenses: Certain expenses for things a disabled person needs because of his or her impairment in order to work may be deducted when counting earnings to determine if the person continues to be eligible. For blind persons who work, the work expenses need not be related to the impairment.

Recovery During Vocational Rehabilitation: If a person recovers while participating in a vocational rehabilitation program that is likely to lead to becoming self-supporting, benefits may continue until the program ends.

Sheltered Workshop Payments: Pay received in a sheltered workshop is treated as earned income, regardless of whether it is considered wages for other purposes. This enables Social Security to exclude more of the sheltered workshop employee's earnings when computing his or her SSI payment.

Disabled Students: Tuition, books, and other expenses related to getting an education may not be counted as income for recipients who go to school or are in a training program.

6

Supplemental Security Income: SSI Benefits

Supplemental Security Income (SSI) is a federal program that assures a minimum monthly income to people who are in severe financial need, have little or no income, extremely limited resources, are 65 years of age or older, or who, regardless of age, are blind or disabled. SSI may also ensure eligibility to receive, in addition to cash benefits, social services managed through state or local agencies.

Although the SSI program is administered through the Social Security Administration, Social Security funds are not used to make SSI payments; the federal portion of these benefits are paid from the Social Security Disability Insurance Trust Fund, financed by those taxes. Many states provide supplements through state sources of taxation.

In this chapter you will find out about SSI benefits, how eligibility is determined, what information you need in order to apply, and how your income and resources affect eligibility. We also cover retroactive benefits for certain children, the rules that apply to working while collecting SSI benefits, and emergency assistance.

NOTE: Individuals may receive immediate SSI payments for up to 6 months while their claim is being processed if they meet the nonmedical criteria **and** if their medical condition at the time they first file for SSI makes it likely they will qualify for benefits.

Determining Eligibility for SSI

Even if you think you may not qualify for this program, look over the lists of income and resources, particularly those items that are **not** counted as resources—you may find that you are eligible after all. Furthermore, SSI eligibility may entitle you to other programs—private, public, local, state, and federal—which could be very helpful. It can be well worth some extra effort to find out about such programs; often they are not widely advertised or known.

For example, the 1990 federal budget contained a little-noticed provision (left over from the Catastrophic Care bill) for Medicare beneficiaries who were below the federally defined poverty level. Of the 4 million people eligible to have their Medicare premiums picked up by Medicaid, 2.2 million continued to pay those premiums because they didn't know about the Qualified Medicare Beneficiary (QMB) program and did not apply for it. (The QMB program is discussed in more detail in Chapter 7.)

AGE, DISABILITY, AND CITIZENSHIP

In order to get SSI benefits, even before financial need is considered, you must meet the age or disability and citizenship requirements of the program. These stipulate that you must be 65 years of age or older (or any age, if blind or disabled) and a resident and citizen of the United States (or an alien lawfully admitted for permanent residence in the United States).

FINANCIAL NEED

If you meet the conditions above, you must also meet the conditions for financial need. The 2 determining factors are the value of your resources and your income, and there are some fairly complex rules governing what resources and income are counted and what are not in determining eligibility.

Resources

To be eligible for SSI, you as an individual applicant must have resources or assets of less than $2,000. If you are married, you and your spouse must have combined assets of less than $3,000.

Your assets are any resources or things you own that can be converted to cash, such as land, securities, jewelry, and other valuables.

Items Counted As Resources

• Real estate (land or buildings).

• Personal property and household goods (furniture, jewelry, books, appliances, etc.).

• Securities (stocks and bonds).

• Bank accounts (checking and savings).

NOTE: The resources of an applicant's ineligible spouse or parent(s) are also considered in determining SSI eligibility and payments, but not necessarily dollar for dollar.

Items Not Counted As Resources

From the value of the items above, you can deduct, or not count, the following:

• A home and its land that you use as your main living place, regardless of value.

• Personal property or household goods with a total equity value of $2,000 are not counted; equity value in excess of $2,000 *is* counted. (Equity value is the amount you can sell an item for, less the amount of any legal debt against it.)

• For a car, only the amount of market value in excess of $4,500 is counted; the value of 1 car is not counted at all if it is used by the household for special purposes—transportation to a job, transportation to a place of regular treatment for a specific medical problem, or use by a handicapped person. If you own other cars, the equity value of each is counted.

• Life insurance policies having a face value of $1,500 or less per person.

• Any resources or things needed by a blind or disabled person for an approved self-support program.

• Up to $1,500 in burial funds for a person and up to $1,500 in burial funds for a spouse; a burial plot for you and members of your immediate family is also not counted.

• Income-producing property, regardless of value, used in a trade or business (tools of a tradesperson, machinery and livestock of a farmer) essential to self-support.

Excess Resources: If your counted resources exceed the limits listed above, you may still be eligible for SSI. But in order to keep your eligibility for payments, you may be required to sell excess resources within 9 months for real estate and 3 months for personal property. (Under certain conditions, excess real estate can be excluded if it cannot be sold.)

Benefits from SSI you receive while you are selling excess resources may have to be repaid to SSI after you get the sales proceeds. If you refuse to sell excess resources, you will be declared ineligible for benefits and must reimburse SSI for all payments so far received.

INCOME

For 1995, individual income must be less than $1,001 (earned income) or $478 (unearned income) per month, and the income of a couple living alone in their own household must be less than $1,459 (earned) or $707 (unearned). If a couple is separated for 6 months or more, each individual is regarded as a single applicant in terms of income restriction. These figures are for federal amounts; they do not reflect income exclusions or extra SSI payments that are made by state programs.

Income, generally, is defined as earned or unearned, depending on the source, but assistance or compensation in lieu of (instead of) money may also be considered as income.

As with resources, some items count as income and some do not in determining eligibility for SSI.

Items Counted As Income

• Money, which includes cash and checks.

• Food, shelter, and clothing which are provided as compensation in lieu of money.

• Earned income from sources such as wages, net earnings from self-employment, and income from sheltered workshops.

• Unearned income from sources such as Social Security benefits, Workers' Compensation, veterans' benefits, pensions, alimony, annuities, gifts, interest, dividends, and rents.

• Royalties and honorariums even if received for past work.

Items Not Counted As Income

• $20 per month of earned or unearned income (except some types of unearned income based on need, such as certain veterans' pensions).

• $65 per month of earned income plus one-half of earned income over $65 a month, or, if there is no unearned income, $85 a month of earned income plus one-half of the remainder over $85 a month.

• Government refunds of taxes paid on real property or on food purchases.

• Assistance based on need from a state or local political subdivision or Native American tribe; most federal judgment distribution payments and per capita payments of funds held in trust by the Secretary of the Interior which are made to members of Native

American tribes, including purchases made with these payments.

• Amounts for tuition and fees paid from grants, scholarships, and fellowships.

• Homegrown produce consumed by the household.

• Irregular or infrequent earned income totaling no more than $10 a month; irregular or infrequent unearned income totaling no more than $20 a month.

• Foster care payments for a child who is not receiving SSI payments but has been placed in the recipient's household by an approved agency.

• If a child, one-third of any child support payments received from the absent parent.

• Earnings (up to $400 a month, but not more than $1,620 a year) of an unmarried blind or disabled child who is a student under 22.

• If disabled or blind, the amount of income necessary for fulfillment of an approved Plan for Achieving Self-Support (PASS program); if blind, an amount equal to work expenses and if disabled, an amount equal to impairment-related work expenses.

• Food stamp assistance.

• Housing assistance from federal housing programs run by state and local subdivisions.

• Benefits, compensation, or items from ACTION programs run by state and local subdivisions.

• Relocation expense assistance provided because of property acquisition for federal or federally assisted projects or by state or local governments.

• Grants or loans to undergraduate students from the Department of Education's educational programs.

• Assistance furnished in connection with a presidentially declared disaster and any interest earned on the assistance for the first 9 months.

• Interest which is paid on excluded burial funds and left to accumulate.

• Food, clothing, or shelter in a nonprofit retirement home or similar institution that is provided or paid for by a nonprofit organization which is not expressly obligated to do so.

• Food, clothing, shelter, and home energy assistance provided in kind by a private nonprofit organization if the assistance is based on need and is certified by the state; home energy assistance provided by certain home energy suppliers if the assistance is based on need and is certified by the state.

• Money received by a victim of a crime (excluded from resources for 9 months after the month in which payments are received if it can be shown they are compensation for expenses or losses that resulted

from the crime); reparations payments to Holocaust survivors from the Federal Republic of Germany.

• Impairment-related work expenses.

• Federal income tax refunds related to earned income tax credits excluded from income in the month they are received and excluded from resources the following month in order to allow time for the refunds to be used.

ELIGIBILITY FOR TEMPORARY RESIDENTS OF EMERGENCY SHELTERS

Aged, blind, and disabled residents of public shelters for the homeless (as defined by SSA regulations) may be eligible for SSI benefits for as many as 6 months in a 9-month period. Benefits for homeless people in emergency shelters will provide some income to help meet the expenses of seeking a permanent residence.

EMERGENCY AND OTHER ASSISTANCE BY PRIVATE ORGANIZATIONS

A needy aged, blind, or disabled person or a needy family may receive assistance from a private, nonprofit charitable organization without causing a reduction in the recipient's SSI benefits.

Your local SSA office can suggest state and local sources that provide social services to SSI recipients. Your church or synagogue is another source for referrals. Also check in your local telephone book's government listings and seniors pages for help.

Housekeeping services help the aged, the blind, and the disabled with their personal care, chores, and money management. People who can no longer care for themselves in their own homes are helped to make living arrangements in residential or family care facilities. Visiting volunteers and special help for the handicapped are other services available.

NOTE: If you are declared eligible for SSI, you are also probably eligible for Medicaid or for payment of your Medicare premiums. You may qualify for food stamps and other social services as well.

WORKING AND COLLECTING SSI

Special rules make it possible to receive SSI or Social Security benefits, Medicare, or Medicaid while holding a job. In fact, the Social Security Administration encourages people to be independent and helps them to prepare themselves to work.

There is a work incentive program for both SSI and DI recipients, though the rules differ slightly for each program. If you are an SSI beneficiary interested in working, or preparing yourself to go to work, you should see the work incentives specialist at your local Social Security office for more information about the programs. Here's a brief summary of how these apply to SSI recipients:

Continuation of SSI

Disabled or blind SSI recipients who work may continue to receive payments until countable income exceeds SSI limits.

Continuation of Medicaid Eligibility

Medicaid may continue for disabled or blind SSI recipients who earn over the SSI limits if the person cannot afford similar medical care and depends on Medicaid in order to work.

Plan for Achieving Self-Support (PASS)

A disabled or blind SSI recipient may set aside income and resources for up to 48 months toward an approved plan for achieving self-support.

Recovery During Vocational Rehabilitation

If a person recovers while participating in a vocational rehabilitation program and is likely to become self-supporting, benefits may continue until the program ends.

Sheltered Workshop Payments

Pay received in a sheltered workshop is treated as earned income, regardless of whether it is considered wages for other purposes. This enables Social Security to exclude more earnings of a sheltered workshop employee when computing his or her SSI payment.

Disabled Students

Under Age 22: A disabled student receiving SSI in this age group may earn as much as $400 per month in 1994 up to a yearly maximum of $1,620. Higher earnings will result in a reduction or termination of benefits.

Over Age 22: A disabled student in this age group can deduct disability-related expenses from earnings to lower the substantial gainful activity figure that affects his or her benefit amount. These are the same as the deductions for work expenses listed below.

NOTE: These deductions are not available to younger students.

Deductions for Work Expenses

If you are disabled, certain impairment-related work expenses can be deducted from earned income, but the SSA must approve each deduction and the amount. The following work expenses generally are deductible:

• Wheelchairs, respirators, braces, and other medical devices.

• Attendant care services, such as assistance in going to and from work, a reader for the blind, or an interpreter for the deaf.

• Transportation costs that are extraordinary, such as modifications to a vehicle.

• One-handed typewriters, braille devices, telecommunications devices for the deaf, and certain other work-related equipment.

• Regularly prescribed drugs and medical services needed to control an impairment.

• Residential modifications, such as ramps or railings outside the home that improve mobility.

• Expendable medical supplies, costs of keeping a guide dog, and other miscellaneous expenses.

Special Deductions for the Blind

Blind recipients are allowed deductions for certain work expenses in addition to those mentioned above. Examples are federal, state, and Social Security taxes, routine transportation costs to and from work, and union dues. These work expenses will not be counted in determining a blind recipient's eligibility or SSI payment amount.

To assure that blind beneficiaries learn about any changes that may affect their monthly payments, Social Security will either telephone them or send their notices by certified mail if they request this service. In an additional effort to keep blind individuals informed about Social Security programs, the SSA and the Library of Congress have a braille publication and a 3-hour audio-cassette entitled *Social Security Programs and Benefits*. This ''talking book'' is available through all 160 libraries in the Library of Congress national network. The braille booklet can be found in the braille lending libraries that are affiliated with the Library of Congress.

SSI AND SUBSTANCE ABUSE

Nearly 60,000 people now receive SSI payments because of disability resulting from addiction to drugs or alcohol, and the number increases each year. The requirements that the recipients be in treatment and have their benefits paid to a representative are not new, but the Social Security Independence and Program Improvements Act of August 1994 places some further restrictions on payments to substance abusers that do not apply to other SSI recipients. This new legislation covers both disability and SSI.

Eligibility Period

Under both Social Security and SSI, benefits are now limited to 36 months. (Under SSI, the period begins with the first month for which payment is made; for disability, it begins with the first month treatment is available.)

After the 36 month eligibility period, if the beneficiary continues to be medically disabled and meets all other eligibility requirements, Medicare, Medicaid, and dependents' benefits will continue.

NOTE: This provision does *not* affect those whose disability is independent of their substance abuse (for example, a blind person who meets other requirements for disability benefits and also is an alcoholic would continue to receive benefits).

Referral and Monitoring Agency

Under both programs, recipients are required to participate in a treatment program. Compliance with treatment programs is supervised by a Referral and Monitoring Agency (RMA) in each state which issues regulations to define appropriate treatment, oversees compliance and reports to the SSA if a beneficiary is not undergoing treatment or is rehabilitated. In some states, it is the state alcohol and drug abuse agencies which serve as RMA's; other states use private organizations for this purpose.

Representative Payees

Both programs require that beneficiaries whose drug addiction or alcoholism is material to their disability have their benefits paid to a third party (the representative payee) who is responsible for ensuring that the benefits are used for the beneficiary's basic needs (food, shelter, clothing, personal comfort items, and medical care). Qualified agencies appointed as representative payees are allowed to retain up to 10% of the monthly benefit or $50, whichever is less, as a fee for services. (Qualifying organizations acting as payees for beneficiaries other than drug addicts or alcoholics may charge up to 10% of the benefit amount or $25, whichever is less.)

The SSA gives preference to social service agencies or to federal, state, or local government agencies in appointing a representative payee, unless a family member can be shown to be more appropriate.

Benefits

SSI benefits are paid on a monthly basis. Many states cooperate with the federal government by including the state and local share of SSI payments in one check that is issued by the federal government. However, some states administer their own SSI program and issue separate checks. If a combined state and federal check is issued, the total will vary from state to state, since each state sets its own benefit payment limits.

The table at the end of this chapter shows the **federal** monthly payment amounts effective January 1994 for eligible people, both individuals and couples, in different living arrangements. The table does not include Cost-of-Living Adjustments (COLA's) or additions from state SSI programs.

Special payment rates are established for eligible people living in residential or family care facilities for the aged, the blind, the mentally disabled, or the mentally retarded. Check with your local Social Security office to find out more about these payment rates.

It is important to apply for SSI benefits as soon as you believe you are eligible, because these benefits are paid only from the date of application *or* from the date of eligibility, whichever is later.

CHANGES IN INCOME AND RESOURCES

Many people believe that once they have begun receiving SSI benefits, those benefits will not change unless their general economic situation changes—but that is not the case. All the items on the qualifying list are important to the amount of your benefit. That means if **any** of them change, you must report the change. If, for example, your Department of Veterans

Affairs pension is reduced, your SSI payment may go up; or if a relative starts paying your rent, your SSI benefit could go down.

Changes in your spouse's or child's income or resources affect your benefit, and must be reported. Changes in living arrangements, such as having someone move in or out of your home, having someone in your household die, or having a baby, must be reported.

Review the income and resources lists at the beginning of the chapter and the questions on the SSI application form in Appendix C; anything that changes what was on your original application should be reported, to be on the safe side. Penalties for not reporting a change or for making false statements about a change are severe. You may be subject to a fine or imprisonment or both, in addition to having to pay back any overpayment.

Any change must be reported within 10 days after the month it happens, but the change will not affect your check for the first 2 months after the event.

APPEALS OF DECISIONS

If you disagree with the determination made about your eligibility or the amount of your SSI payment, you have the right to appeal the decision. You also may be represented by a lawyer at any stage in your appeals. The procedure for appealing a decision is fully explained in Chapter 9.

Your Application for SSI

You can apply for SSI benefits at your local Social Security office. Parents, guardians, or personal representatives of eligible blind or disabled children under 18, as well as personal representatives of eligible aged people who cannot manage on their own, can apply on behalf of these applicants.

CHECKLIST FOR YOUR APPLICATION

The documents required to make SSI claims are listed below, although not all of these will apply to your situation. When you apply for SSI payments, you will need to take original documents with you to the Social Security office.

• Proof of age, unless that is already established because you are getting Social Security benefits.

• Names of people who contribute to your support, as well as the amount of money they contribute.

• Bank books and statements (both checking and savings), stock certificates, and bonds.

• Latest tax return (federal and state) if you are currently employed.

• Latest tax bill or assessment notice if you own real property other than your home.

• Motor vehicle registration.

• Proof of pension and annuity payments.

• List of doctors, hospitals, or clinics where, if you are under 65, you have received treatment for blindness or disability.

You will be asked to provide the information requested on Form SSA-8000-BK, Application for Supplemental Security Income. A sample copy of this form, for your reference, appears in Appendix C.

After you have read this chapter, and especially if you are interested in applying for SSI, you may wish to obtain a copy of *Understanding SSI,* a 57-page booklet adapted from a training manual developed by the American Association of Retired Persons (AARP) to train its volunteers. It provides detailed information about how SSI affects other government assistance programs such as food stamps, Aid to Families with Dependent Children, and Medicaid. Your local Social Security office also offers an SSI booklet (ask for SSA publication 05-11000), or you can order it from the Government Printing Office.

MAXIMUM MONTHLY BENEFIT UNDER SSI

Effective January 1, 1995

Category	Federal Amount*
Individual living alone	$458
Individual living with others but paying his or her own way	458
Individual living with others and getting support and maintenance	305
Individual living in a public general hospital or Medicare-approved long-term-care facility	30
Couple living alone	687
Couple living with others but paying their own way	687
Couple living with others and getting support and maintenance	458
Couple living in a public general hospital or Medicare-approved long-term-care facility	60

Does not include state payments or Cost-of-Living Adjustment.

7

Medicare

Some Background on the Program

Medicare came into existence in 1965 to provide health insurance for eligible Americans 65 years of age or older. In 1972 it was expanded to cover the severely disabled and people with end-stage renal disease.

Medicare consists of 2 related health insurance plans: Part A compulsory Hospital Insurance (HI), and Part B voluntary Supplementary Medical Insurance (SMI).

It's important, as you become eligible for Medicare insurance, to understand the program so that you can take full advantage of the coverage it offers and, at the same time, protect yourself and your family against the expenses it does not cover.

When you enroll in Medicare, the Social Security Administration sends you a free, 53-page booklet called *The Medicare Handbook*. This booklet provides an official reference explaining what the program does and does not cover, and it answers many other questions you are likely to have about your participation in Medicare.

This chapter provides an overview of the material covered by the handbook and discusses some other Medicare-related topics to supplement the handbook information.

If you have not yet received your booklet, ask the SSA to send you one. Call your local office or 1-800-772-1213. The SSA also publishes other free material on Medicare relating to Medicare coverage for kidney dialysis and transplants, getting a second opinion, and hospice benefits. There is an order form for these special-interest booklets in *The Medicare Handbook*.

Changes in the rules and laws that govern Medicare have occurred regularly in the past and surely more are to come. Many of us are concerned about what may happen to Medicare under a comprehensive health care reform bill.

It seems likely that whatever health care legislation emerges from Congress, the scope and difficulty of reforming such a large part of our economy will require long debate and considerable time. Congress will be most reluctant to tamper with Medicare, and any-

thing done in that quarter will probably be phased in over some period of time.

NOTE: Even if you don't plan to begin collecting Social Security benefits at age 65, you should apply for Medicare shortly before reaching your 65th birthday. Part A is free if you're eligible for benefits whether you draw them or not, and you can be billed quarterly for Part B if you're not yet getting a Social Security check.

MEDICARE AND MEDICAID

Many people confuse Medicare with Medicaid, but they are very different programs. Medicare is an **insurance** program, primarily serving people 65 and older. Medicaid is an **assistance** program for qualified low-income people of any age.

The states administer their own Medicaid programs under broad federal guidelines. Each establishes its own rules for eligibility, amount of services, and fees, so these vary a great deal from state to state. However, there are some situations in which Medicare and Medicaid overlap.

Qualified Medicare Beneficiary (QMB) and Specified Low-Income Medicare Beneficiaries (SLMB)

The QMB program requires states to pay the Medicare Part A and Part B premiums, deductibles, and coinsurance expenses for Medicare beneficiaries who meet the income and resource limits. Under the SLMB program the states pay only the full Medicare Medical Insurance (Part B) monthly premium, though eligibility may be retroactive for up to 3 months.

The rules vary from state to state, but in general, to qualify, your:

• Annual income must be at or below the current national poverty guidelines for the QMB program. For the SLMB program, your annual income must be 110% or less of the current guidelines figures. In 1994, these amounts were $7,360 for one person and $9,840 for a family of 2. (These figures change each year in January. Call the SSA for the latest poverty level figures in use. Under both programs, $20 a month will not be counted toward the limit.

• Resources (such as bank accounts or stocks) may not exceed the current poverty level. Resources generally are things you own. However, not everything is counted. The house you live in, for example, doesn't count, and in some circumstances your car may not count either.

Only your state can decide if you can get help under the QMB and SLMB programs. See Chapter 6 and contact your state or local Medicaid, welfare, or social service agency if you think you should apply.

Spending Down

We all know, or have heard about, people who, requiring long-term care not covered by Medicare, spent all their resources paying for that care. When every-thing was gone, they qualified for Medicaid, which then paid the ongoing nursing home bills.

There are people, too, who voluntarily (or under pressure) divested themselves of their assets *before* this could happen to them, only to find out too late that they did not qualify for Medicaid after all.

In the current push for health care reform, we have been promised there will be cuts and savings in both Medicare and Medicaid—the so-called "spending down" option is an obvious area for change. Certainly it's wrong for people to have to impoverish themselves for nursing home care, but it's also wrong when people buy themselves expensive houses or personal possessions and then let the government (which is us) pay their nursing home bills. Very likely, laws will soon be passed to penalize those who transfer assets not long before applying for Medicaid and impose higher penalties and stiffer enforcement of laws that already exist.

NOTE: If you are advised to "spend down" your assets, get a second opinion before you take any action.

Medicare Part A: Hospital Insurance

Medicare Part A, Hospital Insurance, is financed directly through Social Security taxes. Your local Social Security office provides Medicare information and forms, but the claims themselves are submitted by the hospital or other providing agency to large insurance companies called "intermediaries" which have been designated by the Health Care Financing Administration (HCFA) to process those claims. (For Medicare Part B, the insurance companies are called "carriers.")

It is always the hospital that submits Part A claims to the intermediary. The hospital will send you a list of charges, but it will say on it, "Not a Bill."

Part A helps pay for 4 kinds of medically necessary hospitalization—inpatient hospital care, inpatient care in a skilled nursing facility, home health care, and hospice care—as these types of hospital care are defined by the HCFA.

ELIGIBILITY

You are automatically eligible for hospital insurance:

• **At age 65**, if you are entitled to monthly Social Security benefits, even though you may still be working and not collecting benefits.

• **At age 65**, or over, if your spouse is entitled to Social Security benefits.

• **At age 65**, or over, if you are the widow or widower of a person who was entitled to Social Security benefits.

• **Under 65**, if you have been entitled to Social Security Disability benefits for 24 months.

• **At any age**, if you are fully or currently insured with Social Security (see Chapter 2) and need maintenance dialysis or a kidney transplant (coverage starts the third month after you begin dialysis).

Being automatically eligible does not mean you are automatically covered; **you are not covered until you apply**—which you should do when you first meet any of the conditions above. When you apply for your retirement benefits at age 65, you also apply for both parts of Medicare. If you are fully or conditionally insured, your spouse, at age 65, is eligible for Medicare on your work record, even if you are not yet 65.

If you plan to work past age 65, you should make a separate application for Medicare coverage. You pay no premium for Part A if you are eligible to receive Social Security retirement benefits. There **is** a premium for Part B, and it will be deducted from your Social Security check unless you tell the SSA you don't wish to be covered by Part B.

Voluntary Enrollment in Medicare

If for some reason you are not eligible for Medicare at age 65, you can purchase it through voluntary enrollment. To qualify for voluntary enrollment, you must be 65 or over, live in the United States, and be a U.S. citizen. Aliens are also eligible, if legally admitted and residing in the United States continuously for 5 years immediately prior to Medicare enrollment.

If you voluntarily enroll in Part A, you must also take Part B, the supplementary Medical Insurance. However, you can enroll in Part B without taking Part A.

The form used for voluntary enrollment in Medicare is HCFA-18-F5, available from your Social Security office. It is reproduced in Appendix C so that you can become familiar with the questions it asks.

The 1995 monthly premium for voluntary enrollees in Medicare Part A is $261; the HCFA will bill you for this coverage on a monthly basis.

NOTE: "Coverage" as we use the term means that Medicare will pay some, but not necessarily all, of your provider's bill.

SERVICES COVERED BY PART A

The first table at the end of this chapter gives an overview of the services and limitations of Medicare Part A. The figures here are for 1995, but be aware that the amounts of the deductibles and coinsurance you pay change each year. Some of the program services may change as well. For the most current information, always check with your Social Security office.

Basically, Medicare Hospital Insurance covers these services: hospital, skilled nursing facility, post-hospital home health agency, hospice care, and blood replacement. In addition, Medicare Part A also covers a maximum of 190 days *per lifetime* for inpatient psychiatric hospital care. Drug and alcohol rehabilitation may be covered under this psychiatric provision, or it may be covered under regular hospitalization or disability provisions, depending on the circumstances of admission.

To be covered, services must be provided by facilities and organizations that have been certified as quali-fied providers and that have agreed to participate in the Medicare program. Some exceptions to this rule may be made for emergency services.

Benefit Periods and Reserve Days

Medicare calculates use of its hospital coverage in "benefit periods" and "reserve days." Understanding these terms helps to untangle the rules governing the length and frequency of hospital stays and the deductibles that apply to different situations.

Benefit Periods: A benefit period begins on the day you enter the hospital and ends when you have been out of the hospital (or other covered facility) for 60 consecutive days. For example, if you are admitted to the hospital on March 3 and discharged on March 15, Medicare pays all but $716 of the bill. You pay the rest —the $716 you pay is your deductible—and you will have used 12 days of that benefit period.

Then, if you are readmitted to the hospital on April 1 for 4 days, you will be within the same benefit period and will use up another 4 days of it, but will not have to pay the $716 for that benefit period again.

If, however, you are not readmitted until August (more than 60 days after you left the hospital), the benefit period will not be the same as the one that began in March, and you will have to pay the $716 for a new benefit period.

Reserve Days: With the exception of hospice care, there are no limits on the number of benefit periods that you may use, but if you have to stay in the hospital for more than 90 days, the days beyond the 90th day fall into a special category called "reserve days."

During each and every benefit period that you use, Medicare will pay one amount (all but the $716 mentioned above for 1995) toward the first 60 days of a hospital stay and a lesser amount toward the next 30 days. After that you may use some or all of your reserve days, for which Medicare pays another amount. The Part A table at the end of the chapter gives the 1995 payment amounts for different lengths of hospital and skilled nursing facility care.

As a Medicare beneficiary, you are entitled to only 60 reserve days in a lifetime. Though you may use them a few days at a time, once they are used up, these reserve days are not renewable. You may decide whether or not you want to use any of your reserve days in any given situation; if you decide you do not want to use them, you must notify the hospital **in writing** before the 90th day, or any days beyond 90 automatically will be considered reserve days.

Diagnosis Related Groups

Hospitals are paid by Medicare, not on the basis of what they charge, but by what is called the Prospective Payment System (PPS). Under this system, there is a predetermined standard rate, or average cost, for particular categories of treatment. The fixed fees vary among the 9 regions of the nation and between rural and urban facilities, but a single payment is made for each type of case, as it is identified by the Diagnosis Related Group or DRG. There are 468 groups designated for classification of particular cases.

The DRG system was instituted to cut costs, but there is considerable opposition to it, and it may be modified in the future. Paying a hospital with the DRG system is like paying a worker by the job instead of by the hour. If the hospital keeps you longer than the DRG for your condition allows, the hospital bears the extra cost. If you are released before your DRG time limit is up, the hospital is still paid the same amount.

Safeguards Against Abuses

Peer Review Organizations have been set up by the HCFA to review complaints regarding Medicare admissions, discharges of patients, and performance of medical procedures. These PRO's, as they are called, have the authority to hold hospitals and doctors responsible for violating rules regarding admissions, premature discharges, and performance (or lack of performance) of medical procedures.

Certainly there are instances of fraud in the system, and many more of outright waste. We all pay for it ultimately, so it deserves reporting. The PRO for your area is listed in *The Medicare Handbook* along with full instructions for reporting abuses. Addresses for reporting fraud and abuses also appear in Appendix B.

Appeals Relating to Hospital, Hospice, or Home Care

Should you and your physician believe Medicare is terminating your hospital, hospice, or home care too soon, you can appeal this decision to your PRO when Medicare sends you a Notice of Noncoverage. If you request the review by noon of the first day after receipt of the notice, your Medicare coverage is automatically extended and you will not have to pay until the PRO makes its decision. If, however, the PRO is reviewing the matter for a second time, you may have to pay for the time you spend in the hospital or hospice while the

decision is being made—usually no more than a day. Chapter 9 outlines the steps to take for making an appeal.

SERVICES NOT COVERED BY PART A

Medicare will not pay for anything that isn't "medically reasonable and necessary." For example, Medicare will not pay for your television or telephone fees while you are in the hospital. For the most part, your doctor determines what is medically reasonable and necessary, and the hospital's utilization review committee and the area Peer Review Organization monitor the doctor's decision.

There are some other things, as well, for which Medicare hospital insurance will **not** pay:

• Custodial care as provided by most nursing homes.

• Full-time nursing care in your home.

• Private room and private-duty nursing (unless medically necessary).

• Services paid for by other forms of insurance, such as Workers' Compensation, automobile or other liability insurance, or employer health plans.

• Charges for services in excess of the Medicare standards.

• Items or services for which you are not legally obligated to pay. There are some charges for services which Medicare may refuse to pay that you do not have to pay either. See "When You Don't Have to Pay" farther along in this chapter.

• Drugs and treatments the Food and Drug Administration has not found "safe and effective."

• Hospital treatment in a foreign country. The exception to this is for treatment of an emergency that occurred in the United States and the foreign hospital is closer than one in the United States, or if the emergency occurred in transit between the continental United States and Alaska.

NOTE: Several of the 10 new Medigap (supplementary health insurance) policies described on page 62 have some provision for medical care abroad, though most other health insurance plans don't cover it at all. It is possible for you to buy special temporary health insurance for foreign trips. Your travel agent can supply details.

If you have a question about whether or not any item is covered, you can telephone the insurance intermediary for your area and ask. Or you can submit the claim and see what happens.

COPAYMENTS AND DEDUCTIBLES FOR PART A

Copayments are the payments that you, or whatever health insurance you carry in addition to Medicare, must make to cover expenses that Medicare does not pay. Charges for the Medicare-approved services (such as the $716 of the hospital bill at the beginning of a benefit period you have to cover before Medicare begins paying) count toward your deductible.

SIGNING UP FOR MEDICARE, PARTS A AND B: ENROLLMENT PERIODS

You must decide whether or not you want Medicare coverage and enroll during one of 3 enrollment periods.

The first opportunity is called the "initial enrollment period." This period begins 3 months before the month you become eligible and ends 3 months after that—7 months in all. For example, if your 65th birthday is in August, you become eligible in July, so your initial enrollment period would run from April 1 through October 31 of that same year. If you sign up in April, May, or June, your medical insurance begins in July. If you enroll between July and the end of October, coverage starts 1 to 3 months after you have enrolled.

Should you decide later that you want Medicare coverage and your initial enrollment period has passed, you have a second opportunity: you can sign up during the "general enrollment period," which runs from January 1 through March 31 of each year. Your coverage will not begin until the following July, and you will have to pay a surcharge: your monthly premium will go up 10% for every year you were eligible and did not enroll.

If you work past 65 and have employer health coverage, or if you are 65 and your spouse is a worker of any age, the third opportunity to enroll is during a "special enrollment period" consisting of the 7 months beginning with the month your group coverage ends, or the month employment ends, whichever is first. You do not have to wait for a general enrollment period or pay the surcharge, but you have to meet certain requirements. Check with your Social Security office or your employer's benefits office

Medicare Part B: Medical Insurance

Medicare Part B, medical insurance, is also called voluntary Supplementary Medical Insurance (SMI) and is financed by payments from the federal government and by monthly premiums paid by people enrolled in the plan. Part B helps pay for doctors' bills and other medical services and supplies not covered by Part A.

"Helps pay" is the key phrase here, as Part B involves a premium, requires a deductible, limits the amount payable for each service, and in all but a few situations pays 80%—not all—of the Medicare-approved amount.

PART B ENROLLMENT AND APPLICATION FORMS

You can enroll for Part B medical insurance in 3 different ways:
• You are automatically enrolled if you apply for and receive Social Security benefits or Railroad Retirement benefits. You must pay a monthly premium for this coverage. However, if you do not wish to have the coverage, you must say so at the time you become eligible for hospital insurance (Medicare Part A).
• You can voluntarily enroll for Part B, but only if you are over 65. You do not have to be entitled to Social Security benefits in order to get this coverage, but you must pay monthly premiums for it, and you have to enroll for *both* Parts A and B.

Enrollment for Medicare Part B is automatic only if you apply for and receive Social Security benefits. Otherwise, you have to apply for enrollment in medical insurance if:
• You plan to work past 65.
• You are 65 but ineligible for hospital insurance.
• You have permanent kidney failure.
• You are a disabled widow or widower between 50 and 65 and you are not receiving disability checks.

Sample application forms for Medicare Part B (HCFA-18-F5 and HCFA-40B, a shorter version) are reproduced for your information in Appendix C. Note that items 16 and 17 on Form HCFA-18 pertain to medical insurance.

NOTE: There are "enrollment periods" for Medicare (both or either parts), during which you must sign up or pay a penalty in the form of a higher premium if you are late. Exceptions to these rules are made for some situations in which there is coverage from employment, or when that coverage changes. See your *Medicare Handbook* for details, or call your Medicare insurance carrier.

PART B PREMIUMS

The monthly Part B premium for 1995 is $46.10. This premium is deducted from your Social Security check. If you do not receive a benefit check, you are billed for the premium on a monthly basis.

NOTE: If you find you are unable to pay your premium, call your local Social Security office and give the reason for your nonpayment. If your explanation is accepted, you will be given a grace period—usually 90 days—in which to pay the premium. However, if you do not pay within the grace period, your coverage will be canceled and future reinstatement will result in a higher premium. You might also look into the QMB and SLMB programs discussed at the beginning of this chapter.

REQUIREMENTS FOR DEDUCTIBLE AND APPROVED CHARGES

In order to receive medical insurance benefits from Medicare, you must first pay the annual deductible, and Medicare must have approved the charge for each category of service you have received.

Deductible for Part B

For calendar year 1995, you must pay the first $100 —the deductible—of your doctor or medical bills. (Your other health insurance may pay some or all of this deductible; it may also have its own deductible.) Don't wait until your bills total the amount of the Medicare deductible; submit individual bills as you pay them so they will be applied to your deductible. Meeting this deductible is a one-time requirement for each calendar year.

You also have an annual blood deductible; you can either pay for the blood or replace the blood that was used. Blood is covered under both Parts A and B, but the deductible has to be met only once under either part in a calendar year.

Coinsurance (Cost Sharing)

After the deductible is met, Medicare still pays only part of the bill; you or your other insurance must pay the rest. Broadly speaking, the coinsurance for Part A is the specified amount that you (or your other insurance) pay after Medicare has paid its limit in each benefit period. For Part B, your share of the cost is the amount beyond Medicare's 80% of the approved charge; that is, you are responsible for 20% plus anything else you are obliged to pay beyond the approved charge.

Recognized, Approved, or Allowable Charges

After you have paid the deductible for the calendar year, Medicare Part B will make 80% of the payments toward certain expenses above the deductible. These payments are not based on your doctors' bills or your medical suppliers' charges, but are based instead on what Medicare defines as reasonable, allowable, or the "approved charge" under the new fee schedule.

There are limits to (or "caps" on) the amount a Medicare patient can be charged for certain services, if a doctor or supplier "does not accept assignment." Accepting assignment means agreeing to take the amount Medicare specifies for a given service as full payment for that service.

Resource-Based Relative-Value System (RBRV)

Finding a way to arrive at fair and reasonable approved charges for physicians is an ongoing struggle; the introduction (January 1, 1992) of a new fee schedule called the Resource-Based Relative-Value system, or RBRV, is the latest attempt to satisfy all parties. It has drawn a great deal of criticism from the American Medical Association.

The purpose of the plan is to equalize payments among different kinds of physicians. The new fee schedule is expected to have the effect of giving more money to general practitioners and less to specialists. It also cuts Medicare expenditures. The HCFA believes that the doctors whose fees are cut by this plan will make up the difference by offering more services, but many doctors disagree.

Under the RBRV plan, a number is assigned to a treatment (from 1 for an office visit to 119 for a liver transplant) with a dollar figure tied to the number. The more complex the treatment is, the higher the number. The doctor's or other provider's overhead and liability insurance premiums are also figured into this system.

Medicare is not the only form of insurance this fee schedule will affect. Most large health insurance carriers have indicated an intention to adopt the new fee schedule as well.

As long as medical costs continue to rise faster than the overall inflation rate, and as long as a large percentage of Americans cannot afford adequate medical care—or the insurance to pay for it—there will be controversy about how health providers are paid. This controversy will express itself in frequent policy changes in Medicare, changes that will affect the entire American health care system.

SUBMITTING PART B MEDICARE CLAIMS

Medicare providers under Part B are now required to prepare and submit Medicare claims for their patients. They have to do this whether or not the provider of the services or supplies accepts assignment. The providers are also prohibited by law from charging any fee for filling out and submitting these claims.

The provider submits the claim to the insurance carrier, and the carrier pays 80% of the approved charge directly to the provider; you are responsible for paying the rest. Claims should be submitted promptly; most providers do so, since it is in their best interest as well as yours. (Most providers now submit Medicare claims electronically, some will also submit Medigap claims at the same time.)

The rule that providers have to handle the submission of claims doesn't mean that you will never have to make a claim yourself. In some cases you may have to do so. The necessary forms can be obtained from your local Social Security office.

Assignment

The easiest way to deal with Medicare is to choose doctors and suppliers who "accept assignment," that is, take the approved Medicare charge as full payment. The patient is then responsible only for the 20% of the charge Medicare does not pay, the deductible, and any services not covered. Not all physicians accept assignment, and there are some who accept assignment only for some services.

Even though your physician or supplier does not accept assignment, there are limits on the amount you can be charged above the set fee for that service. Check with your local Social Security office for the current limits on accepted charges for office and hospital visits, surgery, and other services. Severe penalties are imposed for charging fees above the limits.

NOTE: You can find out which doctors in your area accept assignment of claims by checking the physicians' directory for your state which is published by your area insurance carrier. Your local Social Security office has this book, as do most agencies for seniors. Acceptance of assignment by your doctor will save you money and paperwork.

Primary and Secondary Payers

If you have health insurance through an employer, it is your primary insurance and this insurer pays first; Medicare is the secondary payer. If this is your situation, your provider may not be required (or might not choose) to make the claim for you. Since the primary payer has to pay before Medicare will, you may have to file 1 or both of these claims.

When you have supplementary insurance (Medigap), and Medicare is your primary payer, all providers must prepare the necessary paperwork to support the charges and file the claim with the Medicare carrier. This is the case even if the supplier is not a Medicare participant. Examples of this situation would be a payment for emergency treatment in a Canadian or Mexican hospital, or a U.S. hospital or HMO (Health Maintenance Organization) that is not in the Medicare system. These sorts of suppliers may not make the supplementary claim to your Medigap insurer; you will have to do that yourself.

If the doctor accepts assignment on a Part B claim, and you have signed the form giving that doctor the right to submit claims on your behalf, the Medicare carrier or the doctor may submit claims to your Medigap insurer.

SERVICES COVERED BY PART B

After you have paid the first $100 (the deductible) of approved or recognized charges for the covered services provided, Supplementary Medical Insurance will pay 80% of the covered expenses, subject to the maximum charges of the fee schedule.

Among the services covered are:
• Physician's services, including surgery and anesthesia, either outpatient or inpatient, and supplies furnished as part of the service.
• Diagnostic testing as part of treatment.
• X-ray, radium, and radioactive-isotope therapy.
• Speech, physical, and occupational therapy.

• Pap smears and mammograms to detect cervical and breast cancers (some limitations by age and risk).
• Necessary ambulance service.
• Diagnostic and screening tests for hearing and vision problems.
• Nonroutine vision services.
• One pair of glasses following cataract surgery.
• Some treatment of mental illness (50% of recognized outpatient charges, unless hospital admission would have been necessary without it; then, 80% of recognized charges).
• Certain drugs that cannot be self-administered.
• Rental or purchase of durable medical equipment to be used in the home.
NOTE: This is the least regulated area in the Medicare system and the one in which a great deal of abuse occurs. Be wary of suppliers who try to get you to take equipment by telling you they will accept Medicare's 80% as their full payment and you will not have to pay anything. **Don't agree to accept equipment unless your own doctor has told you that you need it.**
• Home health services (as under Part A, but with payment by either Part A or Part B only).
• Artificial replacements for limbs, eyes, and all or part of internal body organs, including colostomy bags and supplies.
• Braces for limbs, back, or neck.
• Pneumococcal vaccination or immunizations required because of injury or risk of infection.
• Annual physical examinations and flu shots.
• Some heart, kidney, bone marrow, and liver transplants.
• Every-other-year mammograms for women 65 and over, and certain disabled women (limits by age).

• This is a general list, and in most of these categories there are limitations imposed beyond those of approved charges. See *The Medicare Handbook* or check with your Medicare carrier for details.

SERVICES NOT COVERED BY PART B

• Services not medically necessary or reasonable and charges that exceed Medicare-approved charges.
• Eyeglasses (except after cataract surgery), dental care, hearing aids, foot care, and orthopedic shoes.
• Private-duty nursing, unless medically necessary.
• Custodial nursing home care.
• Services paid for by other government programs or Workers' Compensation.
• Services performed by a relative or household member.
• Cosmetic surgery, unless to correct accidental injury or to improve function of a malformation.
• Most prescription drugs and medicines taken at home.
• Screening mammography for women under 34.

CLAIM NUMBER AND MEDICARE CARD

When you become a Medicare enrollee, you will be sent a card showing what your coverage is (Parts A and B, either or both) and a number—your Social Security number plus a letter. This is your claim number, and no claim will be processed without it. Always carry your Medicare card with you; you will be asked to show it anytime you go for medical services.

What Can Go Wrong and What You Can Do

Though Medicare is not exactly "user friendly," the chief cause of problems people have with it comes from not understanding what is covered and what is not. You can save yourself (and everyone else involved) lots of aggravation by taking the trouble to become familiar with Medicare's basic coverage and the supplementary coverage of your Medigap policy.
NOTE: If you are in doubt about whether or not a particular service is covered, don't hesitate to call the SSA's toll-free number, your insurance intermediary, or your insurance carrier and ask.

There are some other problems that might arise, most simply due to the volume of paperwork involved.
A provider has a year within which to submit a claim to Medicare. If a claim is not submitted promptly, it may cause a problem for you if you have paid the bill yourself and are waiting for its submission to get your money back.
What you can do in this situation is to call the provider, request the backup data for the claim, and offer to file it yourself. If that doesn't work, call (politely) every day until the claim is filed. Ask for a copy.

WHEN A CLAIM IS REJECTED

Usually the first indication that there is a problem is when you receive the Explanation of Medicare Benefits (EOMB). The explanation offered on this form usually is enough to tell you what the problem is, but at times it isn't. You can call the carrier for a fuller explanation. Many carriers have special hotline numbers for just this purpose.

The most common reasons for rejecting claims are that the deductible has not been met, the form is not complete (usually not signed), the claim has already been paid, or there was a duplicate claim. Some of these problems can be avoided by keeping very careful, chronological records of all medical services and then tracking all the deductibles, claims applications, and payments for each one. It also helps to have a clear understanding of what services are covered by Medicare and what services are covered by any other insurance you may have.

WHEN YOU DON'T HAVE TO PAY

Often Medicare will refuse to pay all, or part, of a bill, but there are times when you do not have to pay either.

You do not have to pay more than Medicare pays if the provider has agreed to accept assignment.

You do not have to pay for a service that Medicare does not cover unless you can reasonably have been expected to know that the service was not covered, or was not (medically) reasonable and necessary. This means you have to have been told in writing from an appropriate source that the service was not covered.

NOTE: This source could be a prior notice from your provider or insurance company, but your *Medicare Handbook* is also considered an appropriate source.

REFUNDS FOR OVERCHARGES

A new federal law, passed at the end of 1994, gives the HCFA power to order doctors who overcharge Medicare patients to rescind the charge or refund the overcharge. Physicians who refuse can face penalties of up to $2,000.

"Nonparticipating physicians," or those who do not accept the approved Medicare fee for a given service, are allowed to add an additional 15% above the ap-proved fee to their bills for Medicare patients, but no more than that. Although this was true under the old law, the new law adds that the patient *is not required to pay* more than the 15% above the approved charge and also requires insurance companies to monitor every Medicare claim for overcharges.

SOME TIPS FOR FILING ALL MEDICAL INSURANCE CLAIMS

• Read the forms carefully before you fill them out, and be sure all of the bills you are including are complete. The form from the provider's office should show:

• Name, address, and telephone number of the provider. If it is a group practice, **circle your doctor's name.**

• Date and place of service.

• Your name and Medicare (and/or other insurance) number.

• Itemized and totaled charges for services performed.

• Specific diagnosis or description of services performed—this may be a number code.

• Do not pay bills as soon as you receive them—wait for Medicare.

• Submit **copies** of bills unless the originals are required. If there are many bills, copy several on 1 page, and circle charges with a colored pen.

• Submit your bills separately from your spouse's. A claim may include more than 1 service, or services performed on several dates, but there must be only 1 person per claim.

• Find out whether you have to bill your Medigap policy yourself.

• For Medigap (not Medicare) that pays for prescription drugs, be sure to circle the **refill** date on the receipt. A rejection can result here if the processor sees only the original date and finds it has already been paid.

• Mail the correct claim to the correct address.

• Keep written records of all problems; keep all files for 5 years, including canceled checks.

• Be prompt—reply to all requests for more information as soon as possible.

• Read, process, and save your EOMB's, matching dates of services from bills with them.

• Be sure everything that requires a signature is, in fact, signed.

Other Insurance to Supplement Medicare

Many people have, or will want to have, other insurance to pay for things Medicare does not cover. Some people are covered by a group plan (such as an HMO), their employer's health plan either as a worker or retiree, or as the spouse of a worker or retiree.

Medicare considers such plans to be primary payers with Medicare as a secondary payer. With new data-sharing capabilities, Medicare can now check to see if you are covered by such a plan.

Employment-related plans can be quite comprehensive and frequently offer enough benefits to round out Medicare coverage. Even if you have to pay some of the premium, it is often a bargain. The best thing to do is have a clear understanding of what both the employer and Medicare plans cover, and then check to see if anything important to you is left uncovered. If so, you may want to look around for additional insurance. Many company plans have charts that will show you exactly how their coverage works with Medicare.

Medicare also considers the following to be primary insurance: veterans' health care, Workers' Compensation, automobile medical, no-fault, and any other liability insurance.

NOTE: For liability insurance when Medicare is the secondary payer, you must file your claim with Medicare **first.** Medicare will make a conditional payment of the claim, but will recover its conditional payment to you when a settlement with the primary payer has been reached.

MEDIGAP INSURANCE

Many people buy extra insurance to cover Medicare's deductible and coinsurance costs and to pick up some of the other nonpayable charges medical care can generate. This coverage is called "Medigap" insurance, and it comes in many forms. So many different policies were developed, and confusion and abuse were so prevalent, that Congress passed a law standardizing this coverage and governing its sale.

There are now 10 packages of Medigap insurance, offering everything from a basic plan with limited coverage through a comprehensive policy. Insurers can sell these policies—and **only** these policies—as Medigap insurance.

All companies must offer the most basic policy, though they don't have to carry the others, and not all

plans may be available in all states or may not be available immediately.

The plans (identified with a letter, "A" for the simplest through "J" for the most comprehensive) are all the same, regardless of which company offers them, but the premiums for the same policy may vary from company to company or in different areas of the country. Of course, the more coverage you want, the higher premium you will pay, regardless of where you buy it.

NOTE: New Medicare enrollees, aged 65 and older, cannot be rejected for Medigap insurance if they sign up for it within 6 months of enrolling in Medicare. This is a new law—before, Medigap insurers were free to reject applicants for health reasons.

The Medigap summary table at the end of this chapter shows what these policies cover. Any Medigap policy must offer the following basic benefits:

• Payment of the patient's share of Medicare-approved amounts for physician services (usually 20%) after the patient meets the $100 annual Part B deductible.

• Payment of Medicare's Part A coinsurance charges for long hospital stays up to a lifetime total of 365 days of inpatient hospital coverage.

• You will see that **none** of these plans covers extended nursing home care or home care for chronic conditions such as Alzheimer's disease. You may want to look into another policy for long-term care. Be aware, however, that this is an area which has not yet been standardized by government regulation, though it is expected to be in the near future.

You may not want to get one of these new policies if you already have Medigap coverage that includes amenities such as private rooms and private-duty nurses. These are benefits the new policies don't cover.

Medicare SELECT is a new (and less expensive) kind of Medigap insurance, available through 1994 in 15 states. The difference between Medicare SELECT and Medigap policies is that a Medicare SELECT policy may limit benefits (except in emergencies) to selected health care professionals. Medicare SELECT policies must meet federal standards and are regulated by the states in which they are approved. Medicare SELECT premiums are expected to be lower than comparable Medigap policies that do not have the selected care provider feature.

The states in which Medicare SELECT policies are

known to be permitted so far are Alabama, Arizona, California, Florida, Illinois, Indiana, Kentucky, Massachusetts, Minnesota, Missouri, North Dakota, Ohio, Texas, Washington, and Wisconsin.

NOTE: If you have more than one Medigap policy, you are paying for some duplicate coverage. Compare what you have with the benefits available under the new policies, and cancel at least one of them.

Law forbids the sale of more than one Medigap policy to a person, and there is a $25,000 fine for doing so.

If you are new to the Medigap market, decide what coverage you need and do some comparison shopping. The current turmoil in the insurance industry suggests that it would be prudent to buy your policy from a well-established, reputable company.

NOTE: If you are receiving Medicaid, you don't need a Medigap policy—Medicaid covers it all.

ANOTHER ALTERNATIVE: PREPAID HEALTH CARE PLANS

In response to rising health care costs, Health Maintenance Organizations (HMO's) and other forms of managed health care offering medical services on a prepayment basis have come into being. By charging a monthly fee to people who enroll, these plans can provide, theoretically, a number of treatment and diagnostic services for less money than would be charged on a per-case or per-visit basis.

Services provided by these umbrella organizations include those covered under both Part A and Part B of Medicare, with some plans providing services Medicare doesn't cover at all.

If you are a Medicare beneficiary, you may enroll in a prepaid health care plan, but you must be sure that it is Medicare eligible. If the plan is eligible, you are entitled to receive all the services and supplies to which you are entitled under Medicare coverage. Medicare makes direct payments to the organization for the services it provides.

In addition to a set monthly prepayment for services in one of these plans, you may also be required to pay a deductible and any coinsurance you would have been expected to pay for equivalent Medicare services if you were not enrolled.

NOTE: Since there may be several prepayment plans in your area, you will need to do some comparison shopping to find out what each offers and what combination of services best meets your needs. Look in the classified section of your local telephone directory under "Health Maintenance Organizations."

Advance Health Care Directives

As of December 1991, all adult patients admitted to a hospital or nursing home, or receiving medical attention from a home health agency or treatment covered by Medicare or Medicaid, must be informed of their options with respect to life-sustaining treatment. This includes the option of executing a living will. These patients also must be given a description of the current state law governing these situations and the hospital's own internal policies on patients' rights. For this reason, most doctors, as well as hospitals and nursing homes, now have forms they give out routinely.

There are 2 basic kinds of documents, known as advance directives, that outline a patient's wishes for treatment: durable powers of attorney and living wills. They are **not** the same.

A durable power of attorney for health care is a document which names a person and an alternate to make health care decisions for you should you not be able to do it yourself. It can also tell, either in a general manner or in specific ways, how you wish to be cared for so that anyone named to act on your behalf will have your guidance.

The living will is a document intended to give your physician information and general instructions about how you want to be treated. If you have strong feelings about specific treatments, in most states you are free to go into detail about which ones you would prefer not be used.

Whatever the document you decide upon, your doctor should have a copy on file as part of your medical record, and your family should know where a copy can be located.

It's a good idea to execute documents such as these before, or early in the course of, an illness. Even more than a durable power of attorney, having a living will means that **you**—rather than a member of your family, the state, or a medical committee—take the responsibility for deciding if extraordinary means should be employed in your medical treatment.

Extraordinary means could include cardiac resuscitation, mechanical respiration, or artificial nutrition and hydration, and a number of other procedures you may or may not want.

If you are mentally competent, you have the right—in principle at least—to refuse to continue treatment; the right to refuse to *begin* treatment is better established. But if you are not mentally competent, or not conscious, recent court decisions suggest that the wishes you expressed when you were should be respected.

More than 40 states now have laws recognizing living wills, and the remaining states have similar laws under review. In the meantime, if you want to address this question for yourself and your family, consult an attorney or legal aid service and arrange to provide legal means to express your wishes. It is wise to have legal advice because the laws governing this matter differ greatly from state to state. An attorney can help you to provide for the changes in your document that might be required because of either new medical technology or new laws.

You can get more information on your state's advance directives for health care by contacting your State Attorney General's Office or the Society for the Right to Die, 250 West 57th Street, New York, NY 10107, 212-366-5540.

Medicare Forms

The forms you need to apply for Medicare benefits (both Part A and Part B) and the forms providers use to apply for payments are reproduced in Appendix C so you can see what information is required. **These forms are sample forms only. Do not use them for actual filing of claims.**

Although Social Security does not administer Medicare, you apply for your Medicare coverage at your local Social Security office. This office can also answer questions you might have about Medicare, direct you to someone who can, and either give you, or order for you, any special information you may need about the Medicare program.

MEDICARE PART A SUMMARY
HOSPITAL INSURANCE—COVERED SERVICES PER BENEFIT PERIOD

Service	Benefit	Medicare Pays	You Pay
Hospitalization Semiprivate room and board, general nursing, miscellaneous hospital services and supplies	First 60 days 61st to 90th day 91st to 150th day Beyond 150 days	All but $716 All but $179/day All but $358/day Nothing	$716 $179/day $358/day All costs
Post-Hospital Skilled Nursing Facility Care You must have been in a hospital for at least 3 days and enter facility within 30 days after hospital discharge	First 20 days Additional 80 days Beyond 100 days	100% of approved amount All but $89.50/day Nothing	Nothing $89.50/day All costs
Home Health Care	Part-time or intermittent care for as long as you meet Medicare requirements	100% of approved services, 80% of approved amount for durable medical equipment	Nothing for services, 20% approved amount for durable medical equipment
Hospice Care	As long as doctor certifies need	All, but limits on costs for outpatient drugs and inpatient respite care	Limited cost for outpatient drugs and respite care
Blood	Unlimited if medically necessary	All but 1st 3 pints per calendar year	For 1st 3 pints (or replace)

Benefit period begins 1st hospital day, ends 60 days after release from facility.
These figures are for 1995 and are subject to change each year.
Facility must be approved by Medicare.
Reserve days (60), nonrenewable.
Neither Medicare nor Medigap will pay for custodial care; you must pay for such care or buy special insurance.
Blood deductible for a calendar year may be met under either A or B.

MEDICARE PART B SUMMARY

MEDICAL INSURANCE—COVERED SERVICES PER CALENDAR YEAR

Service	Benefit	Medicare Pays	You Pay
Medical Expenses Doctors' services, inpatient and outpatient medical and surgical supplies, physical and speech therapy, ambulance, diagnostic tests, and more	Medicare pays for medical services in or out of the hospital	80% of approved amount after $100 deductible	$100 deductible plus 20% of approved amount and limited charges above approved amount
Clinical Laboratory Services Blood tests, biopsies, urinalyses, and more	Unlimited if medically necessary	100% of approved amount	Nothing for services
Home Health Care Medically necessary skilled care	Part-time or intermittent skilled care for as long as you meet conditions for benefits	100% of approved amounts, 80% of approved amount for durable medical equipment	Nothing for services, 20% of approved amount for durable medical equipment
Outpatient Hospital Treatment Services for the diagnosis or treatment of illness or injury	Unlimited if medically necessary	80% of approved amount after $100 deductible	$100 deductible plus 20% of billed charges
Blood	Unlimited if medically necessary	80% of approved amount after $100 deductible and starting with 4th pint	First 3 pints plus 20% of approved amount for additional pints after $100 deductible

These figures are for 1995 and are subject to change each year.
Once you have had $100 of expenses for covered expenses in 1995, the Part B deductible does not apply to any further covered services you receive for the rest of the year.

MEDIGAP INSURANCE BENEFITS SUMMARY

The National Association of Insurance Commissioners has developed 10 standard Medigap policies to simplify supplementary health insurance offerings for Medicare beneficiaries. Insurance companies supplying Medigap policies do not have to offer all 10 plans, but all companies must offer Policy A, and all plans must offer the basic benefits described in detail on page 62.

Coverage	A	B	C	D	E	F	G	H	I	J
Basic benefits	X	X	X	X	X	X	X	X	X	X
Skilled nursing coinsurance			X	X	X	X	X	X	X	X
Part A deductible		X	X	X	X	X	X	X	X	X
Part B deductible			X			X				
Part B excess 100%						X			X	X
Part B excess 80%							X			
Foreign travel emergency			X	X	X	X	X	X	X	X
At-home recovery				X			X		X	X
Basic drugs $1,250 limit								X	X	
Extended drugs $3,000 limit										X
Preventive Care					X					X
Estimated yearly premium*	$400– 600	$500– 700	$500– 700	$500– 800	$550– 850	$650– 900	$600– 700	$700– 900	$850– 1,400	$1,200– 1,800

* Varies widely from state to state.

8

Some Questions, Answers, and Examples

This chapter contains some of the questions from our reader mail over the years. Some of these questions are frequently asked; some go into detail on more obscure points. The questions are divided into broad topics indicated by headings. For more in-depth information, see the chapter devoted to the topic, and use the Index to find all the places in the text where the subject is mentioned.

GENERAL TOPICS

If I have never worked, can I get any Social Security benefits?

If you have no work record of your own with Social Security, you would have to qualify on someone else's record to get benefits. You would have to be eligible as a spouse, widow or widower, divorced spouse, or the dependent parent or child of a covered worker to draw benefits on that worker's record.

What should I do if I don't get my Social Security check when it's due?

Checks are mailed by the Treasury Department so that you get them on the 3rd day of the month following the month for which the check is due. For example, checks for the month of April should be received on May 3rd; if the 3rd falls on a weekend, then on the previous Friday.

If you do not get your check in the mail by the 6th of the month and if you believe that it is lost or stolen, notify the local Social Security office immediately and also the district office of the Treasury Department. Give this office your name, Social Security number, address, and month for which the check was issued.

Can I still get benefits if I move outside the United States?

If you are a U.S. citizen and plan to be outside the United States more than 3 months, your checks will be mailed to your new address. Or, you can have the checks sent to your bank for automatic deposit. You will still be covered by Medicare, but Medicare will not pay for treatment outside the U.S.

If you are not a U.S. citizen, your check will be stopped after you are outside the United States for 6 months. And checks are not sent to anyone in certain restricted countries—Cambodia, Cuba, North Korea, many of the former republics of the U.S.S.R., or Vietnam. See your local Social Security office for a current list of restricted countries.

When I call the Social Security Administration, will the questions I ask and the information I give be treated as confidential? Why are there sometimes 2 representatives on the telephone?

The confidentiality of your dealings with the Social Security Administration is covered under the Privacy Act, but you should be aware that the SSA will match computer records with other government agencies, such as the Department of Veterans Affairs and the Internal Revenue Service. All this is stated on the back of every Social Security form under "Privacy Act Notice." Sometimes there is a supervisor on the line for telephone calls to monitor the service of the representative who is helping you.

I have gotten several different answers to the same question from Social Security. What do I do?

Submit your question in writing and get a written answer to it. If you do not believe the answer is correct, then appeal the decision, using the directions in Chapter 9.

I worked 2 jobs last year and ended up having more than the maximum FICA tax withheld from my wages. Can I get that money back?

You can receive a credit on your federal income tax for the extra FICA taxes you paid. There is a place to request it on your income tax return form.

Why aren't Social Security benefits paid on the basis of need rather than on what a person earned?

In a sense they are, because benefits are defined as a percentage of earnings and calculated on the basis of how much of a worker's salary the benefit replaces. For those with the very lowest earnings, benefits replace 59% of their income, compared to a 27% replacement value for those with the very highest earnings.

I have lost my Social Security card. What do I have to do to get a replacement?

You fill out and submit Form SS-5, Application for a Social Security Number Card. This same form is used to apply for an original number card and to register a name change with the SSA.

RETIREMENT BENEFITS

I will get money from a company pension when I retire. Will that income affect my Social Security benefits?

Pension money is *not* considered earnings or earned income. The only income that affects your Social Security benefits is "earned income." Earned income is defined as wages, tips, or self-employment earnings reported and reflected on your work record, plus any earnings from noncovered work. Your Social Security benefits might affect your pension, though. Some plans consider Social Security benefits as a "replacement" for pension funds and will deduct an amount equal to any benefit you receive from the SSA from your pension payment. Check your pension plan.

I am getting Social Security benefits and am worried about reduction of those benefits because of other money coming in. What can I get that won't reduce my benefits?

These kinds of income defined as "unearned" do not reduce benefits: payments for retirement, death, sickness, or accident; disability payments; medical or hospital expenses reimbursed in connection with sickness, accident, or disability; income from annuities or IRA or Keogh accounts; gifts and inheritances; rental income; royalties from preretirement patents or copyrights; interest on bank accounts or from bonds; dividends from stocks and capital gains from sales of securities; jury duty pay; and income from a limited partnership.

Does the income earned by my wife and children reduce the Social Security benefit I get as a retired worker?

No. Only your earnings are considered, based on your own work record. The income of a dependent does not affect your benefit.

Can I make voluntary contributions or deposits to Social Security in order to boost my benefit when I retire?

No. Your Social Security work record is not like a savings account at a bank—contributions are based solely on your earnings. You can, however, work past "Normal Retirement Age" for your year of birth, and if you replace some of your low-earning years on your work record with higher-earning years, that will increase your benefit.

Is it true that you actually have to pay taxes on Social Security benefits?

Fewer than one-sixth of the people who receive Social Security retirement benefits have high enough incomes to have to pay taxes on Social Security benefits, even after the 1992 tax law was passed. These taxes help make the distribution of benefits a bit fairer and contribute to the system as well, since the money is paid into the Social Security trust funds. The Social Security Benefit Statement, sent to you at the end of each year after you begin receiving benefits, and the instructions that accompany your IRS 1040 tax form, will tell you if your benefits are subject to tax.

Can I collect a reduced benefit on my own work record at age 62 and then switch at 65 and collect a higher benefit on my husband's work record as his spouse?

Yes, you can switch. By comparing your Personal Earnings and Benefit Estimate Statement with your husband's, you will be able to tell whether it will be to your advantage to do so.

The SSA has made an error in counting my pension payments as earned income because the IRS taxes those payments. What should I do?

The IRS may tax your pension retirement benefits, but they are still exempt earnings for the purpose of calculating your Social Security benefits. File an immediate complaint in writing with your local Social Security office, requesting a review of the action taken in reducing your benefits. It is better to go to the office in person with the written complaint, and have the representative stamp your copy of the complaint with the date the complaint was filed and any index number placed on it, so you can keep track of the action on your case.

SURVIVORS' BENEFITS

My husband just died. He was fully covered under Social Security. I am 63 and am getting a check based on my own work record, but it is low. Am I entitled to a higher benefit as his widow?

You are entitled to the higher benefit under either record, but you should explore all the options. You can take your widow's benefit now, but it will be reduced because you are not yet 65. Discuss your situation with a representative at your local SSA office.

When someone dies, whose responsibility is it to report the death to the SSA?

There is a special form that mortuaries are required to file with the Social Security Administration when someone dies. However, if the death will mean a change in your own benefit check, you should also make a report. You will also want to file an application for the lump-sum death benefit.

My wife was killed in an accident; she was only 35, and I am left to care for 3 children. I have been told I am eligible for benefits now, even though I am nowhere near 65, and I've heard that our children are eligible as well. Is this true?

If your wife had sufficient quarters of credit on her work record (as few as 6 QC's in the last 3 years), you and your children under 18 are eligible for Social Security survivors' benefits. These benefits are subject to certain limitations, however. Anything you earn above $8,040 a year will reduce your benefit by $1 for each $2 above this amount. Your earnings will not affect the children's benefits, but if they earn money, the same rule applies. The benefits paid to your family are also subject to the family maximum rule.

I am 63, drawing Social Security benefits as a widow. I would like to marry again, but I don't want to lose my Social Security check.

You would not lose your eligibility for Social Security benefits, as after age 60 (50 if you are disabled), remarriage will not stop your widow's benefit. At age 62 or older, you are also eligible to get benefits on the record of your new spouse, if they are higher.

SUPPLEMENTAL SECURITY INCOME

I have qualified for SSI benefits; can I also get Medicaid?

If you have qualified for SSI, you will probably also be eligible for Medicaid as well as other federal, state, or county social services. You can get more information about this at your local social services department or Medicaid or public welfare office.

Does living in an institution make me ineligible for SSI benefits?

It depends on what sort of institution it is. If you are otherwise eligible for SSI, you can still receive SSI benefits if you live in:
• A publicly operated community residence serving no more than 16 people.
• A public institution in order to attend approved educational or job training.
• A public emergency shelter for the homeless.
• A public or private institution and Medicaid is paying more than half the cost of your care. In this case, your monthly check will be limited to $30, unless your state adds to this amount.

People who live in city or county rest homes, halfway houses, or other public institutions are usually not eligible for SSI.

If I get a Social Security benefit, can I also get one from SSI?

It depends. In some cases a person may be eligible for retirement, disability, or survivors' benefits as well as SSI. The rules that determine disability are the same for SSI as those for Social Security, but the waiting periods are different—it's 5 months for disability insurance, but you can get SSI benefits as soon as you apply. The rules about returning to work also differ between disability insurance and SSI.

Do you have to be 65 to qualify for SSI?

Yes, with a few exceptions. You are eligible for SSI at any age if you meet the income and resources rules and also qualify as blind or disabled. Children as well as adults can get benefits because of blindness or disability.

My state seems to have different amounts and rules for SSI eligibility than your book mentions. Why is that?

We only give the federal amounts for SSI and some states add on to those amounts to pay higher benefits. In the states where the SSI benefits are higher, the income and resources limitations are higher as well.

DISABILITY BENEFITS

Do I have to be out of work 12 months before I file for disability benefits?

No. Disability benefits are paid if you are unable to work in any job due to a disability that is expected to last 12 months or more or that is expected to result in death. If you believe you meet 1 of these conditions, you should apply at once to the SSA.

Is the definition of disability the same for children and adults?

No. Until 1991 the definition of disability applied to children was based on the "listing of impairment" provisions of the SSA. Now, however, adult requirements do not apply to children. A child's ability to function will be determined by comparing his or her ability to that of children in the same age group.

How disabled does one have to be to qualify for disability benefits?

Social Security disability benefits are not intended for temporary conditions—the disability must be serious and long-term, or expected to result in death. Unlike some private pension plans or even other government disability programs, Social Security does not pay for partial disability. If you qualify for disability from some other program, or have a statement from a doctor saying that you are disabled, it doesn't necessarily mean you will be eligible for Social Security disability payments.

I get Workers' Compensation payments for disability. Does this mean I am ineligible for Social Security disability benefits?

You may be eligible, but your Social Security disability payment could be reduced because of the benefit you receive from Workers' Compensation. The law says that all your disability payments combined cannot exceed 80% of your earnings averaged over a period of time shortly before you became disabled.

How does the government monitor these programs to make sure, for example, that money is not being paid to people who have recovered?

The SSA reviews disability cases periodically to determine if beneficiaries are still disabled. When these reviews take place, a person receiving benefits may be asked to submit new medical evidence or undergo more medical examinations or tests.

MEDICARE BENEFITS

I am close to 65 and will soon be entitled to Social Security retirement benefits, but I plan to continue working and will be earning too much to get a benefit check. Does this mean I can't get Medicare coverage?

Your Medicare eligibility is not affected by high income. If you wish to be covered by Medicare, sign up for it at your local Social Security office 3 months before you become 65. You will be told about the enrollment periods, get your Medicare card, and you will be billed monthly for your Medicare Part B premium.

What happens if someone covered by Medicare dies leaving unpaid hospital or medical bills?

Any hospital insurance Part A payments for covered charges will be made directly to the hospital, skilled nursing facility, home health care agency, or hospice that provided the service. Any deductible or coinsurance payments that may be due are still owed and must be paid by the person who is responsible for the debts of the deceased. Payments for Part B covered services (if the supplier did not accept assignment) will be sent to the legal representative, executor, or administrator of the estate, or a survivor of the person who died. If the bills for these services were paid by a third party, proof of payment must be presented. Claims can be made for Part B medical insurance payments from Medicare either before or after the bills have been paid.

What is the difference between Medicare and Medicaid?

They are different health insurance programs. Medicare mainly covers people 65 and older and many disabled people. Medicaid is for people with low income and limited resources. It is possible to be eligible for both.

Do you have to be unable to work because of kidney disease to qualify for Medicare? What treatment for kidney disease does Medicare cover?

You do not need to be work disabled to qualify for Medicare if you have kidney disease, but you do need to require dialysis or a transplant because of permanent kidney failure. Medicare will cover dialysis and a transplant; it will also cover the kidney donor's care.

I have made a living will, but how can we be sure my wishes will be honored if I should be in an accident and be mentally incapacitated?

There is now a federal law, the Patient Self-Determination Act, which requires most hospitals, nursing facilities, hospices, and HMO's to inform patients on admission of their right to create advance directives for their medical care. Many of these providers have forms they will give you for this purpose, as do physicians in private practice. You can also get forms from your local or state medical societies.

There are basically 2 kinds of advance directives: the living will (the form these must take will differ from state to state) and the durable power of attorney for health care. A living will generally states the kind of medical care you want—or do not want—in varying degrees of detail (for example, what sort of life-prolonging or life-sustaining procedures you would not want if you became incompetent or had an incurable or irreversible condition). A durable power of attorney for health care names someone else to make these decisions for you if you are not able to make them yourself.

Having a single copy of one of these documents is not enough; make sure your attorney and your physician have a copy on file and that your family knows where your copy is.

9

Your Right to Appeal

If you feel that a decision the Social Security Administration has made about a claim is wrong—for instance, if you have been denied eligibility or if your benefit has been reduced or eliminated—you have the right to appeal.

Certain rules have to be followed, and you have to be sure that what is at stake is worth the effort. Usually it is, since in many situations, nothing more is required than getting a chance to explain something you've already explained before to a different person.

Persistence in these matters is often as important as patience. If you have kept good records, you have already done most of the work necessary for an appeal.

General Procedure

The first step is to be sure you have most, if not all, of the papers necessary, including (in writing) the decision you wish to appeal. Begin to gather any other documents you may need; you may have to wait a long time, but you also may have to respond quickly. Then you need to think about whether or not you need legal representation. In the early stages, and especially if the matter is not a complicated one, you probably do not.

REQUEST FOR RECONSIDERATION

Your local Social Security office has a form for the Request for Reconsideration, or you can make the request with a letter or on the telephone. Give the date, your name, and your Social Security and/or claim number. Keep a copy of the request, if you make it in writing (the best way). All the evidence submitted for the original decision and any new evidence you include will be considered.

Your papers will be reviewed by someone other than the person who made the decision with which you disagree. This person may ask for more information, and you may ask to speak with him or her to present your case, but since this is not a formal hearing you do not have to appear in person.

Reconsideration requests (except those involving disability, which take considerably longer) should be processed within 30 days after you have submitted all the information required of you. You should receive the SSA's decision in writing within that time, and if you don't agree with it, you have 60 days after the time you receive it to take your appeal further by requesting an administrative hearing.

REQUEST FOR ADMINISTRATIVE HEARING

The Social Security Administration also has a form for filing your request for an administrative hearing, or you may send a letter. At this point, you may want to think again about legal representation, though you do not have to have it. Instead, you may be able to get the help you need from state and area agencies for the aging, or one of the church, business, union, or social groups having advocacy programs.

Even your local Social Security office will provide information about people who can represent you, should you feel you need help. If you decide to get help from a lawyer, be sure he or she specializes in Social Security matters; you can find legal specialists in this area either through one of the programs mentioned above, or from your state or local bar association.

If you are going to have representation in the appeals process, you must fill out a special form naming this person as your representative and file the form with your Social Security office.

Administrative hearings usually are not scheduled for several months, but notice of the exact date may not come until about 2 weeks before it is to be held.

Use the time wisely. Be sure your personal records are in order. Line up any witnesses you may need, and take advantage of your right to examine the file the SSA has kept on this matter. It is especially important to be sure that nothing is missing from that file and that you fully understand why your claim is being denied.

You can arrange to see your file by getting the telephone number of the hearing office from your local Social Security office and calling the hearing office for an appointment.

The hearing is held before an administrative law judge (a lawyer who works for the SSA), who had nothing to do with the first two decisions. The proceedings will be recorded. You or the person you have officially designated will present your evidence, including documents, reports, and testimony of witnesses.

You can explain in your own words, or have your representative explain for you, why you think your claim is valid. If you are representing yourself and have questions about procedures, the administrative law judge will help you.

If you are not going to attend the hearing, you must notify Social Security in writing. Though unless the judge believes a decision can't be made without you, he or she will usually decide the case based on the information in your file plus any new information provided at this time.

The judge will issue a written decision on your appeal within a few weeks of the hearing. If you win the appeal, you may be entitled to receive benefits retroactive to the time you filed your original claim. If your appeal is denied, you have 60 days from the date you received your written notice of denial to file a further appeal.

APPEALS TO THE APPEALS COUNCIL

This is an appeal for a review of your case by the SSA's Appeals Council in Falls Church, Virginia. It is filed on a special form or by letter. The Appeals Council hears very few appeals and decides most cases on the basis of the files and written statements submitted. The Council considers all review requests but may deny a request if it decides the hearing decision is correct. If the Council decides your case should be reviewed, it may decide the case or return it to an administrative law judge for further action. It is rare for a decision to be reversed by this body, but you must have its denial in writing before you can take the next step, suing in federal court. You will be told how much time you have to make that appeal.

BRINGING SUIT IN FEDERAL COURT

If you have exhausted all the Social Security Administration's appeals procedures, you are entitled to sue the SSA in a Federal District Court. You must file in writing within 60 days after receiving the notice from the Appeals Council. Suing the SSA is a complicated and expensive process and you will certainly want expert legal assistance, if you haven't gotten it before this stage.

Again, be sure you have a lawyer who specializes in Social Security law, and find out what the legal fees will be. You should feel you have a good chance of winning the case and that the benefits at stake are worth the cost of going after them.

NOTE: The appeals process is likely to change at any time and without warning. If you need to appeal, check with your local Social Security office for the latest regulations.

DISABILITY APPEALS

The general procedures outlined above will apply to appeals of SSI and retirement program decisions; the methods for disability appeals are slightly different due to some changes made in 1992. These include beginning the reconsideration process for disability claims with a hearing with an administrative law judge (skipping the first level of appeal) and holding a face-to-face hearing for disability claims when they are reconsidered at the federal level.

Along with cutbacks in staffing, general budget tightening, and the rapidly increasing number of applications for disability in the last few years, a large number of claims for disability have been denied and many benefits already in place have been reduced or eliminated. As a result, there have been a number of appeals, so this part of the system is particularly slow with decisions on all levels.

If you need to enter a disability appeal because you believe that the SSA has made a mistake, you are of course entitled to appeal and you should not hesitate to do so. Be sure you fully understand why your claim was denied, your benefit reduced or eliminated, or whatever the problem is. Be prepared to present additional evidence to support your argument. New evidence can include results of tests done since your original claim, medical proof that your condition has not been improved by further treatment, and/or that your condition has gotten worse. You should also have records of all prescription drugs and medical treatments you have received since making your original claim.

The problem in disability appeals is that the process can be long and frustrating, and hard to pursue when one is not in the best of health. Patience and persistence will often be rewarded, however.

NOTE: Disability benefits continue through the hearing level of an appeal, but disability payments are subject to recovery if it is found that the person making the appeal is not disabled.

Disability Decisions

The legal criteria the SSA must follow to process disability claims are quite strict, compared to what is required in many other disability programs. Social Security's claims examiners must consider certain nonmedical criteria when they decide if a person is disabled. In other words, in addition to having an impairment that's expected to last a year or more, or one that might result in death, your condition must be so severe that it is expected to keep you from doing any substantial work.

If your claim is denied initially, you'll receive a letter that explains the decision and the reasons for it. The letter also tells you how to appeal and how much time you have to do it. If you disagree with the decision and decide to appeal, you must notify Social Security in writing, normally within 60 days of the date you receive the notice.

Any appeal, at any level, is made before someone who has not been involved with the previous appeal.

Medicare Appeals

DENIAL OF A HOSPITAL BILL CLAIM—PART A

If you want to appeal a denial of your hospital bill claim, be aware that the procedure differs from other Social Security appeals. First, be sure you fully understand why your claim is being denied. Usually Part A claims are denied for 1 of 3 reasons: services were deemed not medically necessary; services could have been provided to you outside a hospital; or your stay in the hospital was for custodial rather than medical reasons.

These decisions are made by the area's Peer Review Organization (PRO). To avoid the possibility of having to appeal in the first place, discuss Medicare coverage with your doctor in advance of your admission to the hospital. If your doctor believes that the treatment is necessary for your condition and will be covered by Medicare, he or she should be able to help you by writing the letters and furnishing additional information to support the claims you are appealing.

Appealing Decisions Made by Peer Review Organizations

The Peer Review Organization for your state is responsible for making decisions on the need for hospital care. Any time you are admitted to a Medicare-participating hospital, you will be given a statement called "An Important Message from Medicare." It describes briefly your rights as a Medicare hospital patient and tells you what to do if you think you are being asked to leave the hospital too soon, and how to request a review of a Notice of Noncoverage. This statement will also give the name, address, and phone number of the PRO for your state.

The Notice of Noncoverage is the written explanation of why you are being asked to leave the hospital. You must have it in order to request a review by the PRO.

Once you have asked for a review of the Notice of Noncoverage, Medicare will continue to cover your stay in the hospital while the appeal is pending—even if you lose the appeal.

All you need to do is follow the procedures described on the notice you receive. Briefly, the first step will be to request a reconsideration by the PRO. If you disagree with the reconsideration decision and the amount in question is $200 or more, you can request a hearing by an administrative law judge. If the amount is $2,000 or more, it can be appealed in a federal court.

NOTE: The procedure for appealing a part of your hospital bill is the same as that for appealing the whole bill.

APPEALING ALL OTHER HOSPITAL INSURANCE DECISIONS

Appeals of decisions on skilled nursing facility care, home health care, hospice services, and some inpatient hospital matters not handled by PRO's are handled by Medicare intermediaries (insurance companies). The notice you receive from Medicare that tells you of the decision made on these claims will also tell you the specific steps to take if you wish to appeal.

If you disagree with the intermediary's initial decision, you can request a reconsideration. This request is submitted directly to the intermediary, or through your Social Security office. If you disagree with the reconsideration decision and the amount in question is $100 or more, you can request a hearing by an administrative law judge. Cases involving $1,000 or more can be appealed, eventually, to a federal court.

Appealing Decisions by Health Maintenance Organizations (HMO's) and Competitive Medical Plans (CMP's)

Appeal rights for members of Medicare-certified HMO's and CMP's are the same as for any other Medicare beneficiaries. Federal law requires that these organizations provide a written explanation of appeal rights to all members at the time of enrollment.

DENIAL OF A MEDICAL CLAIM—PART B

Although you do have the right to appeal a Medicare Part B decision, this process has strict limitations. It is entirely in the hands of the Medicare carrier (insurance company), and few decisions are reversed.

The first step is to ask the carrier for reconsideration. Within 6 months of having received your Explanation of Medicare Benefits notice, you should file a written request for review by sending a letter to the insurance company named on your notice. Give your full name, the Medicare claim number, and say what you believe the error is or why you think the decision is wrong. Send copies of any pertinent information that may not have been available when the decision was made. The insurance company will then check its files for miscalculations, taking into account any new information you send. If yours is a complex situation, you may have to go to the next step.

If your claim is for $100 or more, the next step is to request an appeal hearing. This hearing is conducted by the insurance company, but may be held at your local Social Security office. You must request this hearing within 6 months of receiving the decision on your reconsideration, and you may present your evidence and bring witnesses to testify for you. Usually, the most important new evidence you can present is from your doctor, whose cooperation is crucial to any

appeal. The hearing officer, a professional health care specialist employed by the insurance carrier, will notify you by mail of the decision.

If the amount in dispute is $500 or more, and you disagree with the decision made by the hearing officer who represents the carrier, you have 60 days from the date you receive the decision to request a hearing before an administrative law judge.

This is as far as a Medicare Part B claim can go. The Social Security Act does not provide for an appeal to a Federal District Court for review of a decision concerning the amount of benefit payable under Medicare Part B.

ALL MEDICARE APPEALS

For any appeal relating to Medicare, these 3 points are essential:

• You must have a clear and detailed understanding of why your claim has been denied.

• You must have an equally clear and persuasive reason why you think Medicare should pay.

• You must have the full cooperation of your doctor.

NOTE: Medicare protection and disability benefits continue through the hearing level of an appeal. The SSA is entitled to recover disability payments made to you if it is determined that you are not disabled. Medicare payments, however, are not subject to recovery, even if you lose the appeal.

FAIR TREATMENT FOR ALL CLAIMANTS

To ensure that all claimants and their representatives receive fair and unbiased treatment in the appeals process, the SSA provides an opportunity to report alleged bias or misconduct at any stage during the hearings and appeals process. Anyone who has a complaint about the way a case is handled or how he or she is treated should be aware that all complaints are reviewed or investigated by someone who has not been involved in the case.

If you make a complaint, the SSA must promptly acknowledge it in writing and inform you or your representative how it will be handled, review or investigate your complaint in a timely manner, and send a written notice of the results of the investigation or review to all those involved.

Complete complaint procedures are available by writing to the Social Security Office of Hearings and Appeals, PO Box 3200, Arlington, VA 22203.

MORE INFORMATION ON APPEALS

If you have questions about your appeal rights, call the SSA's toll-free number, 1-800-772-1213, or your local Social Security office. Ask for the free fact sheet *The Appeals Process.* If you need information about having a representative, ask for the free fact sheet *Social Security and Your Right to Representation.*

Any Social Security office can help you prepare your appeal, or you may ask a lawyer, friend, or someone else to help you. This representative cannot charge or collect a fee from you without first getting written approval from the SSA. He or she will receive a copy of any decisions made about your claim.

Appendix A

Definitions

When you apply for benefits, it helps to be familiar with the terms and acronyms that are used frequently by the Social Security Administration. The Index will also help you find more information about the terms you may encounter.

Advance Directive A document which either names in detail the measures you would (or would not) want used to prolong your life if you should be in a situation in which you could not make your wishes known, or names someone to make these decisions for you.

AIDS Acquired Immune Deficiency Syndrome, a viral disease transmitted by bodily fluids for which there is, as yet, no known cure.

AIME Average Indexed Monthly Earnings. The AIME is calculated from a worker's Social Security covered wages for years after 1950, indexed to compare with the National Average Earnings level at the time of eligibility. Wages for each year up to the "indexing year" (the second year before the worker reaches age 62, or dies, or becomes disabled before 62) are used. The worker's AIME is the basis for determining the Primary Insurance Amount (PIA).

Approved Charge The amount determined by law to be a reasonable charge for a medical fee or service under Medicare. This set amount may be less than the provider's actual charge. You are also responsible for paying any amount above and beyond the approved charge.

ARC AIDS-Related Complex, a group of conditions and diseases which develop as a result of a deficiency of immune cells caused by AIDS.

Auxiliary/Auxiliary Benefits A person who, through his or her relationship to the covered worker, may be entitled to receive benefits on that worker's employment record. Benefits derived from a worker's record but paid to another (spouse, dependent child, grandchild, parent, etc.) are called auxiliary benefits.

Balance-Billing Adopted as a part of Medicare reform, balance-billing protection holds down a patient's out-of-pocket medical costs by limiting the amount a physician can charge over and above what Medicare approves.

Basic Benefit The base figure on which a worker's benefits are calculated. It is determined by the covered wages earned and the amount of time worked over a period of years. It is also called the Primary Insurance Amount (PIA) or the primary benefit.

Bend Points Percentages of the Average Indexed Monthly Earnings used as a formula for computing the Primary Insurance Amount, upon which benefits are based. Bend points are changed for each year's eligible workers according to changes in the national average earnings. Any lowering of the bend points can result in a reduction of the base upon which the benefits are computed. Also called Dollar Bend Points.

Calendar Year Any year from January 1 through December 31, as opposed to a fiscal (accounting) year, which begins at any date in the calendar year and ends a year later.

Carriers The private organizations—usually insurance companies—that have a contract with the government to review, then approve or deny claims and process the paperwork for Medicare Part B (medical insurance). For Medicare Part A, these companies are called intermediaries.

Catastrophic Illness As used in the Medicare Catastrophic Protection Act passed by Congress in July 1988, this term referred to a prolonged and acute illness requiring long hospital stays and expensive treatment. The 1988 legislation provided for expanded coverage to be financed entirely by payments from Medicare beneficiaries, but this plan was so unpopular that Congress repealed the legislation in October 1989.

CDC The Centers for Disease Control, the federal agency located in Atlanta, Georgia. The CDC issues definitions of diseases and the conditions that determine eligibility for state, federal, and/or private benefit programs.

CDR Continuing Disability Review. People receiving disability benefits have their cases reviewed on a periodic basis to determine if disability still exists.

CMP Competitive Medical Plan, a form of pre-payment group medical practice providing health services to enrollees. See also HMO.

Coinsurance When Medicare pays a portion of an approved charge and you (or an insurance company) pay a portion of that charge, the part that is *not* paid by Medicare is called coinsurance. The amount paid in coinsurance is counted toward your deductible. Also called cost sharing.

COLA A Cost-of-Living Adjustment (COLA) increases benefits by a set percentage of a worker's primary benefit. Congress bases the percentage for an adjustment on increases in the Consumer Price Index (CPI) and usually grants a COLA when the CPI increases between the third quarter of one year and the third quarter of the next year.

Common Law Marriage Generally, for a common law marriage to be valid in states where they are recognized, the couple must have the intention to marry and consider themselves husband and wife. Both must be legally capable of entering into a valid marriage (of legal age and not married to someone else). A state's Attorney General's Office will furnish information about specific requirements for that state.

Coordinated Care Plan Health care plans contracting with the Medicare program to provide services for Medicare beneficiaries. But instead of paying for each service when it is delivered, Medicare prepays these groups on a monthly basis for each enrollee. This term encompasses both HMO's and CMP's.

Covered Employment/Covered Worker Basically, any work is considered covered employment, and any worker with taxable earnings is considered a covered worker, if an employer-employee relationship exists and if compensation is paid in the form of wages, salaries, tips, fees, commissions, etc. A covered worker may be self-employed or may be employed in private or government work. Self-employed workers include independent contractors, professionals, farmers, and domestic workers.

Credited Earnings Credited earnings are the basis for Social Security benefits. These earnings represent no more than the maximum amount of money that is taxable each year, whether the worker is employed by an employer or is self-employed. The maximum amount of taxable earnings increases each year.

CSRS The Civil Service Retirement System, a federal civil service retirement program. Generally speaking, federal employees hired before January 1, 1984 are covered by CSRS and those hired after that date are covered under the Federal Employees' Retirement System (FERS).

Currently Insured This term applies to workers (and their beneficiaries and survivors) who become disabled or die before earning enough work credits to be fully insured. A worker is considered currently insured if he or she worked at least half the time between age 21 and death or disability. The SSA requires 6 quarters of coverage earned during the 13 quarters ending with the calendar quarter in which the covered worker dies or becomes entitled to disability or retirement benefits.

Custodial Care Assistance that does not require medical or paramedical training. It consists of help with activities of daily living—bathing, dressing, eating, getting in and out of bed, walking, taking medication, going to the bathroom, etc. Such care is not covered by Medicare, with the exception of hospice care.

DDS Disability Determination Service, a state office in which a doctor and a disability evaluation specialist examine medical records to determine eligibility for disability benefits prior to the SSA ruling on eligibility. The state DDS office may request more information and/or examinations and tests. If so, the DDS must pay any charges incurred.

Deemed Spouse A person who entered in good faith into a marriage ceremony that was later determined to be invalid. To be eligible for benefits, the deemed spouse must be living in the same household as the covered worker at the time of application, or at the time of the worker's death (if for a survivor's benefit). In the past, such a person was not entitled to benefits if there was a legal spouse. Now, a deemed spouse is also entitled to benefits on the worker's earnings record, and the legal spouse's benefit is paid outside the maximum family benefit. That means benefits paid to a deemed spouse will not affect, or be affected by, benefits paid to others based on the worker's earnings.

Delayed Retirement Credit (DRC) The SSA gives credit toward higher benefits to people who continue working and postpone collecting their benefits beyond the normal retirement age. This is intended to strengthen the system financially by encouraging workers to continue to pay money in, while at the same time postponing taking money out.

For eligible people age 65 in 1994, the credit is an increase of 4.5% of Primary Insurance Amount for each additional year the worker delays retirement after age 65 through age 70. These percentages will increase in the future, as will the Normal Retirement Age.

Dependent   To be considered by the SSA as a dependent of a covered worker and eligible for benefits under that worker's work record, you need not be totally dependent on that worker for your support—but you must fit one of the following categories:

- Spouse, age 62 or older.
- Spouse, under age 62, caring for worker's unmarried child who is under 16 or who became disabled before age 22.
- Disabled survivor of a covered worker.
- Divorced spouse (or deemed spouse), age 62 or older, if the marriage lasted more than 10 years.
- Unmarried child under 18.
- Unmarried child, any age if severely disabled before reaching age 22, for as long as the disability continues.
- Parent or parents of a worker who can demonstrate that the worker contributes more than 50% of his, her, or their actual support.

Dividend   The total of indexed earnings for all the years included in the computation of an individual worker's AIME (the best 35 years of indexed earnings for all born in 1929 or later).

Dollar Bend Points   See Bend Points.

DRG   Diagnostic Related Group. The government's cost-containment program for Medicare, which replaced the cost-plus method of payment in 1983, assigns treatment under Medicare to the appropriate Diagnostic Related Group, or DRG. Medicare pays fixed and limited fees for each of these based on local and average fees for those services.

Dual Eligibles   Refers to people who are eligible for Medicaid as well as Medicare.

Dual Entitlement   When a person is eligible to collect the same type of benefit under 2 different work records. About 4 of every 10 women retiring now are eligible for benefits under their own and their husband's (or former husband's) work record. Dual entitlement rules also apply to men, but only 1 percent of all male Social Security beneficiaries are eligible for a spouse's benefit that is higher than their own retirement benefit. Regardless of the number of work records under which a person is eligible, he or she can receive no more than the amount equal to the highest one.

DVA   The Department of Veterans Affairs.

Earned Income Tax Credit (EITC)   A tax credit available to some low-income workers with 1 or more dependent children (under 19 at the end of the tax year, or full-time student under 24, or permanently and totally disabled). If you qualify, use form Schedule EIC 1040 or 1040A with your tax return.

Earnings Limitation   Refers to the limit set by the SSA on how much you can earn without having your benefits reduced. Also called exempt earnings or retirement test.

EIN   Employer's Identification Number, used by the employer when paying Social Security taxes (FICA) withheld from the employee's wages.

Enrollment Periods   You must decide whether or not you want Medicare coverage and sign up for it, or enroll, during specific periods. Each period has different rules.

Entitlements/Entitlement Programs   Federal programs that transfer money from taxes to specific groups of people who meet certain objective criteria, such as being over age 65 or currently attending public school. Program recipients do not have to be needy to qualify for an entitlement program. Social Security and Medicare are entitlement programs; the Supplemental Security Income (SSI) program is not.

EOMB   Explanation of Medicare Benefits, the document Medicare sends to a beneficiary when a claim is made. It explains Medicare's response to that claim.

Extended Care   Refers to services furnished in a skilled nursing facility that "extend" the care that was given during a hospital stay. Extended care is provided by, or requires the supervision of, nurses or other professionals and is covered by Medicare only when provided in an approved skilled nursing facility.

FDI   Federal Disability Insurance trust fund, from which disability benefits are paid. Since 1956, a portion of each year's FICA payments contributed by workers and employers has been deposited in this fund.

FERS There are 3 parts to the Federal Employees' Retirement System (FERS): Social Security, a federal employee pension plan, and a thrift savings plan. This retirement system covers federal employees hired after January 1, 1984 and those federal employees who joined during the period from July through December 1987.

FHI Federal Hospital Insurance trust fund, now called the HI trust fund. Also see HI.

FICA Federal Insurance Contributions Act. The acronym FICA appears on W-2 wage forms, and shows amounts paid by wage earners into the Social Security trust funds. FICA is also referred to as the payroll tax.

Fiscal Year The 12-month period between the settlement of financial accounts. See Calendar Year.

FSMI Federal Supplementary Medical Insurance trust fund. It generally receives premiums and matching payments made under the supplementary medical insurance program (Medicare Part B).

Fully Insured A worker is considered permanently and fully insured if he or she has 40 quarters (10 years) of coverage throughout any 10 years' work history. A worker is also fully insured if he or she has 1 quarter for each year after the year the worker reaches 21 and before attaining age 62, but at least 6 quarters of coverage during this period.

HCFA Health Care Financing Administration. It is responsible for setting the standards that hospitals, skilled nursing facilities, home health agencies, and hospices must meet to be certified as qualified providers of Medicare services.

HHS The Department of Health and Human Services, the President's Cabinet office under which Social Security is administered.

HI The Hospital Insurance (Medicare Part A) trust fund. It helps pay for inpatient hospital care as well as follow-up outpatient care.

HIV Human Immunodeficiency Virus, the virus that causes AIDS.

HMO Health Maintenance Organization, a type of prepayment group medical practice providing health services either directly to its enrollees in a clinic or through hospitals, skilled nursing facilities, or other health suppliers. An HMO is the most closely controlled form of managed health care.

Hospice Special hospitals which provide the termi-

nally ill with physicians' services, nursing care, medical/social services, homemaker/home health services, short-term inpatient care, outpatient drugs for pain relief, and respite care. Terminally ill Medicare patients may now choose between traditional Medicare coverage or hospice care for the management of terminal illness while retaining regular Medicare coverage for all other illnesses or injuries.

Indexing An inflation adjustment procedure by which the earnings record of a worker is related to the national average earnings in the indexing year. The indexing year is the second year before the year in which the worker becomes 62, is disabled, or dies. For example, if a worker becomes 62 in 1994, the indexing year is 1992.

Insured Status The basis on which a worker meets the qualifications for receiving benefits, which can be done in several ways. See Currently Insured and Fully Insured.

Intermediaries The organizations—usually insurance companies—that have been designated by the Health Care Financing Administration to process claims and make payments to hospitals for Medicare Part A (hospital insurance). For Medicare Part B, these organizations or companies are called carriers.

IPA Independent Practice Associations, which have been called "HMO's without walls," have a roster of member doctors who provide care, usually on a prepaid basis.

MAGI Modified Adjusted Gross Income, the figure used to calculate whether or not taxes are due on Social Security income. The MAGI is the total of the adjusted gross income (line 31 of IRS 1040) plus tax-exempt income and one-half the total of the year's Social Security benefits received by an individual or couple.

Managed Health Care A catchall phrase for plans which exert controls over costs of health care delivery, either by contracting with suppliers to furnish care to groups on a prepaid basis (HMO's) or through traditional insured or employer-paid plans which require review for hospital admission, surgery, etc.

Maximum Allowable Amount Depending on your age, the maximum amount you are allowed to earn without lowering or eliminating your benefit.

Maximum Family Benefit The maximum monthly amount that can be paid to one family on a worker's earnings record, usually between 150%

and 180% of the worker's PIA. Your maximum family benefit is shown on your Personal Earnings and Benefit Estimate Statement.

Means Test Refers to the keying of government benefits to the amount of income and/or assets a person may have.

Medigap Insurance The catchall term for insurance policies which cover health care services not covered by Medicare. Abuse in this area had become so widespread, Congress passed a law governing what can be offered and to whom it can be sold.

Medipards Medipard directories are listings of the physicians and medical suppliers that accept assignment of Medicare payments. Medipard directories can usually be found in local American Association of Retired Persons (AARP) or senior citizen offices, area agencies on aging, or district Social Security offices.

Minimum Benefit A special minimum benefit payable to people in covered employment for many years at very low earnings. This benefit is computed by multiplying the number of years of coverage in excess of 10 years up to 30 by $11.50 (for benefits payable from 1979 onward—before that, it was $9). This minimum is paid if it is greater than the benefit computed under any other method. COLA's are added to this minimum benefit.

Modified Adjusted Gross Income See MAGI.

Monthly Earnings Test In the first year in which you retire, you can receive the full amount of your benefits for any month in which you don't earn the maximum allowable amount, or the exempt earnings, for your age group. If you are self-employed, you may get your full benefit for any month in which you do not perform substantial services—usually, that means work in your business for less than 45 hours during the month. (After the first year, earnings as well as benefits are calculated on a yearly basis.)

Normal Retirement Age (NRA) Age at which the SSA will begin to pay full (unreduced) retirement benefits. Presently, the NRA is 65, but it will begin to rise (affecting those who become 62 in 2000) in 2-month increments over a 22-year period until it reaches age 67.

Notch Some workers born in or before 1916 whose benefits were figured under the method in effect before 1977 receive slightly higher benefits than the workers born between 1917 and 1921 (the so-called "notch babies") who have similar earnings histories and who retired at the same age. Some

definitions extend the notch to 1926. This unintended small windfall for the older workers came about through the introduction of COLA's in 1972.

OHA The Social Security Administration's Office of Hearings and Appeals

OMB The Office of Management and Budget.

Ombudsmen Government-appointed officials whose purpose is to look after the interests and protect the rights of specific groups of people. An example is the Medicare Peer Review Organizations. Some private groups, such as the American Association of Retired Persons (AARP), have special committees that perform similar functions

PASS Plan for Achieving Self-Support, a program to encourage people receiving SSI and disability payments to rejoin the work force through individualized plans for training and support in job placement.

PEBES Personal Earnings and Benefit Estimate Statement. By using computerized records of your past covered earnings and your own information about your expected future earnings, the SSA can give you an estimate of your Social Security benefit at the time you choose to receive it. Your local SSA office has forms on which to request this estimate, or call 1-800-772-1213.

Permitted Disparity Also called Social Security integration. Under federal pension and tax laws, companies paying pensions are specifically allowed to include the amount of a worker's Social Security benefit when calculating total retirement benefit. Currently, the law limits the reduction of a pension to no more that 50% for pension credits earned after December 31, 1988; it can be as much as 100% for credits earned before.

PIA Primary Insurance Amount, also called primary benefit and basic benefit. All (100%) of this amount is paid to an entitled worker when he or she retires at the Normal Retirement Age—or this is the amount that is reduced by a sliding percentage for earlier retirement. This is also the amount on which benefits payable to a worker's dependents and survivors are calculated.

Poverty Level/Poverty Threshold Each year, the government sets figures for income below which the recipients are officially considered to be living in poverty. These income figures are set for incomes of an aged individual, a family of 2 with an aged head, and a family of 4.

PPO Preferred Provider Organization, a more

loosely organized managed health care network, which provides a list of doctors and hospitals. It pays more if you go to a "preferred" provider, less if you don't.

Preventive Medicine Treatment by health care providers which attempts to prevent infirmity and disease rather than treating illness after it has occurred.

Primary Wage Earner One whose earnings record is used to determine benefits payable to himself or herself or to eligible dependents and survivors. A primary wage earner can be an employee or a self-employed worker.

PRO Peer Review Organizations are groups of physicians paid by the federal government to review medical care given to Medicare patients by hospitals and other physicians. PRO's in each state provide a professional group to oversee the cost-cutting goals authorized by Medicare, to maintain standards, and to guard against abuses.

Provider The hospital, nursing facility, or health care professional providing Medicare service or equipment.

Provisional Income An individual's or a married couple's adjusted gross income as reported on the IRS Form 1040, plus 50% of total Social Security benefits received for the year, plus nontaxable interest. If this sum exceeds base amounts (set yearly), federal income tax must be paid on Social Security benefits.

QC Quarter of Coverage, a unit of work credit used by the SSA to calculate benefits. The number of credits you need depends on the kind of benefit you are claiming, as well as your age. Also called quarter and credit.

QMB Qualified Medicare Beneficiary. For certain low-income elderly people who meet income and resource qualifications, state medical assistance (Medicaid) will pay the annual Medicare medical insurance premium, and may also pay the yearly Medicare medical insurance deductible and Medicare coinsurance. People eligible for this assistance are sometimes called "Quimbys."

RBRV The Resource-Based Relative-Value scale establishes the rate Medicare will pay for each service a physician performs. The scale provides a formula based on the time, overhead, and liability insurance premiums of doctors applicable to each service or procedure.

Reasonable Fees and Charges Medicare defines reasonable fees and charges as the **lesser** of:

- Your physician's or supplier's present or actual charge for a specific service.
- The customary fees the physician or supplier charges for a particular service.
- The prevailing charge for the service determined by the Medicare carrier under a procedure prescribed by Medicare law.

The charges and fees deemed reasonable are generally not higher than the charges or fees of 3 out of 4 doctors or suppliers for the same services or supplies in the same area.

Recomputation Refiguring your benefit is called a recomputation. It happens automatically if your reported wages cause the benefit to be decreased or increased, or you can request a recomputation from the SSA.

If you disagree with the amount of benefit you have been assigned, or believe there is an error in your computation, you must make your request for a recomputation in writing. Be sure to include pertinent evidence with your letter; you will have to supply documents to substantiate your claim.

Reconsideration If you are turned down for benefits (that is, if you receive a "disallowance of benefits"), you can request a review of your application. You must fill out a form at your Social Security office, and the form must be filed within 60 days of your receipt of the notice that your claim for benefits has been rejected.

Respite Care Short-term care in a hospital to provide temporary relief to a person who regularly provides home care for a Medicare patient. Respite care is limited to 80 hours a year.

Retirement Test The specific conditions of age and years of covered employment a covered worker must meet to be eligible for Social Security retirement benefits.

Representative Payee An agency or person designated to receive payment of a benefit when the beneficiary is incapable of managing money.

RMA Referral and Monitoring Agency is a state agency which sets standards and regulations for substance abuse treatment, monitors and reports to SSA on DI and SSI beneficiaries' compliance with treatment plans.

Rounding In applying COLA's, the SSA rounds down to the dollar. In applying bend points to compute PIA, the SSA rounds down to the dime.

SECA Self-Employment Insurance Contributions Act, or the Social Security taxes on income made by self-employed people. SECA taxes are paid entirely by the self-employed person and are currently equal to the percentage of wages paid by an employee and the employer combined.

Sequestration This term is used in conjunction with the Gramm-Rudman-Hollings Act, which was passed to force Congress to reduce and eventually eliminate the federal deficit by imposing across-the-board spending cuts. These cuts are made automatically if Congress fails to meet the October deadline for passing a budget that cuts spending enough to meet targeted reductions. Budgets for each government department are reduced (sequestered) by a certain percentage, and the longer Congress delays, the more the percentage increases.

Service Benefits Service benefits are for people in or connected with the uniformed forces on active duty in the U.S. Army, Navy, Marines, Air Force, Coast Guard, and Coast and Geodetic Survey.

Before 1957, uniformed services personnel did not pay Social Security taxes, but earned a credit of $160 for each month of active service. Since 1956, all service-connected personnel have paid Social Security taxes. Their credits are based on basic pay plus noncontributory wage credits of $100 for each $300 of wages received in a year up to $1,200 in any year.

SLMB Specified Low-Income Medicare Beneficiary.

SMI Supplementary Medical Insurance, another name for Medical Insurance, Medicare Part B.

Social Security Integration The law which allows a company to reduce a worker's pension by as much as 50% by deducting the amount the worker receives in Social Security benefits. See Permitted Disparity.

Substantial Gainful Activity The cap set on the amount of earnings allowable while collecting disability insurance. The amount of exempt earnings established by the SSA for an individual is generally considered substantial gainful work for the disabled or blind person receiving benefits.

Substantial Services More than 45 hours of work per month in a trade or business. However, less than 45 hours per month may be considered substantial if it is spent in a highly skilled occupation, or in managing a sizable business.

Survivors' Benefits Payments made to a living spouse or living children of a deceased worker who was covered by Social Security.

Terminal Illness An illness expected to end in death.

Utilization Review Traditional health insurance plans usually require a second opinion for surgery, and a nurse or doctor from the reviewing company will call your physician before approving hospital admissions (except emergencies). They also usually limit the number of days the plan will pay for care, or the amount the company will pay for the care.

The Utilization Review Committee of a hospital decides if a particular service is covered by Medicare or not. Sometimes the PRO or PSRO (Peer Review Organization or Professional Standards Review Organization) is the committee that does this review.

Veterans' Benefits The federal government has more than 40 different benefits and services for veterans of service in the armed forces. The payment procedures under all these programs are complex, particularly when benefits under the Social Security programs also come into play. The Veterans Administration has material explaining these benefits programs; Pamphlet 27-82-2 may be ordered from the VA Compensation Group, Office of Personnel Management, Washington, DC 20415. Fact Sheet IS-I, *Federal Benefits for Veterans and Dependents,* is available from the Government Printing Office, Washington DC 20402.

Voluntary Enrollment for Medical Insurance Anyone age 65 or over and *not* eligible for Medicare hospital insurance (Part A) under Social Security may buy the coverage. For 1994, the basic premium for voluntarily enrollment for Medicare Part A is $245 per month. But if you want to buy hospital insurance, you have to enroll for Part B medical insurance and pay that monthly premium as well. The Part B premium for 1994 is $41.10 per month. Time restrictions for signing up are the same as for those eligible under Social Security coverage. See Enrollment Periods.

Work Record The record kept by the SSA of the wages you have in covered employment and the Social Security taxes you have paid over the years you have worked. The SSA sometimes refers to this record as your "account." Your work record determines your eligibility for benefits and the amount of benefits to which you are entitled, so it pays to be sure it is accurate. Check by requesting a Personal Earnings and Benefits Estimate Statement from the SSA.

Appendix B

Sources of Additional Information and Help

Your local Social Security office is the first place to call or go to for information on Social Security, Medicare, Disability Insurance, and Supplemental Security Income. The people who work there are there to answer your questions and help you with any problems you may have. In addition, the office will have a selection of free pamphlets that explain different aspects of the SSA programs.

This appendix suggests other sources from which you can get additional information about Social Security programs. We have also provided addresses for national, state, and local resources if you need to obtain copies of documents you do not have. Your public library reference department staff can also help by directing you to information in the collection and/or by helping you to find more books or additional information from other sources.

Social Security Telephone Numbers

The toll-free telephone number for Social Security is 1-800-772-1213 (or 1-800-SSA-1213), and automated service is available weekdays from 7 AM to 7 PM. You can get information on applying for a Social Security number, or a request form for a PEBES, or you can order free publications on Social Security, retirement, survivors' and disability benefits, SSI, and Medicare. You can also speak to a Social Security "teleservice representative" using this number.

The telephone number for your local or area SSA office is listed in your local telephone directory. Try to avoid calling at the busiest times, such as the middle of the day, the first half of the week, and the first half of every month.

Any Social Security notice you receive is now required by law to give you the address and telephone number of the office you should call if you have any questions about the notice. (The same law requires that these notices be written in clear and simple language to assure that the information they contain can be easily understood.)

NOTE: One thing the SSA will **not** tell you is someone else's Social Security number: giving out this information is a violation of the Privacy Act. Should you need to get another person's Social Security number, it may be found on copies of previous tax returns, W-2 and 1099 forms, labels on income tax booklets, payroll statements, military and school records, credit union and bank records, and most marriage certificates.

Social Security Regional Offices

Social Security files and records are maintained in the main office in Baltimore, Maryland, and they can usually be accessed by other offices. Regional offices serve specific areas, on a state-by-state basis. When requesting your Personal Earnings and Benefits Estimate Statement, send the form to the regional office for your state. (Please don't send it to us—we don't have your records!)

• If your legal residence is in Alabama, Arkansas, Colorado, Illinois, Iowa, Kansas, Louisiana, Mississippi, Missouri, Nebraska, New Mexico, Oklahoma, Texas, or Wisconsin, your regional office is:

> Social Security Administration
> Albuquerque Data Operations Center
> PO Box 4429
> Albuquerque, NM 87196

• If your legal residence is in Alaska, American Samoa, Arizona, California, Guam, Hawaii, Idaho, Minnesota, Montana, Nevada, North Dakota, Northern Mariana Islands, Oregon, South Dakota, Utah, Washington, or Wyoming, your regional office is:

> Social Security Administration
> Salinas Data Operations Center
> 100 East Alvin Drive
> Salinas, CA 93906

• If your legal residence is in Connecticut, Delaware, the District of Columbia, Florida, Georgia, Indiana, Kentucky, Maine, Maryland, Massachusetts, Michigan, New Hampshire, New Jersey, New York, North Carolina, Ohio, Pennsylvania, Puerto Rico, Rhode Island, South Carolina, Tennessee, Vermont, Virginia, Virgin Islands, West Virginia, or a foreign country, your regional office is:

Social Security Administration
Wilkes-Barre Data Operations Center
PO Box 20
Wilkes-Barre, PA 18703

Ordering Government Publications

In addition to the SSA's booklets and flyers, there are many other government publications that may be of interest to you. Catalogs from the following offices indicate the vast range of information available. Some, but not all, of the publications are free; the catalogs will tell you how to order.

• The catalog listing the free Social Security program pamphlets found at your local SSA office is available from:

Office of Public Affairs, SSA
Distribution Center
PO Box 17743
Baltimore, MD 21235
410-965-1720

• The Office of Research and Statistics for the Social Security Administration has a catalog listing and describing some of the statistical, administrative, and survey data available to non-SSA researchers.

ORS/SSA Publications Staff
Room 209
4301 Connecticut Avenue NW
Washington, DC 20008
202-282-7138

• The Consumer Information Center of the General Services Administration offers a catalog of government publications that are of special interest to consumers. The catalog includes Social Security program publications, along with many other useful and interesting booklets.

Consumer Information Center
PO Box 100
Pueblo, CO 81002
719-948-3334

• If unavailable in your local office, you can order a catalog and/or any of the free "consumer" publications the SSA itself produces by writing to:

Social Security Administration
Office of Public Affairs
Public Information Distribution Center
PO Box 17743
Baltimore, MD 21235

• The Government Printing Office catalog lists all of the publications currently available from the government. You can order what you want from the Printing Office, but it is sometimes easier and faster to order directly from the department that issues the publication. It's even better if you can visit a Government Printing Office bookstore—there are 24 of these around the country—where you can browse through the publications and select what is useful to you.

Government Printing Office
Order Department
Washington, DC 20402-9325
202-783-3238

• A commercial company that also sells publications of the U.S. Government and related agencies is:

Bernan Associates
4611-F Assembly Drive
Lanham, MD 20706-4391
301-459-7666

Medicare and Other Medical Information

When you enroll in Medicare, you will be sent a booklet, *The Medicare Handbook,* which gives a basic description of Medicare services. (There is also a *Social Security Handbook,* but you have to buy that from the Government Printing Office, address listed above.) Here are some useful resources if you need more help with Medicare:

• Your doctor's office or clinic will tell you the name and address of the Medicare carrier and intermediary for your area. You can also get this address from your local or state Office of Aging, which is listed in your phone book. This office is an excellent resource for addresses of various ombudsmen groups, such as the ones for nursing homes, the Medicare Peer Review Organizations, and the state agencies regulating home health care and insurance. The insurance intermediaries and PRO's are also listed in the Medicare booklet.

• Another resource you can write to or call is the Health Care Financing Administration at:

200 Independence Avenue SW
Washington, DC 20201
202-690-6726

The HCFA also has a toll-free number to answer questions about their programs: 1-800-638-6833.

Or, you can write the Department of Health and Human Services, at the same address. The telephone number, however, is 202-690-7000.

• The trade association for health insurers will provide answers to questions on its toll-free hotline about health and disability insurance, long-term care insurance, Medigap coverage, and general health insurance:

Health Insurance Association of America
1025 Connecticut Avenue NW
Washington, DC 20036-3998
1-800-942-4242

• To gain access to your own medical records, first ask the physician who treated you. If that doesn't work, the following resources may help. A free brochure (send a stamped, self-addressed envelope) entitled *Your Health Information Belongs to You* is available from:

American Medical Record Association
919 North Michigan Avenue, Suite 1400
Chicago, IL 60611

Information and advice on obtaining your medical records, including a state-by-state survey of laws governing patient access, is available for $5 from:

Health Research Group
Publications Manager
2000 P Street NW, Suite 700
Washington, DC 20036

For a copy of your Medical Information Bureau record (if one exists), contact:

Medical Information Bureau
Information Office
PO Box 105, Essex Station
Boston, MA 02112
617-426-3660

REPORTING FRAUD AND ABUSES

Phony and Alarmist Mailings About Government Programs

It is illegal to send out mailings which look as though they are from the government and which may use scare tactics such as threatening the loss of Social Security or Medicare benefits. The usual aim of these mailings is to solicit money and add your name to a mailing list that can be sold. If you receive such a mailing, you should report it to:

Chief Postal Inspector
United States Post Office
475 L'Enfant Plaza SW

Washington, DC 20260-2100
202-268-2000

Medicare Fraud and Abuse

One of the reasons for the soaring cost of Medicare is the filing of fraudulent claims, estimated to account for 3% to 10% of the program's total budget. If you have reason to believe that a physician, hospital, or other health care provider is billing for services not performed, or is performing unnecessary or inappropriate services, you should report it.

Begin by contacting the Medicare carrier or intermediary. Then write to:

Office of the Inspector General
Department of Health and Human Services
OIG Hotline
PO Box 17303
Baltimore, MD 21203-7303

This office will want to know the exact nature of the fraud you suspect; the date it occurred; the name and address of the party involved; the name and location of the carrier or intermediary you have reported it to and the date reported; and the name of the person you spoke to there and what that person told you to do.

The OIG currently has a toll-free fraud and abuse hotline (1-800-638-5779; in Maryland, 1-800-638-3986) as do the insurance carriers, but these numbers may be abolished because of budget constraints.

These offices do not handle questions about delayed claims or payments. If you have problems such as these, see the Medicare chapter.

Fair Treatment

The SSA is committed to fair and unbiased treatment of all Social Security claimants and their representatives and has a procedure for reporting alleged bias or misconduct. You can file a complaint at any Social Security office or any of the SSA's Offices of Hearings and Appeals (OHA offices). Your local office can give you a copy of the complete procedures for a complaint, or write to:

Social Security Administration
Office of Hearings and Appeals
PO Box 3200
Arlington, VA 22203

Congressional Representatives

If you want to write or call your congressional representatives about Social Security or Medicare, but don't know how to reach them, look in the government section (usually the blue pages) of your telephone directory. The names of your senators and representatives and their districts are listed under the heading "United States Congress." You can also contact a local or regional League of Women Voters, if there is one in your area.

The Social Security Administration maintains a liaison office for Congress and most members have staff people who specialize in Social Security matters.

VITAL STATISTICS OFFICES

One of the duties of state and local governments is to maintain records of births, deaths, marriages, and divorce. If you no longer have original copies of the documents you need in order to file a claim with the SSA, the city, county, or state where the event was recorded can supply you with certified copies of any required documents. (It is a good idea to get at least 2 copies of anything you have to order; you will usually need them.)

The sources below are arranged alphabetically by state, and include the fees for certified copies, research fees when applicable, and in some cases, how far back the records date. Fees were verified at press time, but they frequently change.

By calling ahead before sending a written request for copies, you can find out whether a special request form is required and check on the current fees. It may even be possible to place a telephone order and charge the fee to your credit card. Calling ahead also saves time because you can provide any special information necessary to locate the records you want.

However, if you write for copies without calling ahead, be sure to include the date of the event you want documented. If you do not know the exact date, give as close an approximate date as possible. These records are kept by year, and some offices will charge extra for each year's files that require a search.

Alabama

Bureau of Vital Statistics
State Department of Public Health
PO Box 5625
Montgomery, AL 36103
205-613-5418

$12 per copy; additional copies at same time, $4 each. Fee for special searches, $3 per hour. Birth and death records since 1908; marriage records since 1936; divorce records since 1950.

Alaska

Bureau of Vital Statistics
Department of Health and Social Services
Alaska Office Building, PO Box 110675
Juneau, AK 99811-0675
907-465-3391

$10 per copy; additional copies at the same time, $2. Records since 1913.

Arizona

Division of Vital Records
State Department of Health
2727 West Glendale
Phoenix, AZ 85015-3887
602-255-3260

$9 per copy for records after 1950; earlier, $12. Records since July 1, 1909; abstracts filed in counties before that date.

Arkansas

Bureau of Vital Statistics
State Department of Health
4815 West Markham
Little Rock, AR 72205
501-661-2336

$5 per copy for birth records; $4 per copy for death records. Records since February 1, 1914; some Little Rock and Fort Smith records from 1881.

California

Vital Statistics
Department of Health Services
304 S Street, PO Box 730241
Sacramento, CA 94244
916-445-2684

$13 per copy for birth record; $9 for death record. Records since July 1, 1905; for earlier records, write to County Recorder in county of event.

Colorado

Health Statistics & Vital Records
State of Colorado Department of Health
4300 Cherry Creek Drive South
Denver, CO 80222
303-692-2000

$12 per copy; additional copies, $6; $14 priority service. Records since January 1, 1910; for earlier records, write to local Registrar in county of event.

Connecticut

Vital Records Unit
Department of Health Services
150 Washington Street
Hartford, CT 06106
203-566-1120

$15 per copy. Records since July 1, 1897; for earlier records, write to Town or City Hall of event.

Delaware

Office of Vital Statistics
Division of Public Health
PO Box 637
Dover, DE 19903-0637
302-739-4721

$5 for first copy; additional copies at the same time, $3 each. Records since 1881.

District of Columbia

Vital Records Branch
Room 3007
613 G Street NW
Washington, DC 20001
202-727-5314

$12 per copy for short form; $18 for long form. Records since 1913.

Florida

Vital Statistics
Department of Health & Rehabilitative Services
PO Box 210
Jacksonville, FL 32231-0210
904-359-6900

$9 per copy; additional copies at the same time, $4 each.

Georgia

Vital Records Service
47 Trinity Avenue SW
Atlanta, GA 30334
404-656-7456

$10 per copy; additional copies, $5. Records since January 1, 1919; for earlier records, write to County Health Department in county of event.

Hawaii

State of Hawaii Research & Statistics Office
Department of Health
PO Box 3378
Honolulu, HI 96801-3378
808-586-4533

$2 per copy. Records since 1853.

Idaho

Vital Statistics
State House
Boise, ID 83720
208-334-5980

$8 per copy. Records since 1911; for earlier records, write to County Recorder in county of event.

Illinois

Division of Vital Records
605 West Jefferson
Springfield, IL 62702
217-782-6553

$10 for short form; $15 for long form; additional copies at the same time, $2 each. Records since January 1, 1916; for earlier records, write to County Clerk in county of event.

Indiana

Division of Vital Records
State Board of Health
1330 West Michigan Street
Indianapolis, IN 46206-1964
317-633-0274

$6 per copy for birth record; $4 for death record; additional copies at the same time, $1 each. Records since October 1, 1907; death records since 1900.

Iowa

Bureau of Vital Records & Statistics
State Department of Health
Lucas State Office Building, 321 East 12th Street
Des Moines, IA 50319-0075
515-281-4944

$10 per copy. Records since July 1, 1880.

Kansas

Vital Statistics
Kansas State Department of Health & Environment
900 Southwest Jackson
Topeka, KS 66612
913-296-1400

$10 per copy; additional copies at the same time, $5. Birth and death records since July 1911; marriage records since 1913.

Kentucky

Office of Vital Statistics
State Department of Health
275 East Main Street
Frankfort, KY 40621
502-564-4212

$7 per copy; death records, $6. Records since January 1, 1911 and earlier for Covington, Lexington, and Louisville.

Louisiana

Vital Records Section
Department of Health & Human Resources
PO Box 60160
New Orleans, LA 70160
504-568-5156

$10 per copy for birth record; $7 for death record or marriage certificate. Records since 1900.

Maine

Office of Vital Records
Department of Human Services
State House Station 11
Augusta, ME 04333
207-287-3184

$10 per copy; additional copies at the same time, $4 each. Records since 1892; for earlier records, write to Town Clerk in town of event.

Maryland

Division of Vital Records
State Department of Health & Mental Hygiene
PO Box 68760
Baltimore, MD 21215
410-225-5988

$4 per copy; additional copies at the same time, $3 each.

Massachusetts
(*except Boston*)

Department of Public Health
Registry of Vital Records & Statistics
Commonwealth of Massachusetts

150 Tremont Street, Room B3
Boston, MA 02111
617-727-0110

$11 per copy. Records since 1896; for earlier records, write to City or Town Clerk in place of event.

Massachusetts
(*Boston*)

Registry Division, Vital Statistics
Commonwealth of Massachusetts
1 City Hall Square
Boston, MA 02201
617-725-4175

$11 per copy. Records since 1639.

Michigan

State Registrar, Health Statistics
Michigan Department of Health
3423 North Logan Boulevard
PO Box 30195
Lansing, MI 48909
517-335-8656

$13 per copy; additional copies at the same time, $4 each. Search more than 3 years, $3 for each additional year. Records since 1867.

Minnesota

Registration, Department of Health
Minnesota Vital Statistics
717 Delaware Street SE
Minneapolis, MN 55414
612-623-5120

$11 per copy for birth record; $8 for death record. Records since 1900. Copies also available from Clerk of District Court in place of event.

Mississippi

Office of Vital Statistics
Department of Public Health
Mississippi State Board of Health
PO Box 1700
Jackson, MS 39215-1700
601-960–7981

$12 per copy for birth record; $7 short form; $10 for death record. Records since November 1, 1912.

Missouri
(*except Kansas City and St. Louis County*)

Bureau of Vital Records
Missouri Department of Health
PO Box 570
Jefferson City, MO 65102-0570
314-751-6387

$10 per copy. Records since January 1910.

Missouri
(*Kansas City*)

Bureau of Vital Statistics
City Hall
414 East 12th, 21st Floor
Kansas City, MO 64106
816-274-1428

$6 per copy.

Missouri
(*St. Louis County*)

Bureau of Vital Statistics
St. Louis County Health Department
111 South Meramec Avenue
Clayton, MO 63105
314-854-6685

$10 per copy for birth and death records.

Montana

Division of Records & Statistics
State Department of Health & Environmental
  Sciences
Cogswell Building
Helena, MT 59620
406-444-2614

$10 per copy. Records since late 1907.

Nebraska

Bureau of Vital Statistics
State Department of Health
PO Box 95007
Lincoln, NE 68509
402-471-2871

$8 per copy for birth record; $7 for death record.
Records since 1904; for earlier records, write to this
office for information.

Nevada

Department of Health, Welfare & Rehabilitation
Division of Health, Section of Vital Statistics
505 King Street
Carson City, NV 89710
702-687-4480

$11 per copy for birth record; $8 for death record.
Records since July 1, 1911; for earlier records, write
to County Recorder in county of event.

New Hampshire

Bureau of Vital Records
Division of Public Health Services
Department of Health & Human Services
6 Hazen Drive
Concord, NH 03301
603-271-4650

$10 per copy. Copies of records may also be ob-
tained from City or Town Clerk in place of event.

New Jersey

Bureau of Vital Statistics
State Department of Health
South Warren & Market Streets
Trenton, NJ 08625
609-292-4087

$4 per copy; additional copies at the same time, $2;
$1 per year for search when date is unknown. Records
since June 1878; for earlier records, write to Archives
and History Bureau, State Library Division, State Department of Education, Trenton, NJ 08625.

New Mexico

Vital Records Bureau
New Mexico Health & Environment Department
1190 St. Francis Drive
Santa Fe, NM 87502
505-827-2338

$10 per copy for birth record; $5 for death record.
Records since 1920; for earlier records, write for information.

New York
(*except New York City*)

Bureau of Biostatistics
Vital Records Section
State Department of Health
Empire State Plaza, Corning Tower Building

Albany, NY 12237
518-474-3077

$15 per copy. Records since 1880. For records prior to 1914 in Albany, Buffalo, and Yonkers, write to Registrar of Vital Statistics in city of event.

New York
(New York City, all boroughs)

Bureau of Vital Records
Department of Health
125 Worth Street
New York, NY 10013
212-788-4520/25

$15 per copy. Records since 1866. For earlier records, write to Municipal Archives and Records Retention Center of New York Public Library, 238 William Street, New York, NY 10038.

North Carolina

Vital Records Branch
Division of Health Services
225 North McDowell Street
Raleigh, NC 27602
919-733-3526

$10 per copy. Records since October 1, 1913 (and some earlier).

North Dakota

Division of Vital Records
North Dakota State Department of Health
600 East Boulevard
Bismarck, ND 58505
701-224-2360

$7 per copy for birth record; $5 for death record. Records since July 1893; records from 1894 to 1920 are incomplete.

Ohio

Division of Vital Statistics
State Department of Health
G-20 State Department Building
PO Box 15098
Columbus, OH 43215
614-466-2531

$7 per copy. Records since December 20, 1908; for earlier records, write to Probate Court in county of event.

Oklahoma

Division of Statistics
State Department of Health
PO Box 53551
Oklahoma City, OK 73152
405-271-4040

$5 per copy. Records since October 1908.

Oregon

Vital Statistics Section
Oregon State Health Division
PO Box 14050
Portland, OR 97214
503-731-4108

$15 per copy. Records since October 1903.

Pennsylvania

Vital Records
512 State Office Building
300 Liberty Avenue
Pittsburgh, PA 15222
412-565-5114

$4 per copy for birth record; $3 for death record. Records since January 1, 1906; for earlier records, write to Register of Wills, Orphans' Court, county seat of event.

Rhode Island

Division of Vital Statistics
State Department of Health
101 Cannon Building
3 Capitol Hill
Providence, RI 02908
401-277-2812

$12 per copy; additional copies, $7 each. Records since 1853; for earlier records, write to Town Clerk in town of event.

South Carolina

Office of Vital Records & Public Health Statistics
Department of Health & Environmental Control
2600 Bull Street
Columbia, SC 29201
803-734-4830

$8 per copy. Records since January 1, 1915; for earlier records, write to City or County Health Department in place of event.

South Dakota

Public Health Statistics
State Department of Health
445 East Capitol
Pierre, SD 57501
605-773-3355

$5 per copy. Records since July 1, 1905; some earlier records.

Tennessee

Office of Vital Records
Tennessee Department of Health & Environment
Cordell Hull Building, C-3
Nashville, TN 37247-0350
615-741-1763

$5 per copy for short form; $10 for long form (marriage, divorce, birth, and death records). No short forms before 1960.

Texas

Bureau of Vital Statistics
Texas Department of Health
1100 West 49th Street
Austin, TX 78756
512-458-7111

$11 per copy for birth records; $9 for death records. Records since 1903.

Utah

Bureau of Vital Statistics
Utah State Department of Health
PO Box 16700
Salt Lake City, UT 84116
801-538-6105

$12 per copy for birth record; $9 for death record; additional copies at the same time, $3 each. Records since 1905; for earlier Salt Lake City or Ogden records, write to City Board of Health in city of event.

Vermont

Agency of Administration
Reference Research Section
State Administration Building
US Route 2, Drawer 33
Montpelier, VT 05633-7601
802-828-3286

$5 per copy. Records 1857–1954 (births, deaths, and marriages) and 1857–1967 (divorces). Recent records are kept by the Division of Public Health Statistics, Vermont Department of Health, PO Box 70, Burlington, VT 05402-0070; 802-862-5701.

Virginia

Division of Vital Records
State Department of Health
PO Box 1000
Richmond, VA 23208-1000
804-786-6228

$5 per copy. Records from January 1853 through December 1896 and since June 4, 1912. For records between these dates, write to Health Department in city of event.

Washington

Vital Records
State Department of Health
PO Box 9709
Olympia, WA 98507
206-753-5936

$11 per copy. Records since July 1, 1907. Seattle, Spokane, and Tacoma City Health Departments also have these records; for earlier records, write to Auditor in county of event.

West Virginia

Division of Vital Statistics
State Department of Health
State Office Building No. 3
Charleston, WV 25305
304-558-2931

$5 per copy. Records since January 1917; for earlier records, write to Clerk of County Court in county of event.

Wisconsin

Center for Health Statistics
Wisconsin Division of Health
PO Box 309
Madison, WI 53701
608-266-1372

$10 per copy for birth records; $7 for death records.

Wyoming

Vital Record Services
Hathaway Building
Cheyenne, WY 82002
307-777-7591

$11 per copy for birth records; $9 for death records.

NATIONAL ARCHIVES AND OTHER FEDERAL OFFICES

The National Archives keeps records of births, deaths, and marriages that take place at U.S. Army facilities, and of American citizens registered at foreign service posts.

For registrations made more than 80 years ago of the births and marriages of American citizens abroad (and for deaths prior to 1955), contact:

Civil Archives Division
National Archives
Washington, DC 20408
202-501-5402

For registrations made less than 80 years ago on births and marriages of American citizens abroad (and for deaths after 1955), apply to Passport Services. The address is given below under "Passport Applications." Records are also kept in the National Archives offices located in or near 10 major cities:

Atlanta

Chief Archives Branch
Federal Archives & Records Center
1557 St. Joseph Avenue
East Point, GA 30344
404-763-7477

Records cover Alabama, Florida, Georgia, Mississippi, North Carolina, South Carolina, and Tennessee. This office also holds the census records for the entire United States.

Boston

National Archives—Boston Branch
Federal Records Center
380 Trapelo Road
Waltham, MA 02150
617-647-8100

Chicago

Chief Archives Branch
Federal Archives & Records Center
7358 South Pulaski Road
Chicago, IL 60629
312-581-7816

Denver

National Archives—Denver Branch
Building 20, Denver Federal Center
Denver, CO 80225
303-236-7817

Kansas City

Chief Archives Branch
Federal Archives & Records Center
2312 East Bannister Road
Kansas City, MO 64132
816-926-7271

Los Angeles

National Archives—Los Angeles Branch
2400 Avila Road
Laguna Niguel, CA 92677
714-643-4241

Records cover Arizona; the southern California counties of Imperial, Inyo, Kern, Los Angeles, Orange, Riverside, San Bernardino, San Diego, San Luis Obispo, Santa Barbara, and Ventura; and Clark County, Nevada.

New York

National Archives—New York Branch
Building 22—MOT Bayonne
Bayonne, NJ 07002-5388
201-823-7252

Records cover New Jersey, New York, Puerto Rico, and the Virgin Islands.

Philadelphia

Chief Archives Branch
Federal Archives 7 Records Center
5000 Wissahickon Avenue
Philadelphia, PA 19144
215-597-3000

Records cover Delaware, the District of Columbia, Maryland, Pennsylvania, Virginia, and West Virginia.

San Francisco

Chief Archives Branch
Federal Archives & Records Center
1000 Commodore Drive

San Bruno, CA 94066
415-876-9009

Records cover California (except counties covered by Los Angeles branch), Hawaii, Nevada, and the Pacific Ocean Area.

Seattle

Chief Archives Branch
Federal Archives & Records Center
6125 Sands Point Way NE
Seattle, WA 98115
206-526-6501

Records cover Alaska, Idaho, Oregon, and Washington.

Census Records

Census records give name, age, state, territory, and country of birth for each person in a counted household. Records are available since 1790 (except for 1890, most of which were destroyed by fire).

United States Bureau of the Census
National Archives Reference Service
Washington, DC Area Office
7th and Pennsylvania Avenues NW
Washington, DC 20408
202-501-5402

Naturalization Records

The Immigration and Naturalization Service of the U.S. Department of Justice maintains records that may be useful. A search of these records requires submission of the Freedom of Information Privacy Act Request Form (G-639). To obtain a copy of the form and the location of the appropriate office(s) to submit it to, write:

U.S. Department of Justice
Immigration & Naturalization Service
Washington, DC 20536

Passport Applications

Passport applications serve as good documentation for date of birth because they show a date based on a review of the applicant's birth certificate. Passport applications from as early as 1791 through 1905 are available from the National Archives. For more recent records, write to:

Passport Services, PS/PC
Department of State
Washington, DC 20524

Military Records

Access to military records is restricted to the veteran himself or herself; next of kin if the veteran is deceased; federal officers for official purposes; or those with release authorization signed by the veteran or his or her next of kin. The form that must be submitted is Request Pertaining to Military Records, #180; it gives all the addresses of the records depositories for the different services. To obtain this form, write to:

National Personnel Records Center
9700 Page Boulevard
St. Louis, MO 63132

SPECIAL RESOURCES FOR SENIORS

Recently, a nationwide information and referral service designed to identify resources available for older people at the state and local levels has been established. Administered in part by the National Association of Area Agencies on Aging, this service is called "Eldercare Locator." By dialing the toll-free number, 1-800-677-1116, callers can be referred to a local resource that will provide information about senior services available in the requested community, such as legal assistance, day care, home health services, financial aid, and nursing homes.

The network covers the United States and its territories and is a collaborative project of the Administration on Aging, the National Association of Area Agencies on Aging, and the National Association of State Units on Aging.

Anyone in the United States, Puerto Rico, and the Virgin Islands can call the toll-free number for assistance. It is a public service available business days between 9 AM and 8 PM Eastern Standard Time. It helps to have the following information when you call:

• Your name and address, with Zip Code, or that of the older person for whom you are calling. (The Zip Code is key, as that is how they locate the nearest sources.)

• A brief, general description of the problem or type of assistance you are seeking.

Appendix C

Forms

The Social Security Administration is rapidly moving toward the elimination of paper forms altogether. Interviewing people, either in person or over the telephone, and entering their answers directly into the computer saves time, minimizes opportunity for error, and requires many fewer people to manage the information. As the population to be served increases and resources shrink, the SSA must become more efficient and computers are the major component of this effort.

In most SSA offices today, the use of computers has eliminated the need for many of the forms that follow, but it is helpful and timesaving to know in advance what questions you will be expected to answer in various situations so you will be able to provide the information when you are asked. For that reason, we continue to reproduce this material.

You should never use these forms to apply for benefits —they are reproduced here as samples only.

COLLECTION AND USE OF INFORMATION FROM YOUR APPLICATION

All SSA forms contain a standard statement about the Privacy Act and the use of the information you provide. You should read it so that you will be aware of the many ways the information you furnish may be shared with other government agencies.

The Privacy Act statement usually appears on the last page of applications. Rather than reproduce it with every form, it appears on pages 135 and 165.

PAPERWORK ACT

In addition to a statement about the Privacy Act, each SSA form meets the requirements of the Paperwork Act by providing a statement that establishes the length of time needed to complete the form.

Regulations also provide that unless for some reason the form is obsolete, all supplies must be used up before new forms are ordered. The number of the form and its date of issue appear in the lower left-hand corner.

RECEIPT FOR CLAIMS

Some forms include a receipt that provides a record of when you filed your application for benefits and tells you approximately when, after you have furnished all the information requested, you will hear from the SSA about your claim. It also gives a telephone number or numbers to call should you need to report some change that may affect your claim.

REPORTING CHANGES

When and how you must report changes in your circumstances are listed on the forms for which this is important. These sections will also explain how much time you have to report a change and what the penalties will be if you fail to do so.

DEPARTMENT OF HEALTH AND HUMAN SERVICES
SOCIAL SECURITY ADMINISTRATION

Form Approved
OMB No. 0960-0066

FORM SS-5 – APPLICATION FOR A SOCIAL SECURITY NUMBER CARD (Original, Replacement or Correction)

Unless the requested information is provided, we may not be able to issue a Social Security Number (20 CFR 422-103(b))

INSTRUCTIONS TO APPLICANT ▶ Before completing this form, please read the instructions on the opposite page. Type or print, using pen with dark blue or black ink. Do not use pencil. SEE PAGE 1 FOR REQUIRED EVIDENCE.

		First	Middle	Last
NAA	NAME TO BE SHOWN ON CARD			
NAB **1**	FULL NAME AT BIRTH (IF OTHER THAN ABOVE)	First	Middle	Last
ONA	OTHER NAME(S) USED			

STT **2**	MAILING ADDRESS	(Street/Apt. No., P.O. Box, Rural Route No.)

CTY	CITY (Do not abbreviate)	STE	STATE	ZIP	ZIP CODE

CSP 3 CITIZENSHIP (Check one only)
- [ ] a. U.S. citizen
- [ ] b. Legal alien allowed to work
- [ ] c. Legal alien not allowed to work
- [ ] d. Other (See instructions on Page 2)

SEX 4 SEX
- [ ] MALE
- [ ] FEMALE

ETB 5 RACE/ETHNIC DESCRIPTION (Check one only) (Voluntary)
- [ ] a. Asian, Asian-American or Pacific Islander (Includes persons of Chinese, Filipino, Japanese, Korean, Samoan, etc., ancestry or descent)
- [ ] b. Hispanic (Includes persons of Chicano, Cuban, Mexican or Mexican-American, Puerto Rican, South or Central American, or other Spanish ancestry or descent)
- [ ] c. Negro or Black (not Hispanic)
- [ ] d. Northern American Indian or Alaskan Native
- [ ] e. White (not Hispanic)

DOB **6** DATE OF BIRTH	MONTH	DAY	YEAR	AGE **7** PRESENT AGE	PLB **8** PLACE OF BIRTH	CITY (Do not abbreviate)	STATE OR FOREIGN COUNTRY (Do not abbreviate)	FCI [ ]

MNA **9** MOTHER'S NAME AT HER BIRTH	First	Middle	Last (Her maiden name)
FNA FATHER'S NAME	First	Middle	Last

PNO 10
a. Has a Social Security number card ever been requested for the person listed in item 1? [ ] YES(2) [ ] NO(1) [ ] Don't know(1)

b. Was a card received for the person listed in item 1? [ ] YES(3) [ ] NO(1) [ ] Don't know(1)

▶ **IF YOU CHECKED YES TO A OR B, COMPLETE ITEMS C THROUGH E; OTHERWISE GO TO ITEM 11.**

SSN c. Enter the Social Security number assigned to the person listed in item 1. [ ][ ][ ] – [ ][ ] – [ ][ ][ ][ ]

NLC d. Enter the name shown on the most recent Social Security card issued for the person listed in item 1.

PDB e. Date of birth correction (See Instruction 10 on page 2) ▶ | MONTH | DAY | YEAR |

DON **11** TODAY'S DATE	MONTH	DAY	YEAR	**12** Telephone number where we can reach you during the day. Please include the area code.	HOME	OTHER

ASD WARNING: Deliberately furnishing (or causing to be furnished) false information on this application is a crime punishable by fine or imprisonment, or both.

IMPORTANT REMINDER: WE CANNOT PROCESS THIS APPLICATION WITHOUT THE REQUIRED EVIDENCE. SEE PAGE 1

13 YOUR SIGNATURE

14 YOUR RELATIONSHIP TO PERSON IN ITEM 1
[ ] Self [ ] Other (Specify) _____

WITNESS (Needed only if signed by mark "X")

WITNESS (Needed only if signed by mark "X")

DO NOT WRITE BELOW THIS LINE (FOR SSA USE ONLY)

DTC (SSA RECEIPT DATE)	NPN	DOC
NTC CAN	BIC	IDN	ITV [ ] MANDATORY IN PERSON INTERVIEW CONDUCTED

TYPE(S) OF EVIDENCE SUBMITTED

SIGNATURE AND TITLE OF EMPLOYEE(S) REVIEWING EVIDENCE AND/OR CONDUCTING INTERVIEW

DATE

DATE

DCL

Form SS-5 (11-86)
5/84, 1/85 and 8/85 editions may be used until supply is exhausted

97

SOCIAL SECURITY ADMINISTRATION

Request for Earnings and Benefit Estimate Statement

To receive a free statement of your earnings covered by Social Security and your estimated future benefits, all you need to do is fill out this form. Please print or type your answers. When you have completed the form, fold it and mail it to us.

1. Name shown on your Social Security card:

   _____
   First   Middle Initial   Last

2. Your Social Security number as shown on your card:

   ☐☐☐-☐☐-☐☐☐☐

3. Your date of birth:

   _____ - _____ - _____
   Month   Day   Year

4. Other Social Security numbers you have used:

   ☐☐☐ - ☐☐ - ☐☐☐☐
   ☐☐☐ - ☐☐ - ☐☐☐☐

5. Your Sex: ☐ Male ☐ Female

6. Other names you have used (including a maiden name):

   _____

7. Show your actual earnings for last year and your estimated earnings for this year. Include only wages and/or net self-employment income covered by Social Security.

   A. Last year's actual earnings:

   $ ☐☐☐,☐☐☐.0 0
     Dollars only

   B. This year's estimated earnings:

   $ ☐☐☐,☐☐☐.0 0
     Dollars only

8. Show the age at which you plan to retire:

   ☐☐ (Show only one age)

9. Below, show the average yearly amount that you think you will earn between now and when you plan to retire. Your estimate of future earnings will be added to those earnings already on our records to give you the best possible estimate.

   Enter a yearly average, not your total future lifetime earnings. Only show earnings covered by Social Security. Do not add cost-of-living, performance or scheduled pay increases or bonuses. The reason for this is that we estimate retirement benefits in today's dollars, but adjust them to account for average wage growth in the national economy.

   However, if you expect to earn significantly more or less in the future due to promotions, job changes, part-time work, or an absence from the work force, enter the amount in today's dollars that most closely reflects your future average yearly earnings.

   Most people should enter the same amount that they are earning now (the amount shown in 7B).

   Your future average yearly earnings:

   $ ☐☐☐,☐☐☐.0 0
     Dollars only

10. Address where you want us to send the statement:

    _____
    Name

    _____
    Street Address (Include Apt. No., P.O. Box, or Rural Route)

    _____
    City   State   Zip Code

I am asking for information about my own Social Security record or the record of a person I am authorized to represent. I understand that if I deliberately request information under false pretenses I may be guilty of a federal crime and could be fined and/or imprisoned. I authorize you to send the statement of earnings and benefit estimates to the person named in item 10 through a contractor.

▲

_____
Please sign your name (Do not print)

_____
Date

(_____) _____
(Area Code) Daytime Telephone No.

Form **SSA-7004-PC-OP1** (9-89) Destroy Prior Edition

DEPARTMENT OF HEALTH AND HUMAN SERVICES
Social Security Administration

☐ TEL   TOE 120/145/155

Form Approved
OMB No. 0960-0007

APPLICATION FOR RETIREMENT INSURANCE BENEFITS

(Do not write in this space)

I apply for all insurance benefits for which I am eligible under Title II (Federal Old-Age, Survivors, and Disability Insurance) and part A of Title XVIII (Health Insurance for the Aged and Disabled) of the Social Security Act, as presently amended.

☐ Supplement. If you have already completed an application entitled "APPLICATION FOR WIFE'S OR HUSBANDS'S INSURANCE BENEFITS", you need complete only the circled items. All other claimants must complete the entire form.

---

1. (a) PRINT your name ⟶ | FIRST NAME, MIDDLE INITIAL, LAST NAME

(b) Enter your name at birth if different from item (a) ⟶ | FIRST NAME, MIDDLE INITIAL, LAST NAME

(c) Check (✓) whether you are ⟶ | ☐ Male   ☐ Female

2. Enter your Social Security Number ⟶ | ___ ___ ___ / ___ ___ / ___ ___ ___ ___

3. (a) Enter your date of birth ⟶ | MONTH, DAY, YEAR

(b) Enter name of State or foreign country where you were born. ⟶

If you have already presented, or if you are now presenting, a public or religious record of your birth established before you were age 5, go on to item 4.

(c) Was a public record or your birth made before you were age 5?   ☐ Yes   ☐ No   ☐ Unknown

(d) Was a religious record of your birth made before you were age 5?   ☐ Yes   ☐ No   ☐ Unknown

4. (a) Have you (or has someone on your behalf) ever filed an application for Social Security benefits, a period of disability under Social Security, supplemental security income, or hospital or medical insurance under Medicare? ⟶

☐ Yes (If "Yes," answer (b) and (c).)   ☐ No (If "No," go on to item 5.)

(b) Enter name of person on whose Social Security record you filed other application. ⟶ | (First name, middle initial, last name)

(c) Enter Social Security Number of person name in (b). (If unknown, so indicate) ⟶ | ___ ___ ___ ___ / ___ ___ / ___ ___ ___ ___

Do not answer 5 if you are age 66 or older. Go on to question 6.

5. (a) Are you so disabled that you cannot work or was there some period during the last 14 months when you were so disabled that you could not work? ⟶   ☐ Yes   ☐ No

(b) If "Yes," enter the dat you became disabled. ⟶ | MONTH, DAY, YEAR

6. (a) Were you in the active military or naval service (including Reserve or National Guard *active* duty or active duty for training) after September 7, 1939 and before 1968? ⟶

☐ Yes (If "Yes," answer (b) and (c).)   ☐ No (If "No," go on to item 7.)

(b) Enter dates of service. ⟶ | From: (Month, year)   To: (Month, year)

(c) Have you *ever* been (or will you be) eligible fo a monthly benefit from a military or civilian Federal agency? (include Veterans Administration benefits *only* if you waived military retirement pay) ⟶   ☐ Yes   ☐ No

7. Have you or your spouse worked in the railroad industry for 7 years or more? ⟶   ☐ Yes   ☐ No

---

FORM **SSA-1-F6** (7-89)
Destroy Prior Editions

8.	(a) Have you ever engaged in work that was covered under the social security system of a country other than the United States? ➡	☐ Yes *(If "Yes," answer (b).)*		☐ No *(If "No," go on to item 9.)*
	(b) If "Yes," list the country(ies). ━━━━━━━➤			

9.	Have you ever been married? ━━━━━━━➤	☐ Yes *(If "Yes," answer item 10.)*		☐ No *(If "No," go to item 12.)*

10.

(a) Give the following information about your current marriage. If not currently married, show your last marriage below.

To whom married		When *(Month, day, year)*	Where *(Name of City and State)*
Your current or last marriage	How marriage ended *(If still in effect, write "Not ended.")*	When *(Month, day, year)*	Where *(Name of City and State)*
	Marriage performed by: ☐ Clergyman or public official ☐ Other *(Explain in Remarks)*	Spouse's date of birth (or age)	If spouse deceased, give date of death
	Spouse's Social Security Number (If none or unknown, so indicate) _ _ _ / _ _ _ _ / _ _ _ _		

(b) Give the following information about each of your previous marriages. **(IF NONE, WRITE "NONE")**

To whom married		When *(Month, day, year)*	Where *(Name of City and State)*
Your previous marraige (Use a separate statement for information about any other marriages.)	How marriage ended	When *(Month, day, year)*	Where *(Name of City and State)*
	Marriage performed by: ☐ Clergyman or public official ☐ Other *(Explain in Remarks)*	Spouse's date of birth (or age)	If spouse deceased, give date of death
	Spouse's Social Security Number (If none or unknown, so indicate) _ _ _ / _ _ / _ _ _ _		

⑪	If you are currently married, answer this question **only** if your spouse is within 3 months of age 62 or older; or has a child-in-care who is eligible on your earnings record. Do you wish this application to protect your spouse's right to Social Security benefits? ☐ Yes ☐ No

⑫	List below FULL NAME OF ALL your children (including natural children, adopted children, and stepchildren) or dependent grandchildren (including stepgrandchildren) who are now or were in the past 6 months UNMARRIED and: • UNDER AGE 18 • AGE 18 TO 19 AND ATTENDING SECONDARY SCHOOL • DISABLED OR HANDICAPPED (age 18 or over and disability began before age 22) Also list any student who is between the ages of 18 to 23 if such student was both: 1. Previously entitled to Social Security benefits on any Social Security record for August 1981, and 2. Was also in full-time attendance at a post-secondary school prior to May 1982. **(IF THERE ARE NO SUCH CHILDREN, WRITE "NONE" BELOW AND GO ON TO ITEM 13.)**

13.	(a) Did you have wages or self-employment income covered under Social Security in **all** years from 1978 through last year?	☐ Yes *(If "Yes," skip to item 14.)*	☐ No *(If "No," answer (b).)*
	(b) List the years from 1978 through last year in which you did **not** have wages or self-employment income covered under Social Security.		

⑭ Enter below the names and addresses of all the persons, companies, or government agencies for whom you have worked this year, last year, and the year before last.
IF NONE, WRITE "NONE" BELOW AND GO ON TO ITEM 16.

(a) NAME AND ADDRESS OF EMPLOYER *(If you had more than one employer, please list them in order beginning with your last (most recent) employer).*	Work Began		Work Ended *(If still working, Show "Not ended")*	
	Month	Year	Month	Year

(b) Are you an officer of a corporation, or are you related to an officer of a corporation? ━━━➤	☐ Yes	☐ No

⑮	May we ask your employers for wage information needed for process your claim? ➤	☐ Yes	☐ No

⑯	THIS ITEM MUST BE COMPLETED, EVEN IF YOU ARE AN EMPLOYEE (a) Were you self-employed this year and last year? ➤	☐ Yes *(If "Yes," answer (b).)* ☐ No *(If "No," skip to item 17.)*

(b) Check the year or years in which you were self-employed	In what kind of trade or business were you self-employed? *(For example, storekeeper, farmer, physician)*	Were your net earnings from your trade or business $400 or more? *(Check "Yes" or "No")*
☐ This year		
☐ Last year		☐ Yes ☐ No
☐ Year before last		☐ Yes ☐ No

17. (a) How much were your total earnings last year? ➤ $

(b) Place an "X" in each block for EACH MONTH of last year in which you did not earn more than *$____ in wages, and did not perform substantial services in self-employment. These months are exempt months. If no months were exempt months, place an "X" in "NONE". If all months were exempt months, place an "X" in "ALL".

*Enter the appropriate monthly limit after reading the instructions, "How Your Earnings Affect Your Benefits".

NONE		ALL	
Jan.	Feb.	Mar.	Apr.
May	Jun.	Jul.	Aug.
Sept.	Oct.	Nov.	Dec.

18. (a) How much do you expect your total earnings to be this year? ➤ $

(b) Place an "X" in each block for EACH MONTH of this year in which you did not or will not earn more than *$____ in wages, and did not or will not perform substantial services in self-employment. These months are exempt months. If no months are or will be exempt months, place an "X" in "NONE". If all months are or will be exempt months, place an "X" in "ALL".

*Enter the appropriate monthly limit after reading the instructions, "How Your Earnings Affect Your Benefits".

NONE		ALL	
Jan.	Feb.	Mar.	Apr.
May	Jun.	Jul.	Aug.
Sept.	Oct.	Nov.	Dec.

19. Answer this item ONLY if you are now in the last 4 months of your taxable year (Sept., Oct., Nov., and Dec., if your taxable year is a calendar year).

(a) How much do you expect to earn next year? ➤ $

(b) Place an "X" in each block for EACH MONTH of next year in which you do not expect to earn more than *$____ in wages, and do not expect to perform substantial services in self-employment. These months will be exempt months. If no months are expected to be exempt months, place an "X" in "NONE". If all months are expected to exempt months, place an "X" in "ALL".

*Enter the appropriate monthly limit after reading the instructions, "How Your Earnings Affect Your Benefits".

NONE		ALL	
Jan.	Feb.	Mar.	Apr.
May	Jun.	Jul.	Aug.
Sept.	Oct.	Nov.	Dec.

An ANNUAL REPORT of earnings must be filed with the Social Security Administration within 3 months and 15 days after the end of any taxable year in which you earn more than the yearly limit, if you are under age 70 for at least 1 full month of that year and receive some benefits during the taxable year. I AGREE TO FILE AN ANNUAL REPORT OF EARNINGS. THE ANNUAL REPORT IS REQUIRED BY LAW AND FAILURE TO REPORT MAY RESULT IN A MONETARY PENALTY.

20. If you use a fiscal year, that is, a taxable year that does not end December 31 (with income tax return due April 15), enter here the month your fiscal year ends. ➤ (Month) _____

IF YOU ARE AGE 65 AND 6 MONTHS, OR OLDER, DO NOT ANSWER ITEM 21. GO ON TO ITEM 22.

PLEASE READ CAREFULLY THE INFORMATION ON THE OPPOSITE PAGE AND ANSWER ONE OF THE FOLLOWING ITEMS. ➤

21. (a) I want benefits beginning with the earliest possible month that will be the most advantageous. ➤ ☐

(b) I am age 65 (or will be age 65 within 4 months) and I want benefits beginning with the earliest possible month that will be the most advantageous providing there is not permanent reduction in my ongoing monthly benefit. ➤ ☐

(c) I want benefits beginning with _____ . I understand that either a higher initial payment or a higher continuing monthly benefit amount may be possible, but I choose not to take it. ➤ ☐

FORM **SSA-1-F6** (7/89)

If this claim is approved and you are still entitled to benefits at age 65, you will automatically have hospital insurance protection under Medicare at age 65. If you are not also eligible for automatic enrollment in the Supplementary Medical Insurance Plan, this application may be used for voluntary enrollment.

COMPLETE THIS ITEM ONLY IF YOU ARE WITHIN 3 MONTHS OF AGE 65 OR OLDER

ENROLLMENT IN MEDICARE'S SUPPLEMENTARY MEDICAL INSURANCE PLAN: The medical insurance benefits plan pays for most of the costs of physicians' and surgeons' services, and related medical services which are not covered by the hospital insurance plan. Coverage under this SUPPLEMENTARY MEDICAL INSURANCE PLAN does not apply to most medical expenses incurred outside the United States. Your Social Security district office will be glad to explain the details of the plan and give you a leaflet which explains what services are covered and how payment is made under the plan.

Once you are enrolled in this plan, you will have to pay a monthly premium to cover part of the cost of your medical insurance protection. The Federal Government contributes an equal amount or more toward the cost of your insurance. Premiums will be deducted from any monthly Social Security, railroad retirement, or civil service benefit checks you receive. If you do not receive such benefits, you will be notified about when, where, and how to pay your premiums. If you are eligible for automatic enrollment, you will be automatically enrolled unless you indicate, by checking the "NO" block below, that you do not want to be enrolled.

22.	DO YOU WANT TO ENROLL IN THE MEDICARE SUPPLEMENTARY MEDICAL INSURANCE PLAN? ⟶	☐ Yes ☐ No

Answer question 23 ONLY if you were born January 2, 1924, or later. Otherwise, go on to question 24.

(23.)	(a) Are you entitled to, or do you expect to become entitled to, a pension or annuity based on your work after 1956 not covered by Social Security?	☐ Yes (If "Yes," answer (b) and (c).)	☐ No (If "No," go on to item 24.)
	(b) ☐ I became entitled, or expect to become entitled, beginning ⟶	MONTH	YEAR
	(c) ☐ I became eligible, or expect to become eligible, beginning ⟶	MONTH	YEAR

I agree to notify the Social Security Administration if I become entitled to a pension or annuity based on my employment after 1956 not covered by Social Security, or if such pension or annuity stops.

24. Check if applicable:
(   ) I am not submitting evidence of earnings that are not yet on my earnings record. I understand that these earnings will be included automatically within 24 months, and any increase in my benefits will be paid with full retroactivity.

REMARKS (You may use this space for any explanations. If you need more space, attach a separate sheet.)

I know that anyone who makes or causes to be made a false statement or representation of material fact in an application or for use in determining a right to payment under the Social Security Act commits a crime punishable under Federal law by fine, imprisonment or both. I affirm that all information I have given in this document is true.

SIGNATURE OF APPLICANT	DATE (Month, day, year)

SIGNATURE (First Name, Middle Initial, Last Name) (Write in ink.)	Telephone Number(s) at Which You May Be Contacted During the Day
SIGN HERE ▶	(Area Code)

FOR OFFICIAL USE ONLY	Direct Deposit Payment Address (Financial Institution)			
	Routing Transit Number	C/S	Depositor Account Number	☐ No Account ☐ Direct Deposit Refused

Applicant's Mailing Address (Number and street, Apt. No., P.O. Box, or Rural Route) (Enter Residence Address in "Remarks," if different.)

City and State	ZIP Code	County (if any) in which you now live

Witnesses are required ONLY if this application has been signed by mark (X) above. If signed by mark (X), two witnesses who know the applicant must sign below, giving their full addresses. Also, print the applicant's name in the Signature block.

1. Signature of Witness	2. Signature of Witness
Address (Number and Street, City, State and ZIP Code)	Address (Number and Street, City, State and ZIP Code)

FORM SSA-1-F6 (7-89)

CHANGES TO BE REPORTED AND HOW TO REPORT
Failure to report may result in overpayments that must be repaid, and in possible monetary penalties

► You change your mailing address for checks or residence. To avoid delay in receipt of checks you should ALSO file a regular change of address notice with your post office.

► You go outside the U.S.A. for 30 consecutive days or longer.

► Any beneficiary dies or becomes unable to handle benefits.

► Work Changes-On your application you told us you except total earnings for 19__ to be $____.

You (are) (are not) earning wages of more than $____ a month.

You (are) (are not) self-employed rendering substantial services in your trade or business.

(Report AT ONCE if above work pattern changes)

► You are confined to jail, prison, penal institution, or correctional facility for conviction of a felony.

► You become entitled to a pension or annuity based on your employment after 1956 not covered by Social Security, or if such pension or annuity stops.

► Custody Change—Report if a person for whom you are filing or who is in your care dies, leaves your care or custody, or changes address.

► Change of Marital Status—Marriage, divorce, annulment of marriage.

HOW TO REPORT

You can make your reports by telephone, mail, or in person, whichever you prefer.

WHEN A CHANGE OCCURS AFTER YOU RECEIVE A NOTICE OF AWARD, YOU SHOULD REPORT BY CALLING THE APPROPRIATE TELEPHONE NUMBER SHOWN NEAR THE TOP OF PAGE 6.

In addition, an annual report of earnings must be filed with the Social Security Administration within 3 months and 15 days after the end of any taxable year in which you earned more than the annual exempt amount.

THE ANNUAL REPORT OF EARNINGS IS REQUIRED BY LAW AND FAILURE TO REPORT MAY RESULT IN A MONETARY PENALTY. EVEN IF YOU FILE A FEDERAL INCOME TAX FORM WITH THE INTERNAL REVENUE SERVICE, YOU STILL NEED TO FILE AN ANNUAL REPORT WITH US IS YOU EARN MORE THAN THE ANNUAL EXEMPT AMOUNT.

PLEASE READ THE FOLLOWING INFORMATION CAREFULLY BEFORE YOU ANSWER QUESTION 21.

Benefits may be payable for some months prior to the month in which you file this claim (but not for any month before the first month you will be age 62 for the entire month) if:

(1) you have a child or spouse entitled to unreduced benefits based on your earnings during any of the past 6 months;

— OR —

(2) you will earn over the exempt amount this year. (For appropriate exempt amount, see the instructions, "How Your Earnings Affect Your Benefits".

If your first month of entitlement is prior to age 65, your benefit rate will be reduced. However if you do not actually receive your full benefit amount for one or more months before age 65 because benefits are withheld due to your earnings, your benefit will be increased at age 65 to give credit for this withholding. Thus, your benefit amount at age 65 will be reduced only if you receive one or more full benefit payments prior to the month you are 65.

☐ TEL

TOE 120/145/155

Form Approved
OMB No. 0960-0008

APPLICATION FOR WIFE'S OR HUSBAND'S INSURANCE BENEFITS

(Do not write in this space)

I apply for all insurance benefits for which I am eligible under Title II (Federal Old-Age, Survivors, and Disability Insurance) and part A of Title XVIII (Health Insurance for the Aged and Disabled) of the Social Security Act, as presently amended.

☐ Supplement. If you have already completed an application entitled "APPLICATION FOR RETIREMENT INSURANCE BENEFITS", you need complete only the circled items. All other claimants must complete the entire form.

1. (a) PRINT Name of Wage Earner or Self-Employed Person (Herein referred to as the "Worker") ➤ | FIRST NAME, MIDDLE INITIAL, LAST NAME

(b) Enter Worker's Social Security Number ➤ | ___ / __ / ____

2. (a) PRINT your name ➤ | FIRST NAME, MIDDLE INITIAL, LAST NAME

(b) Enter your Social Security Number ➤ | ___ / __ / ____

3. Enter your name at birth if different from item 2. ➤ | FIRST NAME, MIDDLE INITIAL, LAST NAME

4. (a) Enter your date of birth ➤ | MONTH, DAY, YEAR

(b) Enter name of State or foreign country where you were born ➤

If you have already presented, or if you are now presenting, a public or religious record of your birth established before you were age 5, go on to item 5.

(c) Was a public record of your birth made before you were age 5? ➤ | ☐ Yes ☐ No ☐ Unknown

(d) Was a religious record of your birth made before you were age 5? ➤ | ☐ Yes ☐ No ☐ Unknown

5. (a) Have you (or has someone on your behalf) ever filed an application for Social Security benefits, a period of disability under Social Security, supplemental security income, or hospital or medical insurance under Medicare? ➤ | ☐ Yes (If "Yes," answer (b) and (c).) ☐ No (If "No," go on to item 6.)

(b) Enter name of person on whose Social Security record you filed other application. ➤ | FIRST NAME, MIDDLE INITIAL, LAST NAME

(c) Enter Social Security Number of person named in (b). (If unknown, write "Unknown") ➤ | ___ / __ / ____

DO NOT ANSWER QUESTION 6 IF YOU ARE AGE 66 OR OLDER. GO ON TO QUESTION 7.

6. (a) Are you so disabled that you cannot work or was there some period during the last 14 months when you were so disabled that you could not work? ➤ | ☐ Yes ☐ No

(b) If "Yes," enter the date you became disabled. ➤ | MONTH, DAY, YEAR

If you are now AGE 62 or older, or you will be AGE 62 in this month or one of the next 4 months, answer item 7. If not, go on to item 8.

7. (a) Were you in the active military or naval service (including Reserve or National Guard active duty or active duty for training) after September 7, 1939 and before 1968? ➤ | ☐ Yes (If "Yes," answer (b).) ☐ No (If "No," go on to item 8.)

(b) Enter dates of service ➤ | From: (Month, year) | To: (Month, year)

8. Did you or the worker work in the railroad industry for 7 years or more? ➤ | ☐ Yes ☐ No

9.	(a) Have you ever engaged in work that was covered under the social security system of a country other than the United States? ➤	☐ Yes ☐ No (If "Yes," answer (b).) (If "No," go on to item 10.)
	(b) If "Yes," list the country(ies). ➤	

⑩	(a) Have you qualified for, or do you expect to qualify for a pension or annuity (or a lump sum in place of a pension or annuity) based on your own employment and earnings for the Federal government of the United States, or one of its States or local subdivisions? *(Social Security benefits are not government pensions.)*	☐ Yes ☐ No (If "Yes," check which (If "No," go of the items in item (b) on to item 11.) applies to you.)
	(b) ☐ I receive a government pension or annuity. ☐ I received a lump sum in place of a government pension or annuity. ☐ I applied for and am awaiting a decision on my pension or lump sum.	☐ I have not applied for but I expect to begin receiving my pension or annuity: _____ (Month, year) (If the date is not known, enter "Unknown".)

I AGREE TO PROMPTLY NOTIFY the Social Security Administration if I begin to receive a government pension or annuity, based on my own earnings, from the Federal government or any State (or any political subdivision thereof) or if my present government pension or annuity amount changes.

11.	Enter below the information requested about each of your marriages. Include information on your marriage to the worker and any other marriages, whether before or after you married the worker.		

	To whom married	When (Month, day, year)	Where (Name of City and State)
Your current or last marriage	How marriage ended (If still in effect, write "Not ended.")	When (Month, day, year)	Where (Name of City and State)
	Marriage performed by: ☐ Clergyman or public official ☐ Other (Explain in Remarks)	Spouse's date of birth (or age)	
	Spouse's Social Security Number (If none or unknown, so indicate)	___ ___ ___ / ___ ___ / ___ ___ ___ ___	

	To whom married	When (Month, day, year)	Where (Name of City and State)
Your previous marriage (If none write "NONE")	How marriage ended	When (Month, day, year)	Where (Name of City and State)
	Marriage performed by: ☐ Clergyman or public official ☐ Other (Explain in Remarks)	Spouse's date of birth (or age)	If spouse deceased, give date of death
	Spouse's Social Security Number (If none or unknown, so indicate)	___ ___ ___ / ___ ___ / ___ ___ ___ ___	

(Use "Remarks" space on page 4 for information about any other marriages.)

If you are now under Age 66, answer item 12. If you are Age 66 or over, go to item 13.

You may receive a wife's or husband's benefit for any month in which you have in your care a child or dependent grandchild of the worker entitled to a child's insurance benefit if the child is:
- under-age 16 or   ● disabled or handicapped (age 16 or over and disability began before age 22).

A divorced spouse cannot be entitled to benefits for months before age 62 even if there is an entitled child in care.

⑫	Has an unmarried child of the worker (including natural child, adopted child, or stepchild) or a dependent grandchild of the worker (including stepgrandchild) who is under 16 or disabled lived with you during any of the last 13 months (counting the present month)? (If "Yes," enter the information requested below.)	☐ Yes ☐ No

Name of child	Months child lived with you (If all, write "All")

13.

(a) How much were your total earnings last year? ⟶ $ _____

(b) Place an "X" in each block for each month of last year in which you did not earn more than * $ _____ in wages, and did not perform substantial services in self-employment. These months are exempt months. If no months were exempt months, place an "X" in "NONE". If all months were exempt months, place an "X" in "ALL".

*Enter the appropriate monthly limit after reading the instructions, "How Your Earnings Affect Your Benefits".

NONE		ALL	
Jan	Feb.	Mar.	Apr.
May	Jun.	Jul.	Aug.
Sept.	Oct.	Nov.	Dec.

14.

(a) How much do you expect your total earnings to be this year? ⟶ $ _____

(b) Place an "X" in each block for each month of this year in which you did not or will not earn more than * $ _____ in wages, and did not or will not perform substantial services in self-employment. These months are exempt months. If no months are or will be exempt months, place an "X" in "NONE". If all months are or will be exempt months, place an "X" in "ALL".

* Enter the appropriate monthly limit after reading the instructions, "How Your Earnings Affect Your Benefits".

NONE		ALL	
Jan.	Feb.	Mar.	Apr.
May	Jun.	Jul.	Aug.
Sept.	Oct.	Nov.	Dec.

15.

Answer this item ONLY if you are now in the last 4 months of your taxable year (Sept., Oct., Nov., and Dec., if your taxable year is a calendar year).

(a) How much do you expect to earn next year? ⟶ $ _____

(b) Place an "X" in each block for each month of next year in which you do not expect to earn more than * $ _____ in wages, and do not expect to perform substantial services in self-employment. These months will be exempt months. If no months are expected to be exempt months, place an "X" in "NONE". If all months are expected to be exempt months, place an "X" in "ALL".

*Enter the appropriate monthly limit after reading the instructions, "How Your Earnings Affect Your Benefits".

NONE		ALL	
Jan.	Feb.	Mar.	Apr.
May	Jun.	Jul.	Aug.
Sept.	Oct.	Nov.	Dec.

If you use a fiscal year, that is, a taxable year that does not end December 31 (with income tax return due April 15), enter here the month your fiscal year ends. ⟶ _____

(Month)

If you are now under AGE 66 and do not have an entitled child in your care, answer item 16.
If you are AGE 66 or older, or you have an entitled child in your care, go on to item 17.

PLEASE READ CAREFULLY THE INFORMATION ON THE OPPOSITE PAGE AND ANSWER ONE OF THE FOLLOWING ITEMS.

16.

(a) I want benefits beginning with the earliest possible month that will be the most advantageous. ⟶ ☐

(b) I am age 65 (or will be age 65 within 4 months) and I want benefits beginning with the earliest possible month that will be the most advantageous, providing that there is no permanent reduction in my ongoing monthly benefit. ⟶ ☐

(c) I want benefits beginning with _____ . I understand that either a higher initial payment or a higher continuing monthly benefit amount may be possible, but I choose not to take it. ⟶ ☐

MEDICARE INFORMATION

If this claim is approved and you are still entitled to benefits at age 65, you will automatically have hospital insurance protection under Medicare at age 65. If you are not also eligible for automatic enrollment in the Supplementary Medical Insurance Plan, this application may be used for voluntary enrollment.

COMPLETE THIS ITEM ONLY IF YOU ARE WITHIN 3 MONTHS OF AGE 65 OR OLDER

ENROLLMENT IN MEDICARE'S SUPPLEMENTARY MEDICAL INSURANCE PLAN: The medical insurance benefits plan pays for most of the costs of physicians' and surgeons' services, and related medical services which are not covered by the hospital insurance plan. Coverage under this SUPPLEMENTARY MEDICAL INSURANCE PLAN does not apply to most medical expenses incurred outside the United States. Your Social Security district office will be glad to explain the details of the plan and give you a leaflet which explains what services are covered and how payment is made under the plan.

Once you are enrolled in this plan, you will have to pay a monthly premium to cover part of the cost of your medical insurance protection. The Federal Government contributes an equal amount or more toward the cost of your insurance. Premiums will be deducted from any monthly Social Security, railroad retirement, or civil service benefit checks you receive. If you do not receive such benefits, you will be notified about when, where, and how to pay your premiums. If you are eligible for automatic enrollment, you will be automatically enrolled unless you indicate, by checking the "NO" block below that you do not want to be enrolled.

17.	DO YOU WANT TO ENROLL IN THE SUPPLEMENTARY MEDICAL INSURANCE PLAN?	☐ Yes	☐ No

PLEASE READ THE FOLLOWING INFORMATION CAREFULLY BEFORE SIGNING THIS APPLICATION.

An ANNUAL REPORT of earnings must be filed with the Social Security Administration within 3 months and 15 days after the end of any taxable year in which you earn more than the yearly limit, if you are under age 70 for at least 1 full month of that year and receive some benefits during the taxable year. I AGREE TO FILE AN ANNUAL REPORT OF EARNINGS. THE ANNUAL REPORT IS REQUIRED BY LAW AND FAILURE TO REPORT MAY RESULT IN A MONETARY PENALTY.

BENEFITS MAY END if any of the following events occur. However, there are certain exceptions which are explained in the informational booklet which you will receive. You must report each of these events even if you believe an exception applies. We will advise you whether additional evidence is needed and how your benefits may be affected.

I AGREE TO PROMPTLY NOTIFY the Social Security Administration and to PROMPTLY RETURN ANY BENEFIT CHECK I receive if the check is for a month in or after the month in which:
- The worker DIES. (You may be entitled to survivor's benefits.)
- I am DIVORCED or my marriage is ANNULLED.
- I MARRY. (If I am entitled as a divorced spouse.)
- I NO LONGER HAVE IN MY CARE the worker's child or dependent grandchild under age 16 or disabled who is entitled to benefits.
- I am confined to jail, prison, penal institution or correctional facility for conviction of a felony.

REMARKS (You may use this space for any explanations. If you need more space, attach a separate sheet.)

_____

_____

_____

I know that anyone who makes or causes to be made a false statement or representation of material fact in an application or for use in determining a right to payment under the Social Security Act commits a crime punishable under Federal law by fine, imprisonment or both. I affirm that all information I have given in this document is true.

SIGNATURE OF APPLICANT	Date (Month, day, year)
Signature (First name, middle initial, last name) (Write in ink) SIGN HERE ➤	Telephone Number(s) at which you may be contacted during the day ___ ___ Area Code

FOR OFFICIAL USE ONLY	Direct Deposit Payment Address (Financial Institution)		
	Routing Transit Number	C/S	Depositor Account Number	☐ No Account ☐ Direct Deposit Refused

Applicant's Mailing Address (Number and street, Apt. No., P.O. Box, or Rural Route) (Enter Residence Address in "Remarks," if different.)

City and State	ZIP Code	County (if any) in which you now live

Witnesses are required ONLY if this application has been signed by mark (X) above. If signed by mark (X), two witnesses who know the applicant must sign below, giving their full addresses. Also, print the applicant's name in the Signature block.

1. Signature of Witness	2. Signature of Witness
Address (Number and Street, City, State and ZIP Code)	Address (Number and Street, City, State and ZIP Code)

Form SSA-2-F6 (7/89)

CHANGES TO BE REPORTED AND HOW TO REPORT
FAILURE TO REPORT MAY RESULT IN OVERPAYMENTS THAT MUST BE REPAID, AND IN POSSIBLE MONETARY PENALTIES

▶ You change your mailing address for checks or residence. To avoid delay in receipt of checks you should ALSO file a regular change of address notice with your post office.

▶ You go outside the U.S.A. for 30 consecutive days or longer.

▶ Any beneficiary dies or becomes unable to handle benefits.

▶ Work Changes—On your application you told us you expect total earnings for 19___ to be $_____.

You (are) (are not) earning wages of more than $_____ a month.

You (are) (are not) self-employed rendering substantial services in your trade or business.

(Report AT ONCE if this work pattern changes.)

▶ Change of Marital Status—Marriage, divorce, annulment of marriage.

▶ You are confined to jail, prison, penal institution or correctional facility for conviction of a felony.

▶ Custody Change or Disability Improves — Report if a person for whom you are filing, or who is in your care dies, leaves your care or custody, changes address, or, if disabled, the condition improves.

▶ You begin to receive a government pension or annuity (from the Federal government or any State or any political subdivision thereof) or present payment changes.

HOW TO REPORT

You can make your reports by telephone, mail, or in person, whichever you prefer.

WHEN A CHANGE OCCURS AFTER YOU RECEIVE A NOTICE OF AWARD, YOU SHOULD REPORT BY CALLING THE APPROPRIATE TELEPHONE NUMBER SHOWN NEAR THE TOP OF PAGE 6.

In addition, an annual report of earnings must be filed with the Social Security Administration within 3 months and 15 days after the end of any taxable year in which you earned more than the annual exempt amount.

THE ANNUAL REPORT OF EARNINGS IS REQUIRED BY LAW AND FAILURE TO REPORT MAY RESULT IN A MONETARY PENALTY. Even if you file a Federal income tax form with the Internal Revenue Service, you still need to file an annual report with us if you earn more than the yearly limit.

Under a special rule known as the Monthly Earnings Test, you can get a full benefit for any month in which you do not earn wages over the monthly limit and do not perform substantial services in self-employment regardless of how much you earn in the year. For retirement age beneficiaries this special rule can be used only for one taxable year which will usually be the year of retirement. For younger beneficiaries such as young wives and husbands (entitled only by reason of child-in-care), this special rule can be used for two taxable years. The first taxable year in which the monthly earnings test may be used is usually the first year they are entitled to benefits. The second taxable year in which the monthly earnings test can be used is always the year in which their entitlement to benefits stops. In all other years, the total amount of benefits payable will be based solely on your total yearly earnings without regard to monthly earnings or services rendered in self-employment.

PLEASE READ THE FOLLOWING INFORMATION CAREFULLY BEFORE YOU ANSWER QUESTION 16.

Benefits may be payable for some months prior to the month in which you file this claim (but not for any month before the first month you will be age 62 for the entire month) if:

You will earn over the exempt amount this year. For the appropriate exempt amount, see "How Your Earnings Affect Your Benefits."

If your first month of entitlement is prior to age 65, your benefit rate will be reduced (but not for those months in which you have an entitled child under age 16 or disabled in your care). However, if you do not actually receive your full benefit amount for one or more months before age 65 because benefits are withheld due to your earnings, your benefit will be increased at age 65 to give credit for this withholding. Thus your benefit amount at age 65 will only be reduced if you receive one or more full benefit payments prior to the month you are age 65.

Form **SSA-2-F6** (7/89)

☐ TEL   TOE 120/145/155

Form Approved
OMB No. 0960-0004

APPLICATION FOR WIDOW'S OR WIDOWER'S INSURANCE BENEFITS*

(Do not write in this space)

I apply for all insurance benefits for which I am eligible under Title II (Federal Old-Age, Survivors, and Disability Insurance) and Part A of Title XVIII (Health Insurance for the Aged and Disabled) of the Social Security Act, as presently amended. The information you furnish on this application will ordinarily be sufficient for a determination on the lump-sum death payment.

*This may also be considered an application for survivors benefits under the Railroad Retirement Act and for Veterans Administration payments under title 38 U.S.C., Veterans Benefits, Chapter 13 (which is, as such, an application for other types of death benefits under title 38).

If you were receiving benefits as a wife/husband at the time of your spouse's death, you need complete only the circled items. All other claimants must complete the entire form.

(1.) (a) PRINT name of deceased wage earner or self-employed person *(herein referred to as the "deceased")* ➤ | FIRST NAME, MIDDLE INITIAL, LAST NAME

(b) Check (✓) one for the deceased ➤ | ☐ Male   ☐ Female

(c) Enter deceased's Social Security Number ➤ | ___ ___ ___ ___ ___ ___ ___ ___ ___

(2.) (a) PRINT your name ➤ | FIRST NAME, MIDDLE INITIAL, LAST NAME

(b) Enter your Social Security Number ➤ | ___ ___ ___ ___ ___ ___ ___ ___ ___

(c) Enter your name at birth if different from item 2(a) ➤ | FIRST NAME, MIDDLE INITIAL, LAST NAME

PART I -- INFORMATION ABOUT THE DECEASED

3. Enter date of birth of deceased ➤ | MONTH, DAY, YEAR

(4.) (a) Enter date of death ➤ | MONTH, DAY, YEAR

(b) Enter place of death ➤ | CITY AND STATE

(5.) Enter name of the State or foreign country where the deceased had a fixed, permanent home at the time of death. ➤

6. (a) Did the deceased ever file an application for Social Security benefits, a period of disability under Social Security, supplemental security income, or hospital or medical insurance under Medicare? *If unknown, check this block* ☐ ➤ | ☐ Yes *(If "Yes," answer (b) and (c).)*   ☐ No *(If "No," go on to item 7.)*

(b) Enter name(s) of person(s) on whose Social Security record(s) other application was filed. ➤ | FIRST NAME, MIDDLE INITIAL, LAST NAME

(c) Enter Social Security Number(s) of person(s) named in (b). *If unknown, check this block* ☐ ➤ | ___ ___ ___ ___ ___ ___ ___ ___ ___

ANSWER ITEM 7 ONLY IF THE DECEASED DIED PRIOR TO AGE 66 AND WITHIN THE PAST 4 MONTHS.

(7.) (a) Was the deceased unable to work because of a disabling condition at the time of death? ➤ | ☐ Yes *(If "Yes," answer (b).)*   ☐ No *(If "No," go on to item 8.)*

(b) Enter date disability began ➤ | MONTH, DAY, YEAR

8. (a) Was the deceased in the active military or naval service (including Reserve or National Guard *active* duty or active duty for training) after September 7, 1939 and before 1968? ➤ | ☐ Yes *(If "Yes," answer (b) and (c).)*   ☐ No *(If "No," go on to item 9.)*

(b) Enter dates of service ➤ | *(Month, year)* FROM: *(Month, year)* TO:

(c) Has anyone (including the deceased) received, or does anyone expect to receive, a benefit from any other Federal agency? ➤ | ☐ Yes   ☐ No

FORM **SSA-10-BK** (7/89) Destroy prior editions

| 9. | (a) About how much did the deceased earn from employment and self-employment during the year of death? ➤ | Amount $ |
| | (b) About how much did the deceased earn the year before death? ➤ | Amount $ |

| ⑩ | (a) Did the deceased have wages or self-employment income covered under Social Security in all years from 1978 through last year? ➤ | ☐ Yes *(If "Yes," skip to item 11.)* ☐ No *(If "No," answer (b).)* |
| | (b) List the years from 1978 through last year in which the deceased did not have wages or self-employment income covered under Social Security. ➤ | |

11. CHECK IF APPLICABLE:

☐ I am not submitting evidence of the deceased's earnings that are not yet on his/her earnings record. I understand that these earnings will be included automatically within 24 months, and any increase in my benefits will be paid with full retroactivity.

12. Enter below the information requested about each marriage of the deceased, including the marriage to you.

To whom married	When *(Month, Day, and Year)*	Where *(Enter name of City and State)*
Last marriage of the deceased	How marriage ended	When *(Month, Day, and Year)*	Where *(Enter name of City and State)*
	Marriage performed by: ☐ Clergyman or public official ☐ Other *(Explain in Remarks)*	Spouse's date of birth	If spouse deceased, give date of death
	Spouse's Social Security Number *(If none or unknown, so indicate)* ➤		_ _ _ _ _ _ _ _ _

To whom married	When *(Month, Day, and Year)*	Where *(Enter name of City and State)*
Previous marriage of the deceased (IF NONE, WRITE "NONE.")	How marriage ended	When *(Month, Day, and Year)*	Where *(Enter name of City and State)*
	Marriage performed by: ☐ Clergyman or public official ☐ Other *(Explain in Remarks)*	Spouse's date of birth	If spouse deceased, give date of death
	Spouse's Social Security Number *(If none or unknown, so indicate)* ➤		_ _ _ _ _ _ _ _ _

USE "REMARKS" SPACE ON BACK PAGE FOR INFORMATION ABOUT ANY OTHER PREVIOUS MARRIAGE

| ⑬ | Is there a surviving parent (or parents) who was receiving support from the deceased at the time of death or at the time the deceased became disabled under Social Security law? ➤ | ☐ Yes *(If "Yes," enter the name and address in "Remarks.")* ☐ No |

PART II -- INFORMATION ABOUT YOURSELF

14.	(a) Enter name of State or foreign country where you were born. ➤	
	If you have already presented, or if you are now presenting, a public or religious record of your birth established before you were age 5, go on to item 15.	
	(b) Was a public record of your birth made before 5? ➤	☐ Yes ☐ No ☐ Unknown
	(c) Was a religious record of your birth made before age 5? ➤	☐ Yes ☐ No ☐ Unknown

FORM **SSA-10-BK** (7/89)

15. Enter below information about each of your marriages. Indicate your marriage to the deceased by entering deceased's name (if you are applying for widower's benefits, enter the maiden name of the deceased); it is not necessary to repeat other information about this marriage you have already given in item 12. Enter complete information on all other marriages, whether before or after you married the deceased.

Your current or last marriage	To whom married	When (*Month, Day, and Year*)	Where (*Enter name of City and State*)
	How marriage ended	When (*Month, Day, and Year*)	Where (*Enter name of City and State*)
	Marriage performed by: ☐ Clergyman or public official ☐ Other (*Explain in Remarks*)	Spouse's date of birth	If spouse deceased, give date of death
	Spouse's Social Security Number (*If none or unknown, so indicate*) ⟶		___ ___ ___ ___ ___ ___ ___ ___ ___

Your previous marriage (IF NONE, WRITE "NONE.")	To whom married	When (*Month, Day, and Year*)	Where (*Enter name of City and State*)
	How marriage ended	When (*Month, Day, and Year*)	Where (*Enter name of City and State*)
	Marriage performed by: ☐ Clergyman or public official ☐ Other (*Explain in Remarks*)	Spouse's date of birth	If spouse deceased, give date of death
	Spouse's Social Security Number (*If none or unknown, so indicate*) ⟶		___ ___ ___ ___ ___ ___ ___ ___ ___

USE "REMARKS" SPACE FOR INFORMATION ABOUT ANY OTHER MARRIAGE

IF YOU ARE APPLYING FOR SURVIVING DIVORCED SPOUSE'S BENEFITS, OMIT 16 AND GO ON TO ITEM 17.

16. (a) Were you and the deceased living together at the same address when the deceased died? ⟶

☐ Yes (If "Yes," go on to item 17.) ☐ No (If "NO," answer (b).)

(b) If either you or the deceased were away from home (*whether or not temporarily*) when the deceased died, give the following:

Who was away? ⟶ ☐ Deceased ☐ Surviving spouse

Date last at home:	Reason absence began:	Reason you were apart at time of death:

If separated because of illness, enter nature of illness or disabling condition.

17. (a) Have you (or has someone on your behalf) even filed an application for Social Security benefits, a period of disability under Social Security, supplemental security income, or hospital or medical insurance under Medicare? ⟶

☐ Yes (If "Yes," answer (b) and (c).) ☐ No (If "NO," go on to item 18.)

(b) Enter name of person on whose Social Security record you filed other application ⟶

(c) Enter Social Security Number of person named in (b). (*If unknown, so indicate*) ⟶ ___ ___ ___ ___ ___ ___ ___ ___ ___

FORM SSA–10–BK (7/89)

18. (a) Are you so disabled that you cannot work or was there some period during the last 14 months when you were so disabled that you could not work? ➤

☐ Yes
(If "Yes," answer (b) and (c).)

☐ No
(If "No," go on to item 19.)

(b) If "Yes," enter the date you became disabled. ➤

(Month, day, year)

19. Were you in the active military or naval service (including Reserve or National Guard *active* duty or active duty for training) after September 7, 1939 and before 1968? ➤

☐ Yes

☐ No

20. Did you or the deceased work in the railroad industry for 7 years or more? ➤

☐ Yes

☐ No

21. (a) Did you or the deceased ever engage in work that was covered under the Social Security system of a country other than the United States? ➤

☐ Yes
(If "Yes," answer (b).)

☐ No
(If "No," go on to item 22.)

(b) If "Yes," list the country(ies). ➤

22. (a) Have you qualified for, or do you expect to qualify for, a pension or annuity (or a lump sum in place of a pension or annuity) based on your own employment and earnings for the Federal Government of the United States, or one of its States or local subdivision? *(Social Security benefits are not government pensions).* ➤

☐ Yes
(If "Yes," check which of the items in item (b) applies to your.)

☐ No
(If "No," go on to item 23.)

(b) ☐ I receive a government pension or annuity.

☐ I received a lump sum in place of a government pension or annuity.

☐ I applied for and am awaiting a decision on my pension or lump sum.

☐ I have not applied for but I expect to begin receiving my pension or annuity:

_____
(Month, year)
(If the date is not known, enter "Unknown")

I AGREE TO PROMPTLY NOTIFY the Social Security Administration if I begin to receive a government pension or annuity, based on my own earnings, from the Federal government or any State (or any political subdivision thereof), or if my present government pension or annuity amount changes.

MEDICARE INFORMATION

If this claim is approved and you are still entitled to benefits at age 65, you will automatically have hospital insurance protection under Medicare at age 65. If you are not also eligible for automatic enrollment in the Supplementary Medical Insurance Plan, this application, may be used for voluntary enrollment.

COMPLETE THIS ITEM ONLY IF YOU ARE WITHIN 3 MONTHS OF AGE 65 OR OLDER

Medical insurance under Medicare helps pay your doctor bills. It also helps pay for a number of other medical items and services not covered under the hospital insurance plan does not apply to most medical expenses incurred outside the United States.

If you sign up for medical insurance, you must pay a premium for each month you have this protection. If you get monthly Social Security, railroad retirement, or civil service benefits, your premium will be deducted from your benefit check. If you get none of these benefits, you will be notified how to pay your premium.

The Federal Government contributes to the cost of your insurance. The amount of your premium and the Government's payment are based on the cost of services covered by medical insurance. The Government also makes additional payments when necessary to meet the full cost of the program. (Currently the Government pays about two-thirds of the cost of this program.) You will get advance notice if there is any change in your premium amount.

If you are entitled to hospital insurance as a result of this application, you will be enrolled for medical insurance automatically unless you indicate below that you do not want this protection. If you decline to enroll now, you can get medical insurance protection later only if you sign up for it during specified enrollment periods. Your protection may then be delayed and you may have to pay a higher premium when you decide to sign up.

The date your medical insurance begins and the amount of the premium you must pay depend on the month you filed this application with the Social Security Administration. Any Social Security office will be glad to explain the rules regarding enrollment to you.

23. Do your want to enroll in the Medicare Supplementary Medical Insurance Plan? ➤

☐ Yes

☐ No

FORM **SSA-10-BK** (7/89)

ANSWER ITEM 24 ONLY IF THE DECEASED DIED BEFORE THIS YEAR.

(24.) (a) How much were your total earnings last year? ————————▶ $

(b) Place an "X" in each block for each month of last year in which you <u>did not earn</u> more than *$ _____ in wages, and <u>did not perform</u> substantial services in self-employment. These months are exempt months. If no months were exempt months, place an "X" in "NONE." If all months were exempt months, place an "X" in "ALL."

*Enter the appropriate monthly limit after reading the instructions, "How Your Earnings Affect Your Benefits."

NONE		ALL	
Jan.	Feb.	Mar.	Apr.
May	Jun.	Jul.	Aug.
Sept.	Oct.	Nov.	Dec.

(25.) (a) How much do you expect your total earnings to be this year? ▶ $

(b) Place an "X" in each block for each month of last year in which you <u>did not or will not earn</u> more than *$ _____ in wages, and <u>did not or will not perform</u> substantial services in self-employment. These months are exempt months. If no months are or will be exempt months, place an "X" in "NONE." If all months are or will be exempt months, place an "X" in "ALL."

*Enter the appropriate monthly limit after reading the instructions, "How Your Earnings Affect Your Benefits."

NONE		ALL	
Jan.	Feb.	Mar.	Apr.
May	Jun.	Jul.	Aug.
Sept.	Oct.	Nov.	Dec.

ANSWER ITEM 26 ONLY IF YOU ARE NOW IN THE LAST 4 MONTHS OF YOUR TAXABLE YEAR (SEPT., OCT., NOV., AND DEC., IF YOUR TAXABLE YEAR IS A CALENDAR YEAR).

(26.) (a) How much do you expect to earn next year? ————————▶ $

(b) Place an "X" in each block for each month of next year in which you <u>do not expect to earn</u> more than *$ _____ in wages, and <u>do not expect to perform</u> substantial services in self- employment. These months will be exempt months. If no months are expected to be exempt months, place an "X" in "NONE." If all months are expected to be exempt months, place an "X" in "ALL."

*Enter the appropriate monthly limit after reading the instructions, "How Your Earnings Affect Your Benefits."

NONE		ALL	
Jan.	Feb.	Mar.	Apr.
May	Jun.	Jul.	Aug.
Sept.	Oct.	Nov.	Dec.

(27.) If you use a fiscal year, that is, a taxable year that does not end December 31 (with income tax return due April 15), enter here the month your fiscal year ends. ————————▶ | Month

IF YOU ARE AGE 65 AND 6 MONTHS OR OLDER, GO ON TO PAGE 6. OTHERWISE, PLEASE READ CAREFULLY THE INFORMATION ON PAGE 7 AND ANSWER ONE OF THE FOLLOWING ITEMS.

(28.) (a) I want benefits beginning with the earliest possible month that will be the most advantageous. ————————▶ ☐

(b) I am age 65 (or will be age 65 within 4 months) and I want benefits beginning with the earliest possible month that will be the most advantageous providing that there is no permanent reduction in my ongoing monthly benefits. ———▶ ☐

(c) I want benefits beginning with _____ . I understand that either a higher initial payment or a higher continuing monthly benefit amount may be possible, but I choose not to take it. ————————▶ ☐

ANSWER QUESTION 29 ONLY IF YOU ARE NOW AT LEAST AGE 61 YEARS, 8 MONTHS.

29. Do you wish this application to be considered an application for retirement benefits on your own earnings record? ————————▶ ☐ Yes ☐ No

FORM **SSA-10-BK** (7/89)

An ANNUAL REPORT of earnings must be filed with the Social Security Administration within 3 months and 15 days after the end of any taxable year in which you earn more than the yearly limit, if you are under age 70 for at least 1 full month of that year and receive some benefits during the taxable year. I AGREE TO FILE AN ANNUAL REPORT OF EARNINGS. THE ANNUAL REPORT IS REQUIRED BY LAW AND FAILURE TO REPORT MAY RESULT IN A MONETARY PENALTY.

Remarriage prior to age 60 may terminate your benefits. There are certain exceptions which are explained in the informational booklet which you will receive. You must report if you remarry even if you believe an exception applies. We will advise you whether additional evidence is needed and how your benefits may be affected.

I AGREE TO PROMPTLY NOTIFY the Social Security Administration if I REMARRY and to PROMPTLY RETURN ANY BENEFIT CHECK I receive for the month I marry, and for any later month.

REMARKS *(You may use this space for any explanations. If you need more space, attach a separate sheet.)*

_____

_____

_____

_____

_____

_____

_____

_____

I know that anyone who makes or causes to be made a false statement or representation of material fact in an application or for use in determining a right to payment under the Social Security Act commits a crime punishable under Federal law by fine, imprisonment or both. I affirm that all information I have given in this document is true.

SIGNATURE OF APPLICANT	Date *(Month, day, year)*
Signature *(First name, middle initial, last name) (Write in ink)*	Telephone Number(s) at which you may be contacted during the day
SIGN HERE ▶	__ __ __ __ __ __ AREA CODE

FOR OFFICIAL USE ONLY	Direct Deposit Payment Address *(Financial Institution)*			
	Routing Transit Number	C/S	Depositor Account Number	☐ No Account ☐ Direct Deposit Refused

Applicant's Mailing Address *(Number and street, Apt. No., P.O. Box, or Roural Route) (Enter Residence Address in "Remarks," if different.)*

City and State	ZIP Code	County *(if any)* in which you now live

Witnesses are required ONLY if this application has been signed by mark (X) above. If signed by mark (X), two witnesses to the signing who know the applicant must sign below, giving their full addresses. Also, print the applicant's name in Signature block.

1. Signature of Witness	2. Signature of Witness
Address *(Number and street, City, State and zip Code)*	Address *(Number and street, City, State and zip Code)*

FORM **SSA-10-BK** (7/89)

CHANGES TO BE REPORTED AND HOW TO REPORT
FAILURE TO REPORT MAY RESULT IN OVERPAYMENTS THAT MUST BE REPAID, AND IN POSSIBLE MONETARY PENALTIES

▶ You change your mailing address for checks or residence. To avoid delay in receipt of checks you should ALSO file a regular change of address notice with your post office.

▶ You go outside the U.S.A. for 30 consecutive days or longer.

▶ Any beneficiary dies or becomes unable to handle benefits.

▶ Work Changes---On your application you told us you expect total earnings for 19___ to be $ _____.

You (are) (are not) earning wages of more than $ _____ a month.

You (are) (are not) self-employed rendering substantial services in your trade or business.

(Report at ONCE if this work pattern changes.)

▶ Change of Marital Status---Marriage, divorce, annulment of marriage.

▶ You are confined to jail, prison, penal institution or correctional facility for conviction of a felony.

▶ Custody Change---Report if a person for whom you are filing or who is in your care dies, leaves your care or custody, or changes address.

▶ You begin to receive a government pension or annuity (from the Federal government or any State or any political subdivision thereof) or present payment changes.

Disability Applicants

1. You return to work (as an employee or self-employed) regardless of amount of earnings.

2. Your condition improves.

HOW TO REPORT

You can make your reports by telephone, mail, or in person, whichever you prefer.

WHEN A CHANGE OCCURS AFTER YOU RECEIVE A NOTICE OF AWARD, YOU SHOULD REPORT BY CALLING THE APPROPRIATE TELEPHONE NUMBER SHOWN NEAR THE TOP OF PAGE 8.

In addition, an annual report of earnings must be filed with the Social Security Administration within 3 months and 15 days after the end of any taxable year in which you earned more than the annual exempt amount.

THE ANNUAL REPORT OF EARNINGS IS REQUIRED BY LAW AND FAILURE TO REPORT MAY RESULT IN A MONETARY PENALTY.

Even if you file a Federal income tax form with the Internal Revenue Service you still need to file an annual report with us if you earn more than the yearly limit.

FIGURING YOUR ANNUAL EARNINGS

To figure your total yearly earnings, count all gross wages (before deductions) and net earnings from self-employment which you earn during the entire year. This includes earnings both before and after retirement, and applies to all earned income whether or not covered by Social Security.

In figuring your total yearly earnings, however, DO NOT COUNT ANY AMOUNTS EARNED BEGINNING WITH THE MONTH YOU BECOME AGE 70. Count only amounts earned before the month you become AGE 70.

PLEASE READ THE FOLLOWING INFORMATION CAREFULLY BEFORE ANSWERING QUESTION 28.

Benefits may be payable for some months prior to the month in which you file this claim (but not for any month before you reach age 60 (unless you are disabled)) if:

● YOU WILL EARN OVER THE EXEMPT AMOUNT THIS YEAR.

(For the appropriate exempt amount, see "How Your Earnings Affect Your Benefits.")

If your first month of entitlement is prior to age 65, your benefit rate will be reduced. However, if you do not actually receive your full benefit amount for one or more months before age 65 because benefits are withheld due to your earnings, your benefit will be increased at age 65 to give credit for this withholding. Thus, your benefit amount at age 65 will be reduced only if you receive one or more full benefit payments prior to the month you are age 65.

FORM SSA-10-BK (7/89)

DEPARTMENT OF HEALTH AND HUMAN SERVICES
Social Security Administration

☐ TEL

TOE 120/145/155

Form Approved
OMB No. 0960-0010

APPLICATION FOR CHILD'S INSURANCE BENEFITS

(Do not write in this space)

I apply on behalf of the child or children listed in item 3 below for all insurance benefits for which they may be eligible under title II (Federal Old-Age, Survivors and Disability Insurance) of the Social Security Act, as presently amended. (If you are applying on your own behalf, answer the questions on this form with respect to yourself.)

If you are applying for benefits based on the earnings record of a Deceased Worker, this may also be considered an application for survivors benefits under the Railroad Retirement Act and for Veterans Administration payments under Title 38, U.S.C., Veterans Benefits, Chapter 13 (which is, as such, an application for other types of death benefits under Title 38).

LIFE CLAIM ☐   DEATH CLAIM ☐

1.	(a) PRINT name of Wage Earner or Self-Employed person (herein referred to as the "Worker"). ⟶	FIRST NAME, MIDDLE INITIAL, LAST NAME
	(b) PRINT Worker's Social Security number. ⟶	__ __ __ / __ __ / __ __ __ __

2.	(a) PRINT your name (unless you are the Worker). ⟶	FIRST NAME, MIDDLE INITIAL, LAST NAME
	(b) PRINT your Social Security number. ⟶	__ __ __ / __ __ / __ __ __ __

PART I—INFORMATION ABOUT THE WORKER'S CHILDREN

3. The Worker's children (including natural children, adopted children, and stepchildren) or dependent grandchildren (including stepgrandchildren) may be eligible for benefits based on the earnings record of the Worker. For a living Worker, the information below applies to this month or to any of the past 12 months. For a deceased Worker, the information below applies to the date of death or for any period since the Worker's death. Also list any student who is between the ages of 18 and 23 if the student was both: 1) previously entitled to Social Security benefits on any Social Security record for August 1981, and 2) was also in full-time attendance at a post-secondary school for May 1982.

LIST BELOW ALL SUCH CHILDREN (IN ORDER OF BIRTH BEGINNING WITH THE OLDEST) who are now, or who were at the appropriate time (above), UNMARRIED and: • UNDER AGE 18 • AGE 18 TO 19 (OR TO AGE 23 FOR MONTHS PRIOR TO AUGUST 1982) AND ATTENDING SECONDARY SCHOOL • DISABLED OR HANDICAPPED (age 18 or over and disability began before age 22)	Check (✔) Sex of Child		Date of Birth (Mo., day, yr.)	Check (✔) if Child 17 or Older is:		Check (✔) the Column That Shows Child's Relationship to Worker					CHILD'S SOCIAL SECURITY NUMBER
	M	F		Student	Disabled	Legitimate	Adopted	Stepchild	Dependent Grandchild	Other	
FULL NAME OF CHILD											___ / __ / ____
											___ / __ / ____
											___ / __ / ____
											___ / __ / ____
											___ / __ / ____
											___ / __ / ____

If you do not wish to be payee for any child or dependent grandchild named above, list the child's name and address in "Remarks" on page 5. You may apply for a child even though you do not wish to be payee for the child's benefits.

4.	If any children in item 3 are stepchildren of the Worker, enter the date the Worker married the natural parent. ⟶	MONTH, DAY, YEAR

5.	(a) Is there a legal representative (guardian, conservator, curator, etc.) for any of the children in item 3? ⟶	☐ Yes (If "Yes," complete (b) and (c).)	☐ No (If "No," go on to item 6.)

(b) Write the following information about the legal representative(s):	NAME (First name, middle initial, last name)		TELEPHONE NUMBER (INCLUDE AREA CODE)
	ADDRESS		

(c) Briefly explain the circumstances which led the court to appoint a legal representative.

_____

_____

_____

_____

6. Are you the natural or adoptive parent of the person(s) for whom you are filing?　☐ Yes　☐ No

7. Have any children in item 3 ever been adopted by someone other than the Worker? (If "Yes," enter the following information): ⟶　☐ Yes　☐ No

Name of Child	Date of Adoption	Name of Person Adopting

8. Are all the children in item 3 now living in the same household with you? (If "No," enter the following information about each child not living with you. If uncertain as to the whereabouts of any of these children, explain in "Remarks".) ⟶　☐ Yes　☐ No

Name of Child Not Living With You	Person With Whom Child Now Lives	
	Name and Address	Relationship to Child

9. Has any child in item 3 ever been married? (If "Yes," enter the information requested below.) ⟶　☐ Yes　☐ No

Name of Child	Date of Marriage (Month, day, year)
How Marriage Ended (If still married, write "not ended")	Date Marriage Ended (Month, day, year)

10. Has anyone ever before filed an application with the Social Security Administration for monthly benefits on behalf of any child in item 3? (If "Yes," enter below the name(s) of the child(ren) and the name(s) and Social Security number(s) of the person(s) on whose earnings record any other claim was based.) ⟶　☐ Yes　☐ No

Name of Child	Name of Worker	Social Security Number of Worker
		_ _ _/_ _/_ _ _ _
		_ _ _/_ _/_ _ _ _
		_ _ _/_ _/_ _ _ _
		_ _ _/_ _/_ _ _ _

Form **SSA-4-BK** (7-89)

If you are applying ONLY for a child age 18 or over who is disabled, omit items 11 through 14. In all other cases, answer items 11 through 14.

EARNINGS INFORMATION FOR LAST YEAR (Do not complete if the Worker died this year)

11. (a) Did any child in item 3 earn more than the exempt amount last year?
(If "Yes," answer (b). If "No," go on to item 12.) ➔ ☐ Yes ☐ No

(b)

NAME OF CHILD WHO EARNED OVER THE EXEMPT AMOUNT LAST YEAR	TOTAL EARNINGS OF CHILD	LIST EACH MONTH THAT CHILD DID NOT EARN MORE THAN $ _____ IN WAGES AND DID NOT PERFORM SUBSTANTIAL SERVICES IN SELF-EMPLOYMENT
	$	
	$	
	$	

EARNINGS INFORMATION FOR THIS YEAR

12. (a) Do you expect the total earnings of any child in item 3 to be more than the exempt amount this year? (Count all earnings beginning with the first of this year and all anticipated earnings through the end of this year.) (If "Yes," answer (b). If "No," go on to item 13.) ➔ ☐ Yes ☐ No

(b)

NAME OF CHILD WHO EXPECTS TO EARN OVER THE EXEMPT AMOUNT THIS YEAR	EXPECTED EARNINGS OF CHILD	LIST EACH MONTH (INCLUDING THE PRESENT MONTH) THAT CHILD DID NOT OR WILL NOT EARN MORE THAN $ _____ IN WAGES AND DID NOT OR WILL NOT PERFORM SUBSTANTIAL SERVICES IN SELF-EMPLOYMENT
	$	
	$	
	$	

Complete item 13 ONLY if any child is now in the last 4 months of the child's taxable year (Sept., Oct., Nov., and Dec., if the taxable year is a calendar year).

EARNINGS INFORMATION FOR NEXT YEAR

13. (a) Do you expect the total earnings of any child in item 3 to be more than the exempt amount next year? (If "Yes," answer (b.) If "No," go on to item 14.) ➔ ☐ Yes ☐ No

(b)

NAME OF CHILD WHO EXPECTS TO EARN OVER THE EXEMPT AMOUNT NEXT YEAR	EXPECTED EARNINGS OF CHILD	LIST EACH MONTH THAT CHILD WILL NOT EARN MORE THAN $ _____ IN WAGES AND WILL NOT PERFORM SUBSTANTIAL SERVICES IN SELF-EMPLOYMENT
	$	
	$	
	$	

14. If any of the children for whom you are filing uses a fiscal year (one that does not end on December 31), print here the name of the child and the month the fiscal year ends. ➔

NAME OF CHILD AND MONTH FISCAL YEAR ENDS

Complete items 15 and 16 ONLY if the Worker is living. Otherwise, go on to item 17.

15. If any children in item 3 are children adopted by the Worker, print below the name of each such child and the date of adoption by the Worker.

NAME OF ADOPTED CHILD	DATE OF ADOPTION

Form SSA-4-BK (7-89)

16.	Have all of the children in item 3 lived with the Worker during each of the last 13 months (counting the present month)? _____ (If "No," enter the information requested below.)		☐ Yes	☐ No

NAME OF CHILD WHO DID NOT LIVE WITH THE WORKER IN EACH OF THE LAST 13 MONTHS	LIST EACH MONTH IN WHICH THIS CHILD DID NOT LIVE WITH THE WORKER	PERSON WITH WHOM CHILD LIVED	
		NAME AND ADDRESS	RELATIONSHIP TO CHILD

PART II-INFORMATION ABOUT THE DECEASED. Complete items 17 through 28 ONLY if the Worker is deceased. Otherwise, go on to PART III, item 29 and 30.

17.
(a) Print date of birth of Worker ⟶ MONTH, DAY, YEAR

(b) Print Worker's name at birth if different from item 1(a) ⟶

(c) Check (✔) one for the Worker ⟶ ☐ Male ☐ Female

18.
(a) Print date of death ⟶ MONTH, DAY, YEAR •

(b) Print place of death ⟶ CITY AND STATE

19. Print the name of the state or foreign country where the Worker had a fixed, permanent home at the time of death. ⟶ STATE OR FOREIGN COUNTRY

20. Did the Worker work in the railroad industry for 7 years or more? ⟶ ☐ Yes ☐ No

21.
(a) Was the Worker in the active military or naval service (including Reserve or National Guard active duty or active duty for training) after September 7, 1939 and before 1968? ⟶ ☐ Yes (If "Yes," answer (b) and (c).) ☐ No (If "No," go on to item 22.)

(b) Enter dates of service ⟶ FROM (month – year) | TO (month – year)

(c) Has anyone (including the Worker) received, or does anyone expect to receive, a benefit from any other Federal agency? ⟶ ☐ Yes ☐ No

22.
(a) Did the Worker ever engage in work that was covered under the social security system of a country other than the United States? ⟶ ☐ Yes (If "Yes," answer (b).) ☐ No (If "No," go on to item 23.)

(b) List the country(ies). ⟶

23.
(c.) Did the worker have wages or self-employment income covered under Social Security in all years from 1978 through last year? ⟶ ☐ Yes (If "Yes," skip to item 24.) ☐ No (If "No," answer (b.).)

(b.) List the years from 1978 through last year in which the worker did not have wages or self-employment income covered under Social Security. ⟶

Answer item 24 ONLY if death occurred within the last 2 years.

24.
(a) About how much did the Worker earn from employment and self-employment during the year of death? ⟶ AMOUNT $

(b) About how much did the Worker earn the year before death? ⟶ AMOUNT $

Form **SSA-4-BK** (7-89)

25. Check if applicable:

☐ I am not submitting evidence of the deceased's earnings that are not yet on his/her earnings record. I understand that these earnings will be included automatically within 24 months, and any increase in my benefits will be paid with full retroactivity.

26. **(a)** Did the Worker ever file an application for Social Security benefits, a period of disability under Social Security, Supplemental Security Income, or hospital or medical insurance under Medicare? ⟶

☐ Yes ☐ No ☐ Unknown

(If "Yes," answer (b) and (c).) (If "No" or "Unknown," go on to item 27.)

(b) Enter name of person(s) on whose Social Security record other application was filed. ⟶

(c) Enter Social Security number of person named in (b). (If "Unknown," so indicate.) ⟶

_ _ _ / _ _ / _ _ _ _

Answer item 27 ONLY if the worker died prior to age 66 and within the past 4 months.

27. **(a)** Was the Worker unable to work because of a disabling condition at the time of death? ⟶

☐ Yes ☐ No

(If "Yes," answer (b).)

(b) Enter date disability began ⟶

MONTH, DAY, YEAR

28. Were all the children in item 3 living with the Worker at the time of death? (If "No," enter the following information) ⟶

☐ Yes ☐ No

NAME OF CHILD NOT LIVING WITH THE WORKER	PERSON WITH WHOM CHILD WAS LIVING	
	NAME AND ADDRESS	RELATIONSHIP TO CHILD

PART III—INFORMATION ABOUT THE PAYEE APPLICANT. If you want to be selected as payee for any children in item 3, answer items 29 and 30. Otherwise, go on to the Signature block.

29. Have you ever been convicted of a felony? ⟶

☐ Yes (If "Yes," explain in "Remarks" below.) ☐ No

30. Are you serving, or have your ever served, as representative payee for anyone receiving a Social Security or Supplemental Security income benefit? ⟶

☐ Yes (If "Yes," enter the SSN(s) in "Remarks," below.) ☐ No

REMARKS: (You may use this space for any explanations. If you need more space, attach a separate sheet.)

Form **SSA-4-BK** (7-89)

120

An ANNUAL REPORT of earnings must be filed with the Social Security Administration within 3 months and 15 days after the end of any taxable year in which any child earns more than the yearly limit and receives some benefits in that year.

I AGREE TO FILE AN ANNUAL REPORT OF EARNINGS. THE ANNUAL REPORT IS REQUIRED BY LAW AND FAILURE TO REPORT MAY RESULT IN A MONETARY PENALTY.

BENEFITS MAY END if any of the following events occur. However, there are certain exceptions which are explained in the informational booklet which you will receive. You must report each of these events even if you believe an exception applies. We will advise you whether additional evidence is needed and how the benefits may be affected.

I AGREE TO PROMPTLY NOTIFY the Social Security Administration if any of the following events occur and to PROMPTLY RETURN ANY BENEFIT CHECK I receive to which a child is not entitled if:

- Any child MARRIES, is DIVORCED, or has a marriage ANNULMENT.
- A student, age 18 or over, STOPS ATTENDING SCHOOL, REDUCES SCHOOL ATTENDANCE BELOW FULL-TIME, CHANGES SCHOOLS, OR IS PAID BY AN EMPLOYER TO ATTEND SCHOOL.
- A disabled child, age 18 or over, GOES TO WORK, or the child's DISABLING CONDITION IMPROVES.
- Any child is INCARCERATED FOR CONVICTION OF A FELONY.
- I no longer have responsibility for the care and welfare of any child for whom I am filing.
- Any child for whom I am filing or who is in my care dies, leaves my care or custody, or changes address.

I UNDERSTAND that all payments made to me on behalf of a child must be spent for the child's present needs or (if not presently needed) saved for the child's future needs, and I AGREE to use the benefits that way. I will be held personally liable for repayment of benefits I receive if I misuse the payment or if I am found at fault with respect to an overpayment of such benefits.

I AGREE TO NOTIFY THE SOCIAL SECURITY ADMINISTRATION AS SOON AS I BELIEVE I WILL NO LONGER BE ABLE TO, OR WISH TO, ACT AS A REPRESENTATIVE PAYEE. (SUCH ADVANCE NOTIFICATION WILL ASSIST IN THE DEVELOPMENT OF AN ALTERNATE PAYEE AND WILL AVOID UNNECESSARY SUSPENSION OF PAYMENTS).

I ALSO AGREE TO FILE AN ACCOUNTING REPORT OF THE USE MADE OF THE PAYMENTS WHEN REQUESTED BY THE SOCIAL SECURITY ADMINISTRATION.

I know that anyone who makes or causes to be made a false statement or representation of material fact in an application or for use in determining a right to payment under the Social Security Act commits a crime punishable under Federal law by fine, imprisonment or both. I affirm that all information I have given in this document is true.

SIGNATURE OF APPLICANT	DATE (Month, day, year)
SIGNATURE (First name, middle initial, last name) (Write in ink) SIGN HERE ▶	TELEPHONE NUMBER(S) AT WHICH YOU MAY BE CONTACTED DURING THE DAY (INCLUDE AREA CODE) ___ ___ ___ (AREA CODE)

FOR OFFICIAL USE ONLY	Direct Deposit Payment Address (Financial Institution)			
	Routing Transit Number	C/S	Depositor Account Number	☐ No Account ☐ Direct Deposit Refused

Applicant's Mailing Address (Number and street, Apt. No., P.O. Box, or Rural Route) (Enter Residence Address in "Remarks," if different.)

City and State	ZIP Code	County (if any) in which you now live

Witnesses are required ONLY if this application has been signed by mark (X) above. If signed by mark (X), two witnesses to the signing who know the applicant must sign below giving their full addresses. Also, print the applicant's name in the signature block.

1. SIGNATURE OF WITNESS	2. SIGNATURE OF WITNESS
ADDRESS (Number and Street, City, State, and ZIP Code)	ADDRESS (Number and Street, City, State, and ZIP Code)

TIME IT TAKES TO COMPLETE THIS FORM

We estimate that it will take you about 12.5 minutes to complete this form. This includes the time it will take to read the instructions, gather the necessary facts and fill out the form. If you have comments or suggestions on how long it takes to complete this form or on any other aspect of this form, write to the Social Security Administration. ATTN: Reports Clearance Officer, 1-A-21 Operations Bldg., Baltimore, MD 21235, and to the Office of Management and Budget, Paperwork Reduction Project (0960-0010), Washington, D.C. 20503.

Form SSA-4-BK (7-89)

RECEIPT FOR YOUR CLAIM FOR SOCIAL SECURITY CHILD'S INSURANCE BENEFITS

TELEPHONE NUMBER(S) TO CALL IF YOU HAVE A QUESTION OR SOMETHING TO REPORT	**BEFORE** YOU RECEIVE A NOTICE OF AWARD	SSA OFFICE	DATE CLAIM RECEIVED
	(Area Code)		
	AFTER YOU RECEIVE A NOTICE OF AWARD		
	(Area Code)		

Your application for Social Security benefits on behalf of the child(ren) named below has been received. You will be notified by mail as soon as a decision is made on your claim.

You should hear from us within _____ days after you have given us all the information we requested. Some claims may take longer if additional information is needed.

In the meantime, if you or any child(ren) changes address, or if there is some other change that may affect your claim, you or someone for you should report the change. The changes to be reported are listed below.

Always give us your claim number when writing or telephoning about your claim.

If you have any questions about your claim, we will be glad to help you.

CLAIMANT	SOCIAL SECURITY CLAIM NUMBER

WORKER'S NAME *(If surname differs from name of claimant(s).)*

CHANGES TO BE REPORTED AND HOW TO REPORT

FAILURE TO REPORT MAY RESULT IN OVERPAYMENTS THAT MUST BE REPAID AND IN POSSIBLE MONETARY PENALTIES

▶ You or any child changes mailing address for checks or residence *To avoid delay in receipt of checks you should ALSO file a regular change of address notice with your post office.*

▶ Any beneficiary goes outside the U.S.A. for 30 consecutive days or longer.

▶ Any beneficiary dies or becomes unable to handle benefits

▶ Work Changes—On your application you told us

_____ expected total earnings for 19 ___
(Name of child)
to be $ _____ .

_____ (is) (is not) earning wages of
(Name of child)
more than $ _____ a month.

_____ (is) (is not) self-employed
(Name of child)
rendering substantial services in a trade or business.

(Report AT ONCE if this work pattern changes.)

▶ Custody Change—Report if a child for whom you are filing or who is in your care dies, leaves your care or custody, or changes address.

▶ Change of Marital Status—Marriage, divorce, annulment of marriage of any child

▶ Change in school attendance

▶ Any child is confined to jail, prison, penal institution, or correctional facility for conviction of a felony

▶ Disability Applicants
1. The disabled adult child returns to work (as an employee or self-employed) regardless of amount of earnings
2. The disabled adult child's condition improves
3. The disabled adult child is incarcerated for conviction of a felony

An agency in your State that works with us in administering the Social Security disability program is responsible for making the disability decision on the child's claim. In some cases, it is necessary for them to get additional information about the child's condition or to arrange for the child to have a medical examination at Government expense.

HOW TO REPORT

You can make your reports by telephone, by mail, or in person, whichever you prefer.

WHEN A CHANGE OCCURS AFTER YOU RECEIVE A NOTICE OF AWARD, YOU SHOULD REPORT BY CALLING THE APPROPRIATE TELEPHONE NUMBER SHOWN NEAR THE TOP OF THIS PAGE.

Form SSA-4-BK (7-89)

☐ TEL   TOE 120/145/155   Form Approved
OMB No. 0960-0003

APPLICATION FOR MOTHER'S OR FATHER'S INSURANCE BENEFITS*

I apply for all insurance benefits for which I am eligible under Title II (Federal Old-Age, Survivors, and Disability Insurance) and part A of Title XVIII (Health Insurance for the Aged and Disabled) of the Social Security Act, as presently amended.

The information you furnish on this application will ordinarily be sufficient for a determination on the lump-sum death payment.

*This may also be considered an application for survivors benefits under the Railroad Retirement Act and for Veterans Administration payments under title 38 U.S.C., Veterans Benefits, Chapter 13 (which is, as such, an application for other types of death benefits under title 38).

(Do not write in this space)

1.	(a) PRINT name of deceased wage earner or self-employed person (*herein referred to as the "Deceased."*) ——▶	FIRST NAME, MIDDLE INITIAL, LAST NAME
	(b) Check (✓) one for the Deceased. ——▶	☐ Male ☐ Female
	(c) Enter Deceased's Social Security Number. ——▶	_ _ _ / _ _ / _ _ _ _
2.	(a) PRINT your name. ——▶	FIRST NAME, MIDDLE INITIAL, LAST NAME
	(b) Enter your Social Security number. ——▶	_ _ _ / _ _ / _ _ _ _
3.	Enter your name at birth if different from item 2. ——▶	
4.	(a) Enter your date of birth. ——▶	MONTH, DAY, YEAR
	(b) Enter name of State or foreign country where you were born. ——▶	

Please read carefully before answering item 5

You may receive a mother's or a father's benefit for any month in which you have in your care the Deceased's child or dependent grandchild who is entitled to a child's benefit if the child is:
- under age 16, or
- disabled or handicapped (age 16 or over and disability began before age 22).

If you are filing as a surviving divorced mother or father, such child must be your son, daughter, or legally adopted child who is entitled to child's benefits on the Deceased's earnings record.

Mother's or father's benefits are not payable if the only child in your care is a child age 16 or over who is not disabled.

5.	Has an unmarried child or dependent grandchild of the Deceased, who is under age 16 or disabled, lived with you any time from the month of death through the present month? (Include natural child, adopted child, stepchild, and stepgrandchild.) (*If "Yes," enter the information requested below*) ——▶ ☐ Yes ☐ No

Name of child	Months child lived with you (*If all, write "All"*)

6.	(a) Have you (or has someone on your behalf) ever filed an application for Social Security benefits, a period of disability under Social Security, Supplemental Security Income, or hospital or medical insurance under Medicare? ——▶	☐ Yes (*If "Yes," answer (b) and (c).*) ☐ No (*If "No," go on to item 7.*)
	(b) Enter name of person on whose Social Security record you filed other application. ——▶	
	(c) Enter Social Security number of person named in (b). (*If "Unknown," so indicate.*) ——▶	_ _ _ / _ _ / _ _ _ _

Form **SSA-5-F6** (7/89)Destroy Prior Editions

7. **(a)** Are you so disabled that you can't work, or was there some period during the last 14 months when you were so disabled that you could not work? ⟶

☐ Yes *(If "Yes," answer (b).)* ☐ No *(If "No," go on to item 8.)*

(b) Enter the date you became disabled. ⟶

Month, Day, Year

8. Did you work in the railroad industry for **7 years or more**? ⟶

☐ Yes ☐ No

9. **(a)** Have you ever engaged in work that was covered under the social security system of a country other than the United States? ⟶

☐ Yes *(If "Yes," answer (b).)* ☐ No *(If "No," go on to item 10.)*

(b) List the country(ies). ⟶

10. Is there a surviving parent (or parents) of the Deceased who was receiving support from the Deceased at the time of death or at the time the Deceased become disabled? ⟶

☐ Yes ☐ No *(If "Yes," enter the name and address of the parent(s) in "Remarks".)*

11. Enter below information about each of your marriages. Include information on your marriage to the Deceased and any other marriages, whether before or after you married the Deceased. If you are applying for father's benefits, enter the maiden name of the Deceased.

To whom married		When *(Month, day, year)*	Where *(Name of City and State)*
Your last marriage	How marriage ended	When *(Month, day, year)*	Where *(Name of City and State)*
	Marriage performed by: ☐ Clergyman or public official ☐ Other *(Explain in "Remarks")*	Spouse's date of birth (or age)	If spouse deceased, give date of death
	Spouse's Social Security number *(If "None" or "Unknown," so indicate.)*		__ __ __/__ __/__ __ __ __
To whom married		When *(Month, day, year)*	Where *(Name of City and State)*
Your previous marriage (IF NONE, WRITE "NONE.")	How marriage ended	When *(Month, day, year)*	Where *(Name of City and State)*
	Marriage performed by: ☐ Clergyman or public official ☐ Other *(Explain in "Remarks")*	Spouse's date of birth (or age)	If spouse deceased, give date of death
	Spouse's Social Security number *(If "None" or "Unknown," so indicate.)*		__ __ __/__ __/__ __ __ __

(Use "Remarks" space on back of page for information about any other previous marriage)

12. Enter below the information requested about each marriage of the Deceased, including the marriage to you. (Indicate your marriage to the Deceased by entering your name; it is not necessary to repeat other information about this marriage you have already given in item 11.) Enter complete information on all other marriages.

To whom married		When *(Month, day, year)*	Where *(Name of City and State)*
Last marriage of Deceased	How marriage ended	When *(Month, day, year)*	Where *(Name of City and State)*
	Marriage performed by: ☐ Clergyman or public official ☐ Other *(Explain in "Remarks")*	Spouse's date of birth (or age)	If spouse deceased, give date of death
	Spouse's Social Security number *(If "None" or "Unknown," so indicate.)*		__ __ __/__ __/__ __ __ __
To whom married		When *(Month, day, year)*	Where *(Name of City and State)*
Previous marriage of the Decreased (IF NONE, WRITE "NONE.")	How marriage ended	When *(Month, day, year)*	Where *(Name of City and State)*
	Marriage performed by: ☐ Clergyman or public official ☐ Other *(Explain in "Remarks")*	Spouse's date of birth (or age)	If spouse deceased, give date of death
	Spouse's Social Security number *(If "None" or "Unknown," so indicate.)*		__ __ __/__ __/__ __ __ __

(Use "Remarks" space on back page for information about any other previous marriage)

If you are applying for surviving divorced spouse's benefits, omit 13 and go on to item 14.

13. (a)

Were you and the Deceased living together at the same address when the Deceased died? ➤

☐ Yes
(If "Yes," go on to item 14.)

☐ No
(If "No," answer (b).)

(b) If either you or the Deceased were away from home (whether or not temporarily) when the Deceased died, give the following:

Who was away? ➤ ☐ You ☐ Deceased

Reason absence began ➤

Date last at home ➤

Reason you were apart at time of death ➤

If separated because of illness, enter nature of illness or disabling condition ➤

Answer item 14 ONLY if the Deceased died before this year.

14. (a) How much were your total earnings last year? ➤ $

(b) Place an "X" in each block for EACH MONTH of last year in which you did not earn more than *$_____ in wages and did not perform substantial services in self-employment. These months are exempt months. If no months were exempt months, place an "X" in "NONE." If all months were exempt months, place an "X" in "ALL." ➤

*Enter the appropriate monthly limit after reading the instructions, "How Your Earnings Affect Your Benefits."

NONE		ALL
JAN	FEB	MAR
APR	MAY	JUN
JUL	AUG	SEPT
OCT	NOV	DEC

15. (a) How much do you expect your total earnings to be this year? ➤ $

(b) Place an "X" in each block for EACH MONTH of this year in which you did not or will not earn more than *$_____ in wages and did not or will not perform substantial services in self-employment. These months are exempt months. If no months are or will be exempt months, place an "X" in "NONE." If all months are or will be exempt months, place an "X" in "ALL." ➤

*Enter the appropriate monthly limit after reading the instructions, "How Your Earnings Affect Your Benefits."

NONE		ALL
JAN	FEB	MAR
APR	MAY	JUN
JUL	AUG	SEPT
OCT	NOV	DEC

Answer this item ONLY if you are now in the last 4 months of your taxable year (Sept., Oct., Nov., and Dec., if your taxable year is a calendar year).

16. (a) How much do you expect to earn next year? ➤ $

(b) Place an "X" in each block for EACH MONTH of next year in which you do not expect to earn more than *$_____ in wages and do not expect to perform substantial services in self-employment. These months will be exempt months. If no months are expected to be exempt months, place an "X" in "NONE." If all months are expected to be exempt months, place an "X" in "ALL." ➤

*Enter the appropriate monthly limit after reading the instructions, "How Your Earnings Affect Your Benefits."

NONE		ALL
JAN	FEB	MAR
APR	MAY	JUN
JUL	AUG	SEPT
OCT	NOV	DEC

If you use a fiscal year, that is a taxable year that does not end December 31 (with income tax return due April 15), enter here the month your fiscal year ends. ➤

MONTH

Form **SSA-5-F6** (7/89)

17. (a) Have you qualified for, or do you expect to qualify for, a pension or annuity (or a lump sum in place of a pension or annuity) based on your own employment and earnings for the Federal Government of the United States, or one of its States or local subdivisions? (*Social Security benefits are not government pensions*) ➤

☐ Yes   ☐ No
(*If "Yes," check the box in item (b) that applies.*)
(*If "No," go on to item 18.*)

(b) ☐ I receive a government pension or annuity.

☐ I received a lump sum in place of a government pension or annuity.

☐ I applied for and am awaiting a decision on my pension or lump sum.

☐ I have not applied for but I expect to begin receiving my pension or annuity:
(*If the date is not known, enter "Unknown."*)

Month	Year

18. Check if applicable:

☐ I am not submitting evidence of the deceased's earnings that are not yet on his/her earnings record. I understand that these earnings will be included automatically within 24 months, and any increase in my benefits will be paid with full retroactivity.

I AGREE TO PROMPTLY NOTIFY the Social Security Administration if I begin to receive a government pension or annuity, based on my own earnings, from the Federal government or any State (or any political subdivision thereof), or if my present government pension or annuity amount changes.

An ANNUAL REPORT of earnings must be filed with the Social Security Administration within 3 months and 15 days after the end of any taxable year in which you earn more than the yearly limit and receive some benefits during the taxable year. I AGREE TO FILE AN ANNUAL REPORT OF EARNINGS. THE ANNUAL REPORT IS REQUIRED BY LAW AND FAILURE TO REPORT MAY RESULT IN A MONETARY PENALTY.

BENEFITS MAY END if either of the following events occur. However, there are certain exceptions which are explained in the informational booklet which you will receive. You must report each of these events even if you believe an exception applies. We will advise you whether additional evidence is needed and how your benefits may be affected.

I AGREE TO PROMPTLY NOTIFY the Social Security Administration and to PROMPTLY RETURN ANY BENEFIT CHECK I receive if the check is for a month in or after the month in which:
- I MARRY.
- I NO LONGER HAVE IN MY CARE the Deceased's child or dependent grandchild under age 16 or disabled who is entitled to benefits.
- I am INCARCERATED FOR CONVICTION OF A FELONY.

REMARKS (*You may use this space for any explanations. If you need more space, attach a separate sheet.*)

I know that anyone who makes or causes to be made a false statement or representation of material fact in an application or for use in determining a right to payment under the Social Security Act commits a crime punishable under Federal law by fine, imprisonment or both. I affirm that all information I have given in this document is true.

SIGNATURE OF APPLICANT	Date (*Month, day, year*)
Signature (*First name, middle initial, last name*) (*Write in ink*)	Telephone Number(s) at which you may may be contacted during the day
SIGN HERE ▶	___ ___ ___ (AREA CODE)

FOR OFFICIAL USE ONLY	Direct Deposit Payment Address (*Financial Institution*)			
	Routing Transit Number	C/S	Depositor Account Number	☐ No Account ☐ Direct Deposit Refused

Applicant's Mailing Address (*Number and street, Apt. No., P.O. Box, or Rural Route*) (*Enter Residence Address in "Remarks," if different.*)

City and State	ZIP Code	County (*if any*) in which you now live

Witnesses are required ONLY if this application has been signed by mark (X) above. If signed by mark (X), two witnesses to the signing who know the applicant must sign below, giving their full addresses. Also, print the applicant's name in Signature block.

1. Signature of Witness	2. Signature of Witness
Address (*Number and street, City, State and ZIP Code*)	Address (*Number and street, City, State and ZIP Code*)

Form **SSA-5-F6** (7/89)

126

RECEIPT FOR YOUR CLAIM FOR SOCIAL SECURITY MOTHER'S OR FATHER'S INSURANCE BENEFITS

TELEPHONE NUMBER(S) TO CALL IF YOU HAVE A QUESTION OR SOMETHING TO REPORT	**BEFORE** YOU RECEIVE A NOTICE OF AWARD ___ ___ ___ (AREA CODE) **AFTER** YOU RECEIVE A NOTICE OF AWARD ___ ___ ___ (AREA CODE)	SSA OFFICE	DATE CLAIM RECEIVED

Your application or Social Security benefits has been received and will be processed as quickly as possible.

You should hear from us within _____ days after you have given us all the information we requested. Some claims may take longer if additional information is needed.

In the meantime, if you change your address, or if there is some other change that may affect your claim, you — or someone for you — should report the change. The changes to be reported are listed below.

Always give us your claim number when writing or telephoning about your claim.

If you have any questions about your claim, we will he glad to help you.

CLAIMANT	DECEASED'S SURNAME IF DIFFERENT FROM CLAIMANT'S	SOCIAL SECURITY CLAIM NUMBER

CHANGES TO BE REPORTED AND HOW TO REPORT

Failure to report may result in overpayments that must be repaid and in possible monetary penalties.

▶ You change your mailing address for checks or residence (*To avoid delay in receipt of checks you should ALSO file a regular change of address notice with your post office.*)

▶ You go outside the U.S.A for 30 consecutive days or longer.

▶ Any beneficiary dies or becomes unable to handle benefits

▶ Work Changes — On you application you told us you expect

total earnings for 19_____ to be $ _____ .

You (are) (are not) earning wages of more than

$ _____ a month.

You (are) (are not) self-employed rendering substantial services in your trade or business.

(*Report AT ONCE if this work pattern changes.*)

▶ You are confined to jail, prison, penal institution, or correctional facility for conviction of a felony.

▶ Custody Change or Disabilitly Improves — Report if a person for whom you are filing or who is in your care dies, leaves your care or custody, changes address or, if disabled, the condition improves.

▶ Change of Marital Status — Marriage, divorce, annulment of marriage

▶ You begin to receive a government pension or annuity (from the Federal government or any State or any political subdivision thereof) or present payment changes.

HOW TO REPORT
You can make your reports by telephone, mail, or in person, whichever you prefer.

WHEN A CHANGE OCCURS AFTER YOU RECEIVE A NOTICE OF AWARD, YOU SHOULD REPORT BY CALLING THE APPROPRIATE TELEPHONE NUMBER SHOWN NEAR THE TOP OF THIS PAGE.

Also, an ANNUAL REPORT OF EARNINGS must be filed with the Social Security Administration within 3 months and 15 days after the end of any taxable year in which you earn more than the yearly limit and receive some benefits during the taxable year. THE ANNUAL REPORT IS REQUIRED BY LAW AND FAILURE TO REPORT MAY RESULT IN A MONETARY PENALTY.

Even if you file a Federal income tax form with the Internal Revenue Service, you still need to file an annual report with us if you earn more than the yearly limit.

DEPARTMENT OF HEALTH AND HUMAN SERVICES
Social Security Administration

Form Approved
OMB No. 0960-0013

APPLICATION FOR LUMP-SUM DEATH PAYMENT*

I apply for all insurance benefits for which I am eligible under Title II (Federal Old-Age, Survivors, and Disability Insurance) of the Social Security Act, as presently amended, on the named deceased's Social Security record. (This application must be filed within 2 years after the date of death of the wage earner or self-employed person.)

*This may also be considered an application for insurance benefits payable under the Railroad Retirement Act.

1.	(a) PRINT name of Deceased Wage Earner or Self-Employed Person (herein referred to as the "deceased")	FIRST NAME, MIDDLE INITIAL, LAST NAME
	(b) Check (✓) one for the deceased	☐ Male ☐ Female
	(c) Enter deceased's Social Security Number	__ __ __ / __ __ / __ __ __ __
2.	PRINT your name	FIRST NAME, MIDDLE INITIAL, LAST NAME
3.	Enter date of birth of deceased (Month, day, year)	
4.	(a) Enter date of death (Month, day, year)	
	(b) Enter place of death (City and State)	
5.	(a) Did the deceased ever file an application for Social Security benefits, a period of disability under Social Security, supplemental security income, or hospital or medical insurance under Medicare?	☐ Yes (If "Yes," answer (b) and (c).) ☐ No ☐ Unknown (If "No" or "Unknown," go on to item 6.)
	(b) Enter name(s) of person(s) on whose Social Security record(s) other application was filed.	FIRST NAME, MIDDLE INITIAL, LAST NAME
	(c) Enter Social Security Number(s) of person(s) named in (b). (If unknown, so indicate)	__ __ __ / __ __ / __ __ __ __
6.	ANSWER ITEM 6 **ONLY** IF THE DECEASED WORKED WITHIN THE PAST 2 YEARS.	
	(a) About how much did the deceased earn from employment and self-employment during the year of death?	AMOUNT $
	(b) About how much did the deceased earn the year before death?	AMOUNT $
7.	ANSWER ITEM 7 **ONLY** IF THE DECEASED DIED PRIOR TO AGE 66 AND WITHIN THE PAST 4 MONTHS.	
	(a) Was the deceased unable to work because of a disabling condition at the time of death?	☐ Yes (If "Yes," answer (b).) ☐ No (If "No," go on to item 8.)
	(b) Enter date disability began (Month, day, year)	
8.	(a) Was the deceased in the active military or naval service (including Reserve or National Guard *active* duty or active duty for training) after September 7, 1939 and before 1968?	☐ Yes (If "Yes," answer (b) and (c).) ☐ No (If "No," go on to item 9.)
	(b) Enter dates of service.	From: (Month, Year) To: (Month, Year)
	(c) Has anyone (including the deceased) received, or does anyone expect to receive, a benefit from any other Federal agency?	☐ Yes ☐ No
9.	Did the deceased work in the railroad industry for 7 years or more?	☐ Yes ☐ No

Form **SSA-8-F4** (7/89) Destroy prior editions

10.	(a) Did the deceased ever engage in work that was covered under the social security system of a country other than the United States? ⟶	☐ Yes ☐ No *(If "Yes," answer (b).) (If "No," go on to item 11.)*
	(b) If "Yes," list the country(ies). ⟶	

11.	Is the deceased survived by a spouse or ex-spouse? (If "No," go on to item 12. If "Yes," give the following information about all marriages of the deceased including marriage in effect at time of death.) (If you need more space, use "Remarks" section on back page or attach a separate sheet.)		☐ Yes ☐ No

To whom married *(Name at Birth)*		When *(Month, day, year)*	Where *(Enter name of City and State)*
Last marriage of the deceased	How marriage ended	When *(Month, day, year)*	Where *(Enter name of City and State)*
	Marriage performed by: ☐ Clergyman or public official ☐ Other *(Explain in Remarks)*	Spouse's date of birth (or age)	
	Spouse's Social Security Number *(If none or unknown, so indicate)* ___ ___ / ___ / ___ ___ ___ ___		

To whom married		When *(Month, day, year)*	Where *(Enter name of City and State)*
Previous marriage of the deceased **If none, write "None."**	How marriage ended	When *(Month, day, year)*	Where *(Enter name of City and State)*
	Marriage performed by: ☐ Clergyman or public official ☐ Other *(Explain in Remarks)*	Spouse's date of birth (or age)	If spouse deceased, give date of death
	Spouse's Social Security Number *(If none or unknown, so indicate)* ___ ___ ___ / ___ / ___ ___ ___ ___		

12.	The deceased's surviving children (including natural children, adopted children, and stepchildren) or dependent grandchildren (including stepgrandchildren) may be eligible for benefits based on the earnings record of the deceased.

List below ALL such children who are now or were in the past 12 months UNMARRIED and:
- UNDER AGE 18   • AGE 18 TO 19 AND ATTENDING SECONDARY SCHOOL
- DISABLED OR HANDICAPPED (age 18 or over and disability began before age 22)

(If none, write "None.")

Full Name of Child	Full Name of Child

13.	Is there a surviving parent (or parents) of the deceased who was receiving support from the deceased either at the time the deceased became disabled under the Social Security law or at the time of death? ⟶	☐ Yes ☐ No (If "Yes," enter the name and address of the parent(s) in "Remarks".)
14.	Have you filed for any Social Security benefits on the deceased's earnings record before? ⟶	☐ Yes ☐ No

NOTE: If there is a surviving spouse, continue with item 15. If not, skip items 15 through 18.

15.	If you are not the surviving spouse, enter the surviving spouse's name and address here

16.	(a) Were the deceased and the surviving spouse living together at the same address when the deceased died?	☐ Yes ☐ No (If "Yes," go on to item 17.) (If "No," answer (b).)
	(b) If either the deceased or surviving spouse was away from home (whether or not temporarily) when the deceased died, give the following:	

Who was away? ⟶	☐ Deceased ☐ Surviving spouse

Date last home	Reason absence began	Reason they were apart at time of death

If separated because of illness, enter nature of illness or disabling condition.	

If you are the surviving spouse, and if you are under age 66, answer 17.

17.	(a)	Are you so disabled that you cannot work or was there some period during the last 14 months when you were so disabled that you could not work? ⟶	☐ Yes ☐ No
	(b)	If "Yes," enter the date you became disabled. ⟶	*(Month, day, year)*

Answer 18 ONLY if you are the surviving spouse.

18. Were you married before your marriage to the deceased? *(If "Yes," give the following about each of your previous marriages. If you need more space, use "Remarks" section on back page or attach a separate sheet.)* ⟶   ☐ Yes   ☐ No

To whom married		When *(Month, day, year)*	Where *(Enter name of City and State)*
Your previous marriage	How marriage ended	When *(Month, day, year)*	Where *(Enter name of City and State)*
	Marriage performed by: ☐ Clergyman or public official ☐ Other *(Explain in Remarks)*	Spouse's date of birth (or age)	If spouse deceased, give date of death
	Spouse's Social Security Number *(If none or unknown, so indicate)* ___ __ __/__/____		

Remarks: *(You may use this space for any explanation. If you need more space, attach a separate sheet.)*

_____

_____

_____

_____

_____

_____

_____

_____

_____

I know that anyone who makes or causes to be made a false statement or representation of material fact in an application or for use in determining a right to payment under the Social Security Act commits a crime punishable under Federal law by fine, imprisonment or both. I affirm that all information I have given in this document is true.

SIGNATURE OF APPLICANT	Date *(Month, day, year)*
Signature *(First name, middle initial, last name) (Write in ink)* ▶	Telephone Number(s) at which you may be contacted during the day Area Code

Mailing Address *(Number and street, Apt. No., P.O. Box, or Rural Route)*

City and State	ZIP Code	Enter Name of County (if any) in which you now live

Witnesses are required ONLY if this application has been signed by mark (X) above. If signed by mark (X), two witnesses to the signing who know the applicant must sign below, giving their full addresses.

1. Signature of Witness	2. Signature of Witness
Address *(Number and street, City, State, and ZIP Code)*	Address *(Number and street, City, State, and ZIP Code)*

Form **SSA-8-F4** (7/89)

SOCIAL SECURITY ADMINISTRATION

1993 ANNUAL REPORT OF EARNINGS

The Social Security Administration needs information about your 1993 earnings and your work plans for 1994. I am enclosing your 1993 Annual Report of Earnings which you need to complete to help us make sure that we paid you the correct amount of benefits in 1993. This information will also help us determine how much to pay you in 1994. We hope that you find this form a convenient way to report your earnings.

Why You Need To Complete an Annual Report

Your earnings in 1993 and 1994 may affect your benefits. That is why it is important that you read the information sheet for the annual report and complete each question carefully. If you receive Black Lung benefits and need to file an annual report, you should also use this form.

If your report shows that we owe you money for 1993, we will issue a payment. If your report shows that we paid you too much, we will send you a letter before you have to pay us back. That letter will tell you about the overpayment and what you can do if you think we are wrong.

When To File Your Report

Please be sure to send us your completed annual report no later than **April 15, 1994**. If you do not file your report by then or ask us in writing for an extension, **we may have to stop your checks. And, you may have to pay a substantial penalty.**

Remember, even though you may have sent a Federal income tax return to the Internal Revenue Service (IRS), or asked them for an extension, you still need to file an annual report with us, or ask us in writing for an extension.

If You Have Any Questions

If you have any questions, call us toll-free at 1-800-772-1213. We can answer most questions over the phone. If you prefer to visit or call one of our offices, use the 800 number and we can give you the office address and telephone number. Please have this annual report and your 1993 W-2 form(s) or Federal tax return with you if you call or visit an office. It will help us to answer your questions. If you report this information to SSA by phone or through an office visit, do not mail this form.

Shirley S. Chater
Commissioner
of Social Security

1993 ANNUAL REPORT OF EARNINGS
Information and Worksheet

Below is some information and a worksheet to help you complete your annual report. Please read it **before** you complete the form. Some of this information may not apply to you in 1993, but also keep it in mind when you estimate your 1994 earnings.

The Annual Earnings Limit

Your work will only affect your Social Security benefits if your total earnings are over the limit we show below.

Your Age	Annual Limit	
	1993	1994
Under 65	$ 7,680	$ 8,040
65 - 69	$10,560	$11,160
70 or over	No Limit	

If you earn more than the annual limit we will deduct $1 from your benefits for each $2 you earn over the limit if you are under age 65 for all of 1993. **If you are age 65 or older we will deduct $1 for each $3 over the limit.**

We withhold benefits during the year in whole monthly increments, based on the estimate you give us. When you file your annual report and we know how much you actually earned, we pay you any benefits you are owed, or withhold additional benefits if required.

How Age Affects Your Benefits

As you can see from the chart above, people who are 65 or older have a higher earnings limit than people who are under 65. We consider you to be 65 in 1993 if you turned 65 in any month in 1993 or if you turned 65 on January 1, 1994.

Also, there are special rules for people who turned 70 in 1993, which we discuss in the next section. If you turn 70 in 1994 remember to keep these special rules in mind when you estimate your 1994 earnings.

If You Became 70 In 1993, Please Read This

If you became age 70 in 1993, you are not required to file an annual report if you received no benefits in 1993 for months before you became 70. However, you may be due some benefits and we can determine whether or not you are due benefits only if you return your annual report to us.

If you became 70 years old in 1993, you need to report only your wages and self-employment income for months **before** you turned 70. For example, if you turned 70 in June, in questions 1 and 3 you would report only the total amount of your wages for January through May. You **would not** report your wages for June through December.

If you were self-employed, to determine the amount that is to be reported as self-employment income, you should prorate the amount shown on line 4 of your 1040SE by the number of months in which you were self-employed before age 70. For example, if line 4 of your 1040SE shows $12,000 and you were self-employed all months in the year and you became age 70 in June, the amount of self-employment income to be reported is $5,000 ($12,000 + 12 months = $1,000 x 5 months = $5,000).

If you need help in prorating your self-employment income, contact us. We will help you make sure that you are reporting the correct amount.

If you were born on the first day of a month another special rule affects you. We consider that you turned 70 in the month **before** your birthday. For example, if your birthday is May 1, we treat you as if you turned 70 in April. This means that you only have to report earnings for January through March.

Reporting Your Wages

If any of the following situations apply to you, please contact us **before** you file your report. Also, it would be helpful if you would get a statement from your employer showing how much you actually earned for your work in 1993:

- You plan to report wages that are **less** than the total amount of wages shown on your W-2 form(s).

- Some of the wages shown on your W-2 form(s) for 1993 were earned in an earlier year. This includes bonuses, accumulated vacation or sick pay, severance pay, commissions, or deferred compensation.

- You received retirement payments from an employer pension fund and these payments were included as wages on your W-2 form(s).

Reporting Your Self-Employment Income

If any of the following situations apply to you, please contact us **before** you file your report. We will help you make sure that you are reporting the correct amount of self-employment income:

- You had self-employment income in 1993, but you did not work in your business. This might happen when you have income from a business you own, but your employees completely operate the business. This also might happen when you get agricultural program payments or you have income from carry-over crops.

- The net earnings you show on your annual report are less than the net earnings on your 1993 tax return.

- You are 65 or older in 1993 and you receive royalties on patents or copyrights issued to you before you became 65.

- You report your income on a fiscal year basis.

- You sold or transferred your business in 1993 or your plan to do so in 1994.

- You are a Minister, and/or you receive a W-2 showing income which you report as self-employment.

- You were a director of a corporation and you reported self-employment income this year for services performed in prior years.

Note: Fees for serving as the director of a corporation must be reported on this form in the year the services are performed.

Income You Do Not Have To Report

Generally, you only report income which is earned from employment and self-employment. Here is a list of income you do not have to report to us.

- Social Security, railroad or civil service retirement, veterans, black lung, or public assistance benefits.

- Pensions and other retirement payments which are not reported on your W-2 form.

- Investment income, **unless** you are a dealer in securities.

- Interest from savings accounts.

- Life insurance annuities and dividends

- Gifts or inheritances.

- Gain (or loss) from the sale of capital assets.

- Rental income, **unless** you are a real estate dealer or you rent out a farm and still take part in running the farm in some way.

- Unemployment compensation.

- Jury duty payments.

- Pay for a period when you were sick which you receive more than six months after you stopped working.

- Room and board your employer gives you on his premises for his benefit. For this not to count as income, your employer must require you to live there.

WORKSHEET

Use the worksheet to figure your earnings. In general, you need to report your total earnings from work that you did in 1993. If you had more than one employer, show your earnings from each in the columns below. You may call, write, or visit any Social Security office if you have any questions or problems completing this worksheet. **Do not send this worksheet to Social Security.** You should keep this worksheet for your records, in case there is a question about the amount of your reported earnings. If your estimate for 1994 changes during the year call 1-800-772-1213 to report any changes.

1. **WAGES** — Enter, in the block to the right, your "Social Security Wages" from your 1993 Form W-2(s). If that box is blank, or if it shows the Social Security maximum ($57,600.00), use the amount shown in the, "Wages, tips, other compensation" box instead. State and local employees should include employer "pick-up" plan contributions if made under a salary reduction agreement. If the total wages that you show are less than on your W-2 form(s) please contact us before you file your report. If you were age 70 in 1993, see the instructions on page 1.

2. **TIPS**— *If your entry above was from the "Social Security Wages" box on your W-2,* in the space to the right, enter the amount shown in the "Social Security Tips" box of your W-2. Also show any tips not reported by your employer on your W-2, which you will report on your income tax return.

3. **TAX-DEFERRED SAVINGS CONTRIBUTIONS** — *If your entry in 1, above was from the Wages, tips, other compensation" box on your W-2,* and you made contributions from your salary to a tax-deferred savings plan, show the amount of your contribution in the space to the right.

4. **TOTAL WAGES EARNED IN 1993** — Add the amount in boxes 1, 2, and 3 above. Enter the total in the space to the right and on question 1 of the enclosed annual report form.

5. **SELF-EMPLOYMENT INCOME** — If you operated a trade or business and had net earnings from self-employment show the amount from line 4 of your 1040SE in the space to the right. (Ministers or church employees show the amount on line 6.) Enter this amount in question 2, on the enclosed annual report form. If you had a net loss or net earnings of less than $400 show the amount from schedule C or F. If you were age 70 in 1993, see the instructions on page 1.

"SPECIAL PAYMENTS"

If the earnings on your 1993 W-2 included amounts that you earned in previous years (see "Reporting Your Wages" p. 2), you need to contact your local Social Security office. These amounts will not count in 1993 under the earnings test. Report these payments to your local Social Security office. For your records, show the amount reported in the space to the right.

Note: These payments *may* be shown in the "Nonqualified Plan" box on your W-2.

DO NOT RETURN THIS WORKSHEET TO SOCIAL SECURITY. USE THIS TO HELP YOU COMPLETE YOUR ANNUAL REPORT FORM. KEEP THIS WORKSHEET FOR YOUR RECORDS.

| **Foreign Earnings** | Contact us for special instructions if you had 1993 earnings from work outside the United States and these earnings | were not covered under the U.S. Social Security program (the foreign earnings were not subject to FICA or SECA taxes). |

The Privacy And Paperwork Acts

Social Security is authorized to collect the information on this form by sections 203(h) and 205(a) of the Social Security Act. You are required to file a 1993 annual report if:

● Your earnings from employment and/or self-employment were more than $10,560 (if you were 65 or older) or more than $7,680 (if you were under 65) in 1993;

AND

● You received some Social Security benefits in 1993.

The information you furnish on this form will be used primarily for the purpose of insuring proper payment to you. However, there is a possibility that for the administration of the Social Security program or for the administration of programs requiring coordination with SSA, information may be disclosed to another person or to another government agency. We may also use the information you give us when we match records by computer. Matching programs compare our records with those of other Federal, State, or local government agencies. Many agencies may use matching programs to find or prove that a person qualifies for benefits paid by the Federal government. The law allows us to do this even if you do not agree to it.

Explanations about these and other reasons why information you provide us may be used or given out are available in Social Security offices. If you want to learn more about this, contact any Social Security office.

TIME IT TAKES TO COMPLETE THIS FORM

We estimate that it will take you about 8 minutes to complete this form. This includes the time it will take to read the instructions, gather the necessary facts and fill out the form. If you have comments or suggestions on this estimate, or on any other aspect of this form, write to the Social Security Administration, ATTN: Reports Clearance Officer, 1-A-21 Operations Bldg., Baltimore, MD 21235-0001, and to the Office of Management and Budget, Paperwork Reduction Project (0960-0057), Washington, DC 20503. **Send only comments relating to our estimate or other aspects of this form to the offices listed above. All requests for Social Security cards and other claims-related information should be sent to your local Social Security office, whose address is listed in your telephone directory under the Department of Health and Human Services.**

1993 ANNUAL REPORT OF EARNINGS

TOE 310

Form Approved
OMB No. 0960-0057

Name and Address   **Claim Number-Letter**

Please answer the following questions about your work in 1993 and 1994. Usually, you must report all the money you earn in a year, but there are some exceptions.
Please read the attached sheet before you complete this form to make sure that you report the right amount of earnings, especially if you retired or turned 70 in 1993.

How Much Did You Earn In Wages In 1993?

1 Use the worksheet included in the instructions to determine your total wages for 1993. Show the total from box 4 of the worksheet in the space to the right. If you did not work for wages in 1993, show "0".
If the total wages that you show are less than on your W-2 form(s), please contact us before you file your report. See page 3 "Special Payment".

$_____

How Much Did You Earn In Self-Employment In 1993?

2 In the spaces to the right, write the total net earnings or net loss from self-employment which you will report on your 1993 Federal income tax return (see Worksheet page 3). Do not show wages here. If you were not self-employed, show "0" in the Net Self-Employment Earnings block.
If the total self-employment income that you show is less than you report on your SE tax return, please contact us before you file your report.

$_____
Net Self-Employment Earnings
OR

$_____
Net Loss

Please continue on reverse side ➤

Form **SSA-7770-BK** (12-93)

How Much Do Your Think You Will Earn In 1994?

3 Please estimate how much you plan to earn in 1994 from wages, self-employment or both. Write your answer in the space to the right. If you do not plan to work in 1994, show "0." If your estimate changes during the year, notify us of the change. **If you leave this question blank, we will use your 1993 earnings to decide how much we will pay you in 1994.**

$ _____

Please sign this form in the space below, and mail it to your local Social Security office. If you wish, you may file your annual report by telephone.
Your report must be received by April 15, 1994. If not received by April 15th you may be charged a penalty.

Any person who makes a false statement in connection with this report may be fined, imprisoned or both.

Your Signature ▶	Date
	Daytime Telephone Number
	_____/_____ Area Code

Be sure to include your name, address, and Social Security Claim number at the top, reverse side of this form.

Form Approved
OMB No. 0960-0141

DISABILITY REPORT

PLEASE PRINT, TYPE, OR WRITE CLEARLY AND ANSWER ALL ITEMS TO THE BEST OF YOUR ABILITY. If you are filing on behalf of someone else, enter his or her name and social security number in the space provided and answer all questions. COMPLETE ANSWERS WILL AID IN PROCESSING THE CLAIM.

PRIVACY ACT/PAPERWORK REDUCTION ACT NOTICE: The Social Security Administration is authorized to collect the information on this form under sections 205(a), 223(d) and 1633(a) of the Social Security Act. The information on this form is needed by Social Security to make a decision on your claim. While giving us the information on this form is voluntary, failure to provide all or part of the requested information could prevent an accurate or timely decision on your claim and could result in the loss of benefits. Although the information you furnish on this form is almost never used for any purpose other than making a determination on your disability claim, such information may be disclosed by the Social Security Administration as follows: (1) To enable a third party or agency to assist Social Security in establishing rights to Social Security benefits and/or coverage; (2) to comply with Federal laws requiring the release of information from Social Security records (e.g., to the General Accounting Office and the Veterans Administration); and (3) to facilitate statistical research and audit activities necessary to assure the integrity and improvement of the Social Security programs (e.g., to the Bureau of the Census and private concerns under contract to Social Security). These and other reasons why information about you may be used or given out are explained in the Federal Register. If you would like more information about this, any Social Security office can assist you.

A. NAME OF CLAIMANT	B. SOCIAL SECURITY NUMBER	C. TELEPHONE NUMBER where you can be reached (include area code)
	—— —— —— / —— —— / —— —— —— ——	

D. WHAT IS YOUR DISABLING CONDITION? *(Briefly explain the injury or illness that stops you from working.)*

PART I — INFORMATION ABOUT YOUR CONDITION

	MONTH	DAY	YEAR
1. When did your condition first bother you:			

2A. Did you work after the date shown in item 1? *(If "no" go on to items 3A and 3B.)*	☐ YES	☐ NO

2B. If you did work since the date in item 1, did your condition cause you to change —

Your job or job duties?	☐ YES	☐ NO
Your hours of work?	☐ YES	☐ NO
Your attendance?	☐ YES	☐ NO
Anything else about your work?	☐ YES	☐ NO

(If you answered "no" to **all** of these, go to items 3A and 3B.)

2C. If you answered "yes" to **any** item in 2B, explain below what the changes in your work circumstances were, the dates they occurred, and how your condition made these changes necessary.

	MONTH	DAY	YEAR
3A. When did your condition finally make you stop working?			

3B. Explain how your condition now keeps you from working.

Form **SSA-3368-BK** (1-89)

PART II — INFORMATION ABOUT YOUR MEDICAL RECORDS

4. List the name, address and telephone number of the doctor who has the latest medical records about your disabling condition.		If you have **no** doctor check	☐

NAME	ADDRESS

TELEPHONE NUMBER (include area code)

HOW OFTEN DO YOU SEE THIS DOCTOR?	DATE YOU **FIRST** SAW THIS DOCTOR	DATE YOU **LAST** SAW THIS DOCTOR

REASONS FOR VISITS *(show illness or injury for which you had an examination or treatment)*

TYPE OF TREATMENT OR MEDICINES RECEIVED (such as surgery, chemotherapy, radiation, and the medicines you take for your illness or injury, if known. If no treatment or medicines, show "NONE".)

5A. Have you seen any other doctors since your disabling condition began? If "yes", show the following:	☐ YES ☐ NO

NAME	ADDRESS

TELEPHONE NUMBER (include area code)

HOW OFTEN DO YOU SEE THIS DOCTOR?	DATE YOU **FIRST** SAW THIS DOCTOR	DATE YOU **LAST** SAW THIS DOCTOR

REASONS FOR VISITS *(show illness or injury for which you had an examination or treatment)*

TYPE OF TREATMENT OR MEDICINES RECEIVED (such as surgery, chemotherapy, radiation, and the medicines you take for your illness or injury, if known. If no treatment or medicines, show "NONE".)

5B. Identify below any other doctor you have seen since your illness or injury began.

NAME	ADDRESS

TELEPHONE NUMBER (include area code)

HOW OFTEN DO YOU SEE THIS DOCTOR?	DATE YOU **FIRST** SAW THIS DOCTOR	DATE YOU **LAST** SAW THIS DOCTOR

REASONS FOR VISITS *(show illness or injury for which you had an examination or treatment.)*

TYPE OF TREATMENT OR MEDICINES RECEIVED (such as surgery, chemotherapy, radiation, and the medicines you take for your illness or injury, if known. If no treatment or medicines, show "NONE".)

Form SSA-3368-BK (1-89)

6A. Have you been hospitalized or treated at a clinic for your disabling condition?
  If "yes", show the following: ☐ YES   ☐ NO

NAME OF HOSPITAL OR CLINIC	ADDRESS
PATIENT OR CLINIC NUMBER	

WERE YOU AN INPATIENT? (stayed at least overnight?) ☐ YES ☐ NO *(If "yes", show:)*		WERE YOU AN OUTPATIENT? ☐ YES ☐ NO *(If "yes", show:)*
DATES OF ADMISSIONS	DATES OF DISCHARGES	DATES OF VISITS

REASON FOR HOSPITALIZATION OR CLINIC VISITS *(show illness or injury for which you had an examination or treatment.)*

TYPE OF TREATMENT OR MEDICINES RECEIVED (such as surgery, chemotherapy, radiation, and the medicines you take for your illness or injury, if known. If no treatment or medicines, show "NONE".)

6B. If you have been in other hospital or clinic for your illness or injury, identify it below.

NAME OF HOSPITAL OR CLINIC	ADDRESS
PATIENT OR CLINIC NUMBER	

WERE YOU AN INPATIENT? (stayed at least overnight?) ☐ YES ☐ NO *(If "yes", show:)*		WERE YOU AN OUTPATIENT? ☐ YES ☐ NO *(If "yes", show:)*
DATES OF ADMISSIONS	DATES OF DISCHARGES	DATES OF VISITS

REASON FOR HOSPITALIZATION OR CLINIC VISITS *(show illness or injury for which you had an examination or treatment.)*

TYPE OF TREATMENT OR MEDICINES RECEIVED (such as surgery, chemotherapy, radiation, and the medicines you take for your illness or injury, if known. If no treatment or medicines, show "NONE".)

If you have been in other hospitals or clinics for your illness or injury, list the names, addresses, patient or clinic numbers, dates and reasons for hospitalization or clinic visits in Part VI.

7. Have you been seen by other agencies for your disabling condition?
  (VA, Workmen's Compensation, Vocational Rehabilitation, Welfare, etc.)   ☐ YES   ☐ NO
  (If "yes," show the following:)

NAME OF AGENCY	ADDRESS
YOUR CLAIM NUMBER	

DATE OF VISITS

TYPE OF TREATMENT, EXAMINATION OR MEDICINES RECEIVED (such as surgery, chemotherapy, radiation, and the medicines you take for your illness or injury, if known. If no treatment or medicines, show "NONE".)

If more space is needed, list the other agencies, their addresses, your claim numbers, dates, and treatment received in Part VI.

Form SSA-3368-BK (1-89)

140

8. Have you had any of the following tests in the last year?

TEST	CHECK APPROPRIATE BLOCK OR BLOCKS	IF "YES" SHOW	
		WHERE DONE	WHEN DONE
Electrocardiogram	☐ YES ☐ NO		
Chest X-Ray	☐ YES ☐ NO		
Other X-Ray (name body part here) _____	☐ YES ☐ NO		
Breathing Tests	☐ YES ☐ NO		
Blood Tests	☐ YES ☐ NO		
Other (Specify)	☐ YES ☐ NO		

9. If you have a medicaid card, what is your number (some hospitals and clinics file your records by your medicaid number.)

PART III — INFORMATION ABOUT YOUR ACTIVITIES

10. Has your doctor told you to cut back or limit your activities in any way?   ☐ YES   ☐ NO
If "yes", give the name of the doctor below and tell what he or she told you about cutting back or limiting your activities.

11. Describe your daily activities in the following areas and state what and how much you do of each and how often you do it:
 ● **Household maintenance** (including cooking, cleaning, shopping, and odd jobs around the house as well as any other similar activities):

 ● **Recreational activities and hobbies** (hunting, fishing, bowling, hiking, musical instruments, etc.):

 ● **Social contacts** (visits with friends, relatives, neighbors):

 ● **Other** (drive car, motorcycle, ride bus, etc.)

Form SSA-3368-BK (1-89)

PART IV — INFORMATION ABOUT YOUR EDUCATION

12. What is the highest grade of school that you completed and when?

13. Have you gone to trade or vocational school or had any type of special training? *If "yes", show:* ☐ YES ☐ NO

- ● The type of trade or vocational school or training:

- ● Approximate dates you attended:

- ● How this schooling or training was used in any work you did:

PART V — INFORMATION ABOUT THE WORK YOU DID

14. List all jobs you have had in the last 15 years before you stopped working, beginning with your usual job. Normally, this will be the kind of work you did the longest. (If you have a 6th grade education or less, AND did only heavy unskilled labor for 35 years or more, list all of the jobs you have had since you began to work. If you need more space, use Part VI.)

JOB TITLE (Be sure to begin with your usual job)	TYPE OF BUSINESS	DATES WORKED (Month and Year)		DAYS PER WEEK	RATE OF PAY (Per hour, day, week, month or year)
		FROM	TO		

15A. Provide the following information for your usual job shown in item 14, line 1.

In your job did you:
- ● Use machines, tools, or equipment of any kind? ☐ Yes ☐ No
- ● Use technical knowledge or skills? ☐ Yes ☐ No
- ● Do any writing, complete reports, or perform similar duties? ☐ Yes ☐ No
- ● Have supervisory responsibilities? ☐ Yes ☐ No

15B. Describe your basic duties (explain what you did and how you did it) below. Also, explain all "Yes" answers by giving a FULL DESCRIPTION of: the types of machines, tools, or equipment you used and the exact operation you performed; the technical knowledge or skills involved; the type of writing you did, and the nature of any reports; and the number of people you supervised and the extent of your supervision:

15C. Describe the kind and amount of physical activity this job involved during typical day in terms of:

- **Walking** (circle the number of hours a day spent walking) — 0 1 2 3 4 5 6 7 8

- **Standing** (circle the number of hours a day spent standing) — 0 1 2 3 4 5 6 7 8

- **Sitting** (circle the number of hours a day spent sitting) — 0 1 2 3 4 5 6 7 8

- **Bending** (circle how often a day you had to bend) — Never · Occasionally · Frequently · Constantly

- **Reaching** (circle how often a day you had to reach) — Never · Occasionally · Frequently · Constantly

- **Lifting and Carrying:** Describe below what was lifted, and how far it was carried. Check heaviest weight lifted, and weight frequently lifted and/or carried:

HEAVIEST WEIGHT LIFTED	WEIGHT FREQUENTLY LIFTED/CARRIED
☐ 10 lbs. ☐ 20 lbs. ☐ 50 lbs. ☐ 100 lbs. ☐ Over 100 lbs.	☐ Up to 10 lbs. ☐ Up to 25 lbs. ☐ Up to 50 lbs. ☐ Over 50 lbs.

PART VI — REMARKS

Use this section for additional space to answer any previous questions. Also use this space to give any additional information that you think will be helpful in making a decision in your disability claim, (such as information about other illnesses or injuries not shown in Parts I and II.) Please refer to the previous items by number.

Knowing that anyone making a false statement or representation of a material fact for use in determining a right to payment under the Social Security Act commits a crime punishable under Federal law, I certify that the above statements are true.

NAME (Signature of claimant or person filing on the claimant's behalf)

SIGN HERE ▶   DATE

Witnesses are required ONLY if this statement has been signed by mark (X) above. If signed by mark (X), two witnesses to the signing who know the person making the statement must sign below, giving their full addresses.

1. Signature of Witness	2. Signature of Witness
Address (Number and street, city, state, and ZIP code)	Address (Number and street, city, state, and ZIP code)

Form **SSA-3368-BK** (1-89)

NAME OF CLAIMANT	SOCIAL SECURITY NUMBER
	__ __ __ / __ __ / __ __ __ __

16. Check any of the following categories which apply to this case:

   PRESUMPTIVE DISABILITY CONSIDERATION
   (If any of these boxes are checked, DO's (and DDS's) should be alert to the possibility of a presumptive disability determination in SSI claims per DI 11055.240 and 23535.005.

   A. ☐ Amputation of two limbs

   B. ☐ Amputation of a leg at the hip

   C. ☐ Allegation of total deafness

   D. ☐ Allegation of total blindness

   E. ☐ Allegation of bed confinement or immobility without a wheelchair, walker, or crutches. allegedly due to a longstanding condition — exclude recent accident and recent surgery.

   F. ☐ Allegation of a stroke (cerebral vascular accident) more than 3 months in the past and continued marked difficulty in walking or using a hand or arm.

   G. ☐ Allegation of cerebral palsy, muscular dystrophy or muscular atrophy and marked difficulty in walking (e.g., use of braces), speaking or coordination of the hands or arms.

   H. ☐ Allegation of diabetes with amputation of a foot.

   I. ☐ Allegation of Down's Syndrome (Mongolism).

   J. ☐ An applicant filing on behalf of another individual alleges severe mental deficiency for claimant who is at least 7 years of age. The applicant alleges that the individual attends (or attended) a special school, or special classes in school, because of his mental deficiency, or is unable to attend any type of school (or if beyond school age was unable to attend), and requires care and supervision of routine daily activities.

   L. ☐ Allegation of Acquired Immune Deficiency Syndrome (AIDS)

17A. Does the claimant speak English? .... ☐ Yes ☐ No
   If "no," what language does he speak?

17B. Does the claimant need assistance in prosecuting his or her claim? .... ☐ Yes ☐ No
   If "yes," show name, address, relationship, and telephone number of an interested party willing to assist the claimant.

NAME	ADDRESS	RELATIONSHIP	TELEPHONE NUMBER (area code)

17C. Can the claimant (or his representative) be readily reached by telephone with no communication problems due to language, speech or hearing difficulties? If "no". DO should complete SSA-3369-F6.   ☐ Yes ☐ No

Form SSA-3368-BK (1-89)

18A. Check each item to indicate if any difficulty was observed:

Reading	☐ Yes	☐ No	Using Hands	☐ Yes	☐ No
Writing	☐ Yes	☐ No	Breathing	☐ Yes	☐ No
Answering	☐ Yes	☐ No	Seeing	☐ Yes	☐ No
Hearing	☐ Yes	☐ No	Walking	☐ Yes	☐ No
Sitting	☐ Yes	☐ No			
Understanding	☐ Yes	☐ No	Other (Specify): _____		

18B. If any of the above items were checked "yes," describe the exact difficulty involved:

18C. Describe the claimant fully (e.g., general build, height, weight, behavior, any difficulties that add to or supplement those noted above, etc.):

19. Medical Development — Initiated by District or Branch Office

SOURCE	DATE REQUESTED	DATE(S) OF FOLLOW-UP	CAPABILITY DEVELOPMENT REQUESTED

20. DO or BO curtailed completion of Parts III - V per DI 11005.035 (DI 20501.005)	☐ YES	☐ NO
21. Is capability development by the DDS necessary? If "yes", show "DDS capability development needed" in item 11 of the SSA-831-U5	☐ YES	☐ NO
22. Is development of work activity necessary?	☐ YES	☐ NO
If "yes", is an SSA-820-F4 or SSA-821-F4..	☐ Pending ☐ In File	

23. SSA-3368-BK taken by: ☐ Personal Interview ☐ Telephone ☐ Mail	24. Form supplemented: ☐ Yes ☐ No If "yes" by: ☐ Personal Interview ☐ Telephone ☐ Mail

SIGNATURE OF DO OR BO INTERVIEWER OR REVIEWER	TITLE	DATE

Form **SSA-3368-BK** (1-89)

NUMBER HOLDER

SOCIAL SECURITY NUMBER

EMPLOYEE/CLAIMANT/BENEFICIARY *(If other than Number Holder)*

AUTHORIZATION FOR SOURCE TO RELEASE
INFORMATION TO THE SOCIAL SECURITY ADMINISTRATION (SSA)

INFORMATION ABOUT SOURCE— PLEASE PRINT, TYPE, OR WRITE CLEARLY

NAME AND ADDRESS OF SOURCE *(Include Zip Code)*	RELATIONSHIP TO CLAIMANT/BENEFICIARY

INFORMATION ABOUT CLAIMANT/BENEFICIARY

NAME AND ADDRESS *(If known)* AT TIME CLAIMANT/BENEFICIARY HAD CONTACT WITH SOURCE *(Include Zip Code)*	DATE OF BIRTH	CLAIMANT/BENEFICIARY I.D. NUMBER *(If known and different than SSN)* *(Clinic/Patient No.)*

APPROXIMATE DATES OF CLAIMANT/BENEFICIARY CONTACT WITH SOURCE (e.g., dates of hospital admission, treatment, discharge, etc.)

TO BE COMPLETED BY CLAIMANT/BENEFICIARY OR PERSON AUTHORIZED TO ACT IN HIS/HER BEHALF

GENERAL AND SPECIAL AUTHORIZATION TO RELEASE MEDICAL AND OTHER INFORMATION IN ACCORDANCE WITH THE PROVISIONS OF THE SOCIAL SECURITY LAWS, THE PUBLIC HEALTH SERVICE ACT, SECTIONS 523 AND 527, AND TITLE 38 U.S.C. VETERANS BENEFITS, SECTION 4132.

I hereby authorize the above-named source to release or disclose to the Social Security Administration or State agency the following information for the period(s) identified above:

1) All medical records or other information regarding my treatment, hospitalization, and/or outpatient care for my condition, including psychological or psychiatric impairment, drug abuse and/or alcoholism, or sickle cell anemia, or Acquired Immunodeficiency Syndrome (AIDS), or tests for or infection with Human Immunodeficiency Virus (HIV);

2) Information about how my impairment affects my ability to complete tasks and activities of daily living;

3) Information about how my condition affected my ability to work.

I understand that this authorization, except for action already taken, may be voided by me at anytime. If I do not void this authorization, it will automatically end when a final decision is made on my claim. If I am already receiving benefits, the authorization will end when a final decision is made as to whether I can continue to receive benefits.

READ IMPORTANT INFORMATION ON REVERSE BEFORE SIGNING FORM BELOW.

SIGNATURE OF CLAIMANT/BENEFICIARY OR PERSON AUTHORIZED TO ACT IN HIS/HER BEHALF	RELATIONSHIP TO CLAIMANT/ BENEFICIARY	DATE
STREET ADDRESS		TELEPHONE NUMBER (Area Code)
CITY	STATE	ZIP CODE

The signature and address of a person who either knows the person signing this form or is satisfied as to that person's identity is requested below. This is not required by the Social Security Administration, but without it the source might not honor this authorization.

SIGNATURE OF WITNESS	STREET ADDRESS	
CITY	STATE	ZIP CODE

☐ TEL

Form Approved
OMB No. 0960-0060

TOE 120/145

(Do not write in this space)

APPLICATION FOR DISABILITY INSURANCE BENEFITS

I apply for a period of disability and/or all insurance benefits for which I am eligible under title II and part A of title XVIII of the Social Security Act, as presently amended.

PART I—INFORMATION ABOUT THE DISABLED WORKER

1. (a) PRINT your name ⟶ | FIRST NAME, MIDDLE INITIAL, LAST NAME

(b) Enter your name at birth if different from item (a) ⟶

(c) Check (√) whether you are ⟶ ☐ Male   ☐ Female

2. Enter your Social Security Number ⟶ _ _ _ / _ _ / _ _ _ _

3. (a) Enter your date of birth ⟶ MONTH, DAY, YEAR

(b) Enter name of State or foreign country where your were born. ⟶

If you have already presented, or if you are now presenting, a public or religious record of your birth established before you were age 5, go on to item 4.

(c) Was a public record of your birth made before you were age 5? ☐ Yes ☐ No ☐ Unknown

(d) Was a religious record of your birth made before you were age 5? ☐ Yes ☐ No ☐ Unknown

4. (a) What is your disabling condition? (Briefly describe the injury or illness that prevents, or has prevented, you from working.)

(b) Is your injury or illness related to your work in any way? ⟶ ☐ Yes ☐ No

5. (a) When did you become unable to work because of your disabling condition? ⟶ MONTH, DAY, YEAR

(b) Are you still disabled? (If "Yes," go on to item 6.) (If "No," answer (c).) ⟶ ☐ Yes ☐ No

(c) If you are no longer disabled, enter the date your disability ended. ⟶ MONTH, DAY, YEAR

6. (a) Have you (or has someone on your behalf)ever filed an application for Social Security benefits, a period of disability under Social Security, supplemental security income, or hospital or medical insurance under Medicare? ⟶ ☐ Yes (If "Yes," answer (b) and (c).) ☐ No ☐ Unknown (If "No," or "Unknown" go on to item 7.)

(b) Enter name of person on whose Social Security record you filed other application. ⟶

(c) Enter Social Security Number of person named in (b). If unknown, check this block. ☐ ⟶ _ _ _ / _ _ / _ _ _ _

7. (a) Were you in the active military or naval service (including Reserve or National Guard active duty or active duty for training) after September 7, 1939 and before 1968? ⟶ ☐ Yes (If "Yes," answer (b) and (c).) ☐ No (If "No," go on to item 8.)

(b) Enter dates of service ⟶ FROM: (month, year) | TO: (month, year)

(c) Have you ever been (or will you be) eligible for a monthly benefit from a military or civilian Federal agency? (include Veterans Administration benefits only if you waived military retirement pay) ⟶ ☐ Yes ☐ No

Form SSA-16-F6 (7-89)   Destroy Prior Editions

8.	(a) Have you filed (or do your intend to file) for any other public disability benefits? (Include workers' compensation and Black Lung benefits) ⟶	☐ Yes (If "Yes," answer (b).)	☐ No (If "No," go on to item 9.)

(b) The other public disability benefit(s) you have filed (or intend to file) for is (Check as many as apply):

    ☐ Veterans Administration Benefits   ☐ Welfare

    ☐ Supplemental Security Income   ☐ Other (If "Other," complete a Workers' Compensation/Public Disability Benefit Questionnaire)

9.	(a) Have you ever engaged in work that was covered under the social security system of a country other than the United States? (If "Yes," answer (b).) (If "No," go on to item 10.) ⟶	☐ Yes	☐ No

(b) List the country(ies): ⟶

10.	(a) Are you entitled to, or do you expect to become entitled to, a pension or annuity based on your work after 1956 not covered by Social Security?	☐ Yes (If "Yes," answer (b) and (c).)	☐ No (If "No," go on to item 11.)

		MONTH	YEAR
(b) ☐ I became entitled, or expect to become entitled, beginning			
(c) ☐ I became eligible, or expect to become eligible, beginning			

I agree to notify the Social Security Administration if I become entitled to a pension or annuity based on my employment after 1956 not covered by Social Security, or if such pension of annuity stops.

11.	(a) Did you have wages or self-employment income covered under Social Security in all years from 1978 through last year?	☐ Yes ☐ No (If "Yes," skip to item 12.) (If "No," answer (b).)

(b) List the years from 1978 through last year in which you did not have wages or self-employment income covered under Social Security.

12. Enter below the names and addresses of all the persons, companies, or Government agencies for whom you have worked this year and last year. IF NONE, WRITE "NONE" BELOW AND GO ON TO ITEM 14.

NAME AND ADDRESS OF EMPLOYER (If you had more than one employer, please list them in order beginning with your last (most recent) employer)	Work Began		Work Ended (If still working show "Not ended")	
	MONTH	YEAR	MONTH	YEAR

(If you need more space, use "Remarks" space on page 4.)

13.	May the Social Security Administration or the State agency reviewing your case ask your employers for information needed to process your claim? ⟶	☐ Yes ☐ No

14. THIS ITEM MUST BE COMPLETED, EVEN IF YOU WERE AN EMPLOYEE.

(a) Were you self-employed this year and last year? (If "Yes," answer (b).) (If "No," go on to item 15.) ⟶	☐ Yes ☐ No

(b) Check the year or years in which you were self-employed	In what kind of trade or business were you self-employed? (For example, storekeeper, farmer, physician)	Were your net earnings from your trade or business $400 or more? (Check "Yes" or "No")	
☐ This Year			
☐ Last Year		☐ Yes	☐ No
☐ Year before last		☐ Yes	☐ No

15.	(a) How much were your total earnings last year? (Count both wages and self-employment income. If none, write "None.") ⟶	Amount $ _____
	(b) How much have you earned so far this year? (If none, write "None.") ⟶	Amount $ _____

Form SSA-16-F6 (7-89)

(c) Did you receive any money from an employer(s) on or after the date in item 5(a) when you became unable to work because of your disability? (If "Yes," give amounts and explain in "Remarks" on page 4.) ⟶	☐ Yes ☐ No Amount $ _____
(d) Do you expect to receive any additional money from an employer such as sick pay, vacation pay, other special pay? (If "Yes," please give amounts and explain in "Remarks" on page 4.) ⟶	☐ Yes ☐ No Amount $ _____

PART II—INFORMATION ABOUT THE DISABLED WORKER AND SPOUSE

16.	Have you ever been married? ⟶ (If "Yes," answer item 17.) (If "No," go on to item 18.)	☐ Yes ☐ No

17. (a) Give the following information about your current marriage. If not currently married, show your last marriage below.

To whom married		When (Month, day, year)	Where (Name of City and State)
Your current or last marriage	How marriage ended (If still in effect, write "Not ended.")	When (Month, day, year)	Where (Name of City and State)
	Marriage performed by ☐ Clergyman or public official ☐ Other (Explain in Remarks)	Spouse's date of birth (or age)	If spouse deceased, give date of death
	Spouse's Social Security Number (If none or unknown, so indicate) __ __ __ / __ __ / __ __ __ __		

(b) Give the following information about each of your previous marriages. **(If none, write "NONE.")**

To whom married		When (Month, day, year)	Where (Name of City and State)
Your previous marriage	How marriage ended	When (Month, day, year)	Where (Name of City and State)
	Marriage performed by ☐ Clergyman or public official ☐ Other (Explain in Remarks)	Spouse's date of birth (or age)	If spouse deceased, give date of death
	Spouse's Social Security Number (If none or unknown, so indicate) __ __ __ / __ __ / __ __ __ __		

(Use a separate statement for information about any other marriages.)

18.	Have you or your spouse worked in the railroad industry for 7 years or more? ⟶	☐ Yes ☐ No

PART III—INFORMATION ABOUT THE DEPENDENTS OF THE DISABLED WORKER

19. If your claim for disability benefits is approved, your children (including natural children, adopted children, and stepchildren) or dependent grandchildren (including stepgrandchildren) may be eligible for benefits based on your earnings record.

List below: FULL NAME OF ALL such children who are now or were in the past 12 months UNMARRIED and:
- UNDER AGE 18
- AGE 18 TO 19 AND ATTENDING SECONDARY SCHOOL
- DISABLED OR HANDICAPPED (age 18 or over and disability began before age 22)

(IF THERE ARE NO SUCH CHILDREN, WRITE "NONE" BELOW AND GO ON TO ITEM 20.)

20.	Do you have a dependent parent who was receiving at least one-half support from you when you became unable to work because of your disability? (If "Yes," enter name and address in "Remarks" on page 4.)	☐ Yes ☐ No

Form SSA-16-F6 (7-89)

IMPORTANT INFORMATION ABOUT DISABILITY INSURANCE BENEFITS —
PLEASE READ CAREFULLY

I. SUBMITTING MEDICAL EVIDENCE: I understand that as a claimant for disability benefits, I am responsible for providing medical evidence showing the nature and extent of my disability. I may be asked either to submit the evidence myself or to assist the Social Security Administration in obtaining the evidence. If such evidence is not sufficient to arrive at a determination, I may be requested by the State Disability Determination Service to have an independent examination at the expense of the Social Security Administration.

II. RELEASE OF INFORMATION: I authorize any physician, hospital, agency or other organization to disclose to the Social Security Administration, or to the State Agency that may review my claim or continuing disability, any medical record or other information about my disability.

I also authorize the Social Security Administration to release medical information from my records, only as necessary to process my claim, as follows:

- Copies of medical information may be provided to a physician or medical institution prior to my appearance for an independent medical examination if an examination is necessary.
- Results of any such independent examination may be provided to my personal physician.
- Information may be furnished to any contractor for transcription, typing, record copying, or other related clerical or administrative service performed for the State Disability Determination Service.
- The State Vocational Rehabilitation Agency may review any evidence necessary for determining my eligibility for rehabilitative services.

THIS MUST BE ANSWERED ▶ 21. DO YOU UNDERSTAND AND AGREE WITH THE AUTHORIZATIONS GIVEN ABOVE?

☐ Yes ☐ No (If "No," explain why in "Remarks.")

22. Check if applicable:

( ) I am not submitting evidence of the deceased's earnings that are not yet on his/her earnings record. I understand that these earnings will be included automatically within 24 months, and any increase in my benefits will be paid with full retroactivity.

REMARKS (You may use this space for any explanation. If you need more space, attach a separate sheet.)

_____

_____

_____

III. REPORTING RESPONSIBILITIES: I agree to promptly notify Social Security if:
- My MEDICAL CONDITION IMPROVES so that I would be able to work, even though I have not yet returned to work.
- I GO TO WORK whether as an employee or a self-employed person.
- I apply for or begin to receive a workers' compensation (including black lung benefits) or another public disability benefit, or the amount that I am receiving changes or stops, or I receive a lump-sum settlement.
- I am imprisoned for conviction of a felony.

The above events may affect my eligibility to disability benefits as provided in the Social Security Act, as amended.

I know that anyone who makes or causes to be made a false statement or representation of material fact in an application or for use in determining a right to payment under the Social Security Act commits a crime punishable under Federal law by fine, imprisonment or both. I affirm that all information I have given in this document is true.

SIGNATURE OF APPLICANT	Date (Month, day, year)
Signature (First name, middle initial, last name) (Write in ink)	
SIGN HERE ▶	Telephone Number(s) at which you may be contacted during the day. (Include the area code)

FOR OFFICIAL USE ONLY	Direct Deposit Payment Address (Financial Institution)			
	Routing Transit Number	C/S	Depositor Account Number	☐ No Account
				☐ Direct Deposit Refused

Applicant's Mailing Address (Number and street, Apt. No., P.O. Box, or Rural Route) (Enter Residence Address in "Remarks," if different.)

City and State	ZIP Code	County (if any) in which you now live

Witnesses are required ONLY if this application has been signed by mark (X) above. If signed by mark (X), two witnesses to the signing who know the applicant must sign below, giving their full addresses. Also, print the applicant's name in Signature block.

1. Signature of Witness	2. Signature of Witness
Address (Number and street, City, State and ZIP Code)	Address (Number and street, City, State and ZIP Code)

Form SSA-16-F6 (7-89)

☐ TEL

APPLICATION FOR SUPPLEMENTAL SECURITY INCOME

Do not write in this space

I am/We are applying for Supplemental Security Income and any federally administered State supplementation under title XVI of the Social Security Act, for benefits under the other programs administered by the Social Security Administration, and where applicable, for medical assistance under title XIX of the Social Security Act.

☐ FS-SSA/APP ☐ FS-REFERRED

Filing Date

Month, Day, Year

- -

☐ Actual   or   ☐ Protective

| TYPE OF CLAIM | ☐ Individual with Ineligible Spouse | ☐ Couple | ☐ Individual | ☐ Child | ☐ Child with Parent(s) |

PART I—BASIC ELIGIBILITY—The questions in this section pertain to the period beginning with the first moment of the filing date month through the date this application is signed unless a question specifies a different time period.

1. (a) First Name, Middle Initial, Last Name | Birth *(month, day year)* | Sex ☐ Male ☐ Female | Social Security Number _ _ _ / _ _ / _ _ _ _

   (b) Did you ever use any other names *(including maiden name)* or other Social Security numbers? ➤ ☐ YES Go to (c)   ☐ NO Go to #2

   (c) Other Names and Social Security Numbers Used

2. (a) Are you married? ➤ ☐ YES Go to (b)   ☐ NO Go to #4

   (b) Spouse's Name *(First, middle initial, last)* | Birth *(month, day, year)* | Social Security Number _ _ _ / _ _ / _ _ _ _

   (c) Did your spouse ever use any other names *(including maiden name)* or other Social Security Numbers? ➤ ☐ YES Go to (d)   ☐ NO Go to (e)

   (d) Other Names *(including maiden name)* and Social Security Numbers Used by Spouse

   (e) Are you and your spouse living together? ➤ ☐ YES If your spouse is not filing go to #3; otherwise go to #4.   ☐ NO Go to (f)

   (f) Date you began living apart | Address of spouse or name and address of someone who knows where the spouse is.

   (g) IF YOUR SPOUSE IS NOT FILING FOR SUPPLEMENTAL SECURITY INCOME AND YOU SEPARATED SINCE THE FIRST MOMENT OF THE FILING DATE MONTH GO TO #3. IF YOUR SPOUSE IS FILING FOR SUPPLEMENTAL SECURITY INCOME, GO TO #4.

3. (a) Is your spouse the sponsor of an alien for supplemental security income? ➤ ☐ YES Go to (b)   ☐ NO Go to #4

   (b) Alien's Name | Alien's Social Security Number _ _ _ / _ _ / _ _ _ _

FORM **SSA-8000-BK** (5-90)   Destroy Prior Editions

4.					
(a) Have you been married before? ➔	**You**		**Your Spouse, if filing**	
	☐ YES Go to (b)	☐ NO Go to #5	☐ YES Go to (b)	☐ NO Go to #5

(b) Give the following information about your former spouse. If there was more than one former marriage, show the remaining information in Remarks and go to #5.

	FORMER SPOUSE'S NAME (including maiden name)	SOCIAL SECURITY NUMBER (if none or unknown, so indicate)	DATE OF MARRIAGE	DATE MAR-RIAGE ENDED	HOW MARRIAGE ENDED
You					
Your Spouse					

5.		**You**		**Your Spouse**	
(a) Are you blind or disabled? ➔		☐ YES Go to (b)	☐ NO Go to #6	☐ YES Go to (b)	☐ NO Go to #6

(b) GIVE THE FOLLOWING INFORMATION:	DATE IMPAIRMENT BEGAN	NATURE OF THE IMPAIRMENT
You		
Your Spouse		

6.	**You**	**Your Spouse, if filing**
In what city and State or foreign country were your born? ➔		

7.		**You**		**Your Spouse, if filing**	
Are you a United States citizen by birth? ➔		☐ YES Go to #11	☐ NO Go to #8	☐ YES Go to #11	☐ NO Go to #8

8.					
Are you a naturalized United States citizen? ➔		☐ YES Go to #11	☐ NO Go to #9	☐ YES Go to #11	☐ NO Go to #9

9.					
(a) Are you lawfully admitted for permanent residence in the United States? ➔		☐ YES Go to (b)	☐ NO Go to #10	☐ YES Go to (b)	☐ NO Go to #10
(b) Give the month, day, and year of lawful admission for permanent residence. If date is within 3 years of the filing date, go to (c); otherwise go to #11. ➔		DATE		DATE	
(c) Was your entry into the United States sponsored by any person or promoted by an institution or group? ➔		☐ YES Go to (d)	☐ NO Go to #11	☐ YES Go to (d)	☐ NO Go to #11

(d) Give the following information about the person, institution, or group:

Name	Address	Telephone No. (Include Area Code) (___)-

(e) GO TO #11

10.		**You**		**Your Spouse, if filing**	
(a) Is the Immigration and Naturalization Service (INS) aware of your presence in the United States? ➔		☐ YES Go to (b)	☐ NO Go to #11	☐ YES Go to (b)	☐ NO Go to #11
(b) Through what date will INS allow you to remain in the United States? (If indefinitely, so indicate) ➔		DATE (month, day, year)		DATE (month, day, year)	

11.					
(a) When did you first make your home in the United States? ➔		DATE (month, day, year)		DATE (month, day, year)	
(b) Have you lived outside the United States since then? ➔		☐ YES Go to (c)	☐ NO Go to #12	☐ YES Go to (c)	☐ NO Go to #12
(c) Give dates of residence outside the United States. (Month, day, year) ➔		FROM: ------ TO:		FROM: ------ TO:	

12.					
(a) Have you been outside the United States (the 50 states, District of Columbia and Northern Mariana Islands) 30 days prior to the filing date? ➔		☐ YES Go to (b)	☐ NO Go to #13	☐ YES Go to (b)	☐ NO Go to #13
(b) Give the date (Month, day, year) you left the United States and the date you returned to the United States. ➔		Date Left Date Returned		Date Left Date Returned	

PART II—LIVING ARRANGEMENTS—The questions in this section pertain to the signature date.

13. Check the applicable block to show where you live now:

INSTITUTIONS

☐ House   ☐ Room (commercial establishment)   ☐ Transient   ☐ School   ☐ Rehabilitation Center

☐ Apartment   ☐ Other (Specify)   ☐ Hospital   ☐ Jail

☐ Room (private home)   ☐ Mobile Home   ☐ Rest or Retirement Home   ☐ Other (Specify)

☐ Foster Home   ☐ Nursing Home

_____

IF YOU ARE LIVING IN A FOSTER HOME, AN INSTITUTION, OR ARE A TRANSIENT, EXPLAIN IN REMARKS AND GO TO #21.

14. Do you live alone or with your spouse only? ⟶   ☐ YES Go to #16   ☐ NO Go to #15

15. (a) Give the following information about everyone who lives with you (or with you and your spouse):

NAME	RELATIONSHIP TO YOU OR SPOUSE	SEX M	SEX F	DATE OF BIRTH (Month, day, year)	BLIND OR DISABLED		IF UNDER AGE 22 MARRIED		STUDENT	
					YES	NO	YES	NO	YES	NO

(b) Do all the persons listed in 15(a) receive assistance or income based on need? ⟶   ☐ YES Go to (c)   ☐ NO Go to (c)

(c) Does anyone listed in 15(a) who is not married and under age 18 OR between ages 18-21, not married, and a student receive income? ⟶   ☐ YES Go to (d)   ☐ NO Go to #16

(d) CHILD RECEIVING INCOME	SOURCE & TYPE	MONTHLY AMOUNT
		$
		$
		$

16. (a) Do you (or does anyone who lives with you) own or rent the place where you live? ⟶   ☐ YES Go to #17   ☐ NO Go to (b)

(b) Name and address of person who owns or rents the place where you live: Telephone number, if known (Include Area Code) (_ _ _) -

(c) GO TO #20

17. (a) Are you (or your living with spouse) buying or do you own the place where you live? ⟶   ☐ YES Go to (c)   ☐ NO If you are a child living with parent(s) go to (b); otherwise go to #18.

(b) Are your parent(s) buying or do they own the place where you live? ⟶   ☐ YES Go to (c)   ☐ NO Go to #18

(c) What is the amount and frequency of the mortgage payment? ⟶   Amount $ Frequency of Payment

(d) GO TO #20

FORM SSA-8000-BK (5-90)

18.	(a) Do you (or your living with spouse) have rental liability for the place where you live? ➤	☐ YES Go to (d)	☐ NO	If you are a child living with parent(s) go to (b); otherwise go to (c).
	(b) Do your parent(s) have rental liability? ➤	☐ YES Go to (d)	☐ NO Go to (c)	
	(c) Does anyone who lives with you have rental liability for the place where you live? ➤	☐ YES Give name of person with rental liability in Remarks and go to #19	☐ NO Give name of person with home ownership in Remarks and go to #20.	
	(d) What is the amount and frequency of the rent payment? ➤	Amount $	Frequency of payment	

19.	(a) Are you (or anyone who lives with you) the parent or child of the landlord or the landlord's spouse? ➤	☐ YES Go to (b)	☐ NO Go to #20
	(b) Name of person related to landlord or landlord's spouse:	Relationship	Name and address of landlord (include telephone number and area code, if known):

20.	(a) Does anyone who does NOT live with you provide your household with all or part of the food and shelter (including payment of the bills for food, rent or home mortgage payments, property insurance required by the mortgage holder, real property taxes, heating fuel, gas, electricity, garbage removal, water, or sewerage) or give the household money for these items? ➤	☐ YES Go to (b)	☐ NO Go to (c)

(b) ITEM	CONTRIBUTOR'S NAME AND ADDRESS (TELEPHONE NUMBER AND AREA CODE, IF KNOWN)	MONTHLY AMOUNT	MONTHS RECEIVED
		$	
		$	
		$	
		$	

(c) GO TO (d) IF YOU (OR YOUR LIVING WITH SPOUSE) OWN OR RENT AND LIVE WITH OTHERS (OTHER THAN SPOUSE ONLY) BUT YOU DO NOT LIVE IN A PUBLIC ASSISTANCE HOUSEHOLD; OTHERWISE, GO TO #21.

(d) Does anyone living with you give you (or your living with spouse) money for or help pay for all or part of your food, rent or home mortgage payments, property insurance required by the mortgage holder, real property taxes, heating fuel, gas, electricity, garbage removal, water, or sewer bills? ➤	☐ YES Go to #21	☐ NO Go to #21

21.	(a) Has the information given in items #13 through #20 been the same since the first moment of the filing date month? ➤	☐ YES Go to (b)	☐ NO Explain in Remarks and go to (b).
	(b) Do you expect this information to change? ➤	☐ YES Explain in Remarks and go to #22.	☐ NO Go to #22

PART III—RESOURCES—The questions in this section pertain to the first moment of the filing date month.

22.	(a) Do you own or does your name appear on the title of any vehicles; e.g., cars, trucks, boats, motorcycles, etc.? ➤	You		Your Spouse	
		☐ YES Go to (b)	☐ NO Go to #23	☐ YES Go to (b)	☐ NO Go to #23

(b) OWNER'S NAME	DESCRIPTION (YEAR, MAKE & MODEL)	USED FOR	EQUIPPED FOR HANDICAPPED?		CURRENT MARKET VALUE	AMOUNT OWED
			YES	NO		
					$	$
					$	$
					$	$

23. (a) Do you own or are you buying any life insurance policies? ➔

	You		Your Spouse	
	☐ YES Go to (b)	☐ NO Go to #24	☐ YES Go to (b)	☐ NO Go to #24

(b) Give the following information on each policy:

	OWNER'S NAME	NAME OF INSURED	NAME AND ADDRESS OF INSURANCE COMPANY
Policy (#1)			
Policy (#2)			
Policy (#3)			

	POLICY NUMBER	FACE VALUE	CASH SURRENDER VALUE	DATE PURCHASED	LOANS AGAINST	
					YES	NO
Policy (#1)		$	$		$	
Policy (#2)		$	$		$	
Policy (#3)		$	$		$	

24. (a) Do you (either alone or jointly with any other person) own any:

	You		Your Spouse	
	YES	NO	YES	NO
Life estates or ownership interest in an unprobated estate? ➔				
Household or personal items worth more than $500 each? ➔				

(b) Give the following information for any "Yes" answer in 24(a); otherwise go to #25

OWNER'S NAME	NAME OF ITEM	VALUE	AMOUNT OWED ON ITEM	WHERE APPROPRIATE, GIVE NAME AND ADDRESS OF BANK OR OTHER ORGANIZATION
		$	$	
		$	$	

25. (a) Do you own or does your name appear (either alone or with any other person's name) on any of the following items?

	You		Your Spouse	
	YES	NO	YES	NO
Cash at home, with you, or anywhere else ➔				
Checking Accounts ➔				
Savings Accounts ➔				
Credit Union Accounts ➔				
Christmas Club Accounts ➔				
Certificates of Deposit ➔				
Notes ➔				
Stocks or Mutual Funds ➔				
Bonds ➔				
Other items that can be turned into cash ➔				

(b) Give the following information for any "Yes" answer in 25(a); otherwise go to #26

OWNER'S NAME	NAME OF ITEM	VALUE	NAME AND ADDRESS OF BANK OR OTHER ORGANIZATION IF APPROPRIATE	IDENTIFYING NUMBER
		$		
		$		
		$		
		$		

26.	(a) Do you have any land, houses, buildings, real property, property in foreign countries, equipment, business, mineral rights or other money or property of any kind (including belongings held in safe deposit boxes) that have not been shown elsewhere on the application? (Include assets set aside for an emergency or to provide for your heirs.) ———▶	You		Your Spouse	
		☐ YES Go to (b)	☐ NO Go to #27	☐ YES Go to (b)	☐ NO Go to #27

(b) Give the following information:

DESCRIPTION OF PROPERTY (If real property, include type and size of structure, acreage or lot size, location.)	HOW IS IT USED? (If not used now, when was it last used and what is next planned use.)
Item 1	Item 1
Item 2	Item 2

OWNER'S NAME	ESTIMATED CURRENT MARKET VALUE	TAX ASSESSED VALUE	AMOUNT OF MORTGAGE PAYMENT	AMOUNT OWED ON ITEM
Item 1	$	$	$	$
Item 2	$	$	$	$

27.	(a) Have you sold, transferred title, disposed of or given away any money or other property, including property or money in foreign countries, since the first moment of the filing date month or within the 30 months prior to the filing date month?	You		Your Spouse, if filing	
		☐ YES Go to (b)	☐ NO Go to #28	☐ YES Go to (b)	☐ NO Go to #28

(b) Give the following information:

OWNER'S NAME	DATE OF DISPOSAL	DESCRIPTION OF PROPERTY
Item 1		
Item 2		

IF THE DATE OF DISPOSAL IS BEFORE 7/1/88 <u>AND</u> LESS THAN 24 MONTHS PRIOR TO THE MONTH OF FILING OR IF THE DATE OF DISPOSAL IS AFTER 6/30/88, GO TO 27(c); OTHERWISE GO TO #28.

(c) Give the following about the information in 27(b):

NAME AND ADDRESS OF PURCHASER OR RECIPIENT	RELATIONSHIP TO OWNER	SOLD ON OPEN MARKET	
		YES	NO
Item 1			
Item 2			

VALUE OF PROPERTY AND/OR AMOUNT OF CASH GIFT	SALES PRICE OR OTHER AGREEMENT	ARE ADDITIONAL CONSIDERATIONS OR PROCEEDS EXPECTED? EXPLAIN	DO YOU STILL OWN PART OF THE PROPERTY	
			YES	NO
Item 1 $				
Item 2 $				

28.

(a) Have you acquired any resource since the first moment of the filing date month? ⟶

You		Your Spouse	
☐ YES	☐ NO	☐ YES	☐ NO
Go to (b)	Go to (c)	Go to (b)	Go to (c)

(b) Explain any "Yes" answer given in 28(a)

You	Your Spouse

(c) Has there been any increase or decrease in the value of your resources since the first moment of the filing date month? ⟶

You		Your Spouse	
☐ YES	☐ NO	☐ YES	☐ NO
Go to (d)	Go to #29	Go to (d)	Go to #29

(d) Explain any "Yes" answer given in 28(c)

You	Your Spouse

29.

(a) Do you have any assets set aside for burial expenses such as burial contracts, trusts, agreements, or anything else you intend for your burial expenses? Include any assets mentioned in items #22 through #26 and item #28. ⟶

You		Your Spouse	
☐ YES	☐ NO	☐ YES	☐ NO
Go to (b)	Go to #30	Go to (b)	Go to #30

(b)

DESCRIPTION (Where appropriate, give name and address of organization and account/policy number)	VALUE	WHEN SET ASIDE (Month, Day, Year)	OWNER'S NAME
Item 1	$		
Item 2	$		

FOR WHOSE BURIAL	IS ITEM IRREVOCABLE?	WILL INTEREST EARNED OR APPRECIATION IN VALUE REMAIN IN THE BURIAL FUND?	
Item 1	☐ YES ☐ NO	☐ YES Go to #30	☐ NO Explain in (c)
Item 2	☐ YES ☐ NO	☐ YES Go to #30	☐ NO Explain in (c)

(c) Explanation:

Item 1

Item 2

30.

(a) Do you own any cemetery lots, crypts, caskets, vaults, urns, mausoleums or other repositories for burial or any headstones or markers? ⟶

You		Your Spouse	
☐ YES	☐ NO	☐ YES	☐ NO
Go to (b)	Go to #31	Go to (b)	Go to #31

(b)

OWNER'S NAME	DESCRIPTION	FOR WHOSE BURIAL	RELATIONSHIP TO YOU OR SPOUSE	CURRENT MARKET VALUE (if applicable)
				$
				$

FORM SSA-8000-BK (5-90)

PART IV—INCOME—The questions in this section specify time period.

31.	(a) Since the first moment of the filing date month, have you received or do you expect to receive income in the next 14 months from any of the following sources?	YOU		YOUR SPOUSE	
		YES	NO	YES	NO
	FEDERAL BENEFITS: Social Security				
	Railroad Retirement				
	Veterans Administration (Based on need/not based on need)				
	Office of Personnel Management (Civil Service)				
	Military Pension, Special Pay, or Allowance				
	Black Lung				
	Bureau of Indian Affairs				
	Earned Income Tax Credits				
	STATE/LOCAL BENEFITS: Unemployment Compensation				
	Workers' Compensation				
	State Disability				
	State or Local Pension				
	Aid to Families with Dependent Children				
	State or Local Assistance Based on Need				
	PRIVATE BENEFITS: Employer or Union Pension				
	Insurance or Annuity Payments				
	MISCELLANEOUS: Interest (bank accounts, stocks, CD's, etc.)				
	Rental/Lease Income				
	Dividends/Royalties				
	Alimony				
	Child Support				
	OTHER INCOME NOT PREVIOUSLY MENTIONED				

(b) Give the following information for any "Yes" answer in 31(a); otherwise go to #32.

PERSON RECEIVING	TYPE OF INCOME	AMOUNT	FREQUENCY	DATES EXPECTED OR RECEIVED	SOURCE (Name/Address of Person, Bank, Company, or Organization)	IDENTIFYING NUMBER
You		$		From: To:		
You		$		From: To:		
You		$		From: To:		
Your Spouse		$		From: To:		
Your Spouse		$		From: To:		
Your Spouse		$		From: To:		

32.	Since the first moment of the filing date month, have you received or do you expect to receive any clothing, meals, or other gifts which are not cash? ⟶	**You** ☐ YES Explain in Remarks and go to #33 ☐ NO Go to #33	**Your Spouse** ☐ YES Explain in Remarks and go to #33 ☐ NO Go to #33

| 33. | (a) Have you received wages since the first moment of the filing date month through the current month? ⟶ | **You** ☐ YES Go to (b) ☐ NO Go to (d) | **Your Spouse** ☐ YES Go to (b) ☐ NO Go to (d) |

(b) Name and Address of Employer *(include telephone number and area code, if known)*

You	**Your Spouse**

(c) Total wages received (before any deductions) for each month:

You	Month(s)							
	Amounts							
Your Spouse	Month(s)							
	Amounts							

(d) Do you expect to receive any wages in the next 14 months? ⟶	**You** ☐ YES Go to (e) ☐ NO Go to #34	**Your Spouse** ☐ YES Go to (e) ☐ NO Go to #34

(e) Name and address of employer if different from 33(b) *(include telephone number and area code, if known)*

You	**Your Spouse**

(f) Give the following information:

	RATE OF PAY	AMOUNT WORKED PER PAY PERIOD	HOW OFTEN PAID	PAY DAY OR DATE PAID	DATE LAST PAID *(Month, day, year)*
You	$ per				
Your Spouse	$ per				

(g) Do you expect any change in wage information provided in 33(f)? ⟶	**You** ☐ YES Go to (h) ☐ NO Go to #34	**Your Spouse** ☐ YES Go to (h) ☐ NO Go to #34

(h) Explain change:

You	**Your Spouse**

34.	(a) Have you been self-employed at any time since the beginning of the taxable year in which the filing date month occurs or do you expect to be self-employed in the current taxable year?	**You** ☐ YES Go to (b) ☐ NO Go to #35	**Your Spouse** ☐ YES Go to (b) ☐ NO Go to #35

(b) Give the following information:

	TYPE OF BUSINESS	LAST YEAR'S: GROSS INCOME	LAST YEAR'S: NET INCOME	LAST YEAR'S: NET LOSS	THIS YEAR'S: GROSS INCOME	THIS YEAR'S: NET INCOME	THIS YEAR'S: NET LOSS	DATES OF SELF-EMPLOYMENT
You		$	$	$	$	$	$	
		$	$	$	$	$	$	
Your Spouse		$	$	$	$	$	$	
		$	$	$	$	$	$	

FORM **SSA-8000-BK** (5-90)

159

IF YOU OR YOUR SPOUSE ARE DISABLED AND RECEIVE WAGES OR EXPECT TO RECEIVE WAGES OR ARE SELF-EMPLOYED OR EXPECT TO BE SELF-EMPLOYED, ANSWER #35: OTHERWISE, GO TO #36.

35.		You	Your Spouse
	Do you have any special expenses related to your illness or injury that you paid which are necessary for you to work? →	☐ YES Describe in Remarks and go to #36 ☐ NO Go to #36	☐ YES Describe in Remarks and go to #36 ☐ NO Go to #36

IF YOU ARE FILING AS A CHILD, AND YOU ARE EMPLOYED OR AGE 18-22 (WHETHER EMPLOYED OR NOT), GO TO #36; OTHERWISE, GO TO #37.

36.			
(a)	Have you attended school regularly since the filing date month? ➔	☐ YES Go to (d)	☐ NO Go to (b)
(b)	Have you been out of school for more than 4 calendar months? ➔	☐ YES Go to (c)	☐ NO Go to (c)
(c)	Do you plan to attend school regularly during the next 4 months? ➔	☐ YES Explain absence in Remarks and go to (d)	☐ NO Go to #37

(d) Give the following information:

NAME AND ADDRESS OF SCHOOL	NAME OF PERSON AT SCHOOL WE MAY CONTACT	DATES OF ATTENDANCE	COURSE OF STUDY
	NAME	FROM | TO	
	PHONE (include area code) (_ _ _) -	HOURS ATTENDING OR PLANNING TO ATTEND:	

PART V—POTENTIAL ELIGIBILITY FOR OTHER BENEFITS/FOOD STAMPS/MEDICAL ASSISTANCE

37. (a) Have you or a former spouse (or if you are filing as a child, have you or your parents) ever:	YOU		YOUR SPOUSE	
	YES	NO	YES	NO
Worked for a railroad?				
Been in military service?				
Worked for the Federal government?				
Worked for a State or local government?				
Worked for an employer or belonged to a union with a pension plan?				
Done work that was covered under the Social Security system or pension plan of a country other than the United States?				

(b) Explain and include dates (if appropriate) for any "Yes" answer given in 37(a); otherwise go to #38.

YOU	YOUR SPOUSE

38.	(a) Are you currently receiving food stamps or has a food stamp application been filed for you within the past 60 days on which there has not been a decision? ⟶	You		Your Spouse, if filing	
		☐ YES Go to #39	☐ NO Go to (b)	☐ YES Go to #39	☐ NO Go to (b)
	(b) Do you wish to apply for food stamps? ⟶	☐ YES	☐ NO	☐ YES	☐ NO

39.	Where this application is an application for Title XIX under the Social Security Act, I/we understand that if I/we refuse to assign my/our rights to medical support and payments for medical care from any individual or private, group, or government health insurance, or refuse to cooperate in giving information regarding any health insurance I/we may have, that the Social Security Administration cannot determine whether I am/we are eligible for Medicaid and that I/we must then apply for Medicaid at the Medicaid agency. I/we also understand that as a condition to become eligible for Medicaid, I/we must cooperate with the Medicaid agency in establishing paternity and in obtaining medical support and payments from third party payers.

IN STATES WITH AUTOMATIC ASSIGNMENT OF RIGHTS LAWS, GO TO 39(b).

		You		Your Spouse, if filing	
(a)	Do you agree to assign your rights (or the rights of anyone for whom you can legally assign rights) to payments for medical support and other medical care to the State Medicaid agency? ⟶	☐ YES Go to (b)	☐ NO Go to #40	☐ YES Go to (b)	☐ NO Go to #40
(b)	Do you, your spouse, parent or step-parent have any private, group, or government health insurance that pays the cost of your medical care? (Do not include Medicare or Medicaid) ⟶	☐ YES	☐ NO	☐ YES	☐ NO
(c)	Do you have any unpaid medical expenses for the 3 months prior to the filing date month? ⟶	☐ YES	☐ NO	☐ YES	☐ NO

PART VI—MISCELLANEOUS

ANSWER #40 ONLY IF YOU ARE REQUESTING BENEFITS ON BEHALF OF SOMEONE ELSE; OTHERWISE, GO TO #41.

40.	(a) Name of Person Requesting Benefits	Relationship to Claimant	Your Social Security Number
			__ __ __/__ __/__ __ __ __

(b)	Do you wish to be selected as the claimant's representative payee? ⟶	☐ YES	If you are applying on behalf of a child go to (c); otherwise go to #41.	☐ NO	Explain in Remarks and go to #41.
(c)	Are you the natural or adoptive parent with custody? ⟶	☐ YES	Go to (d)	☐ NO	Go to (d)
(d)	Have you ever been convicted of a felony? ⟶	☐ YES	Explain in Remarks and go to (e)	☐ NO	Go to (e)
(e)	Are you serving, or have you ever served, as representative payee for anyone receiving a Social Security or Supplemental Security Income benefit? ⟶	☐ YES	Enter SSN's in Remarks and go to (f)	☐ NO	Go to (f)
(f)	Does the claimant have a legal representative or a legal guardian appointed by a court? ⟶	☐ YES	If you are NOT the legal rep/guardian, go to (g); otherwise go to (h).	☐ NO	Go to #41

(g) Give the following information about the legal representative or legal guardian:

Name	Address	Telephone Number (Include area code, if known)
		(___)

(h) Explain what led the court to appoint a legal representative or a legal guardian.

IMPORTANT INFORMATION—PLEASE READ CAREFULLY

▶ Failure to report any change within 10 days after the end of the month in which the change occurs could result in a penalty deduction.

▶ The Social Security Administration will check your statements and compare its records with records from other State and Federal agencies, including the Internal Revenue Service, to make sure you are paid the correct amount.

▶ If you are disabled or blind, you must accept any appropriate vocational rehabilitation services offered to you by the State agency to which we refer you.

PART VIII—SIGNATURES

I/We understand that anyone who knowingly lies or misrepresents the truth or arranges for someone to knowingly lie or misrepresent the truth is committing a crime which can be punished under Federal law, State law, or both. Everything on this application is the truth as best I/we know it.

41.	Your Signature *(First name, middle initial, last name) (Write in ink)*	Date *(Month, day, year)*
	SIGN HERE ▶	Telephone number(s) at which you may be contacted during the day (___)___–____ AREA CODE

42.	Spouse's Signature *(First name, middle initial, last name) (Write in ink)* **(Sign only if applying for payments.)**
	SIGN HERE ▶

43. **FOR OFFICIAL USE ONLY**

DIRECT DEPOSIT PAYMENT ADDRESS *(FINANCIAL INSTITUTION)*

Routing Transit Number	C/S	Depositor Account Number	
			☐ No Account ☐ Direct Deposit Refused

44. Applicant's Mailing Address *(Number and Street, Apt. No., P.O. Box or Rural Route)*

City and State	ZIP Code	Enter name of county *(if any)* in which you live

45. Claimant's Residence Address *(If different from applicant's mailing address)*

City and State	ZIP Code	Enter name of county *(if any)* in which the claimant lives

WITNESSES

46. Your application does not ordinarily have to be witnessed. If, however, you have signed by mark (X), two witnesses to the signing who know you must sign below giving their full addresses.

1. Signature of Witness	2. Signature of Witness
Address *(Number and Street, City, State, and ZIP Code)*	Address *(Number and Street, City, State, and ZIP Code)*

FORM **SSA-8000-BK** (5-90)

CHANGES TO REPORT

☑ **WHERE YOU LIVE — You must report to Social Security if:**

- You move.
- You (or your spouse) leave your household for a calendar month or longer. For example, you enter a hospital or visit a relative.
- You leave the United States for 30 days or more.
- You are released from a hospital, nursing home, etc.
- You are no longer a legal resident of the United States.

☑ **HOW YOU LIVE — You must report to Social Security if:**

- Someone moves into or out of your household.
- The amount of money you pay toward household expenses changes.
- Births and deaths of any people with whom you live.
- Your marital status changes:
  - You get married, separated, divorced, or your marriage is annulled.
  - You separate from your spouse or start living together again after a separation.
  - You begin living with someone as husband and wife.

☑ **INCOME — You must report to Social Security if:**

- The amount of money (or checks or any other type of payment) you receive from someone or someplace goes up or down or you start to receive money (or checks or any other type of payment).
- You start work or stop work.
- Your earnings go up or down.

☑ **HELP YOU GET FROM OTHERS — You must report to Social Security if:**

- The amount of help (money, food, clothing, or payment of household expenses) you receive goes up or down.
- Someone stops helping you.
- Someone starts helping you.

☑ **THINGS OF VALUE THAT YOU OWN — You must report to Social Security if:**

- The value of your resources goes over $2,000 when you add them all together ($3,000 if you are married and live with your spouse).
- You sell or give any things of value away.
- You buy or are given anything of value.

☐ **YOU ARE BLIND OR DISABLED — You must report to Social Security if:**

- Your condition improves or your doctor says you can return to work.
- You go to work.
- You stop going to or refuse any vocational rehabilitation services.
- You stop going to or refuse treatment for drug addiction or alcoholism.

☐ **YOU ARE UNMARRIED AND UNDER AGE 22 — A report to Social Security must be made if:**

- If you are under age 18 and live with your parent(s), ask your parent(s) to report if they have a change in income, a change in their marriage, a change in the value of anything they own, or either has a change in residence.
- You start or stop school.
- You get married.

☐ **YOUR IMMIGRATION AND NATURALIZATION SERVICE (INS) STATUS CHANGES—You must report any change to Social Security.**

☐ **YOU ARE SELECTED AS A REPRESENTATIVE PAYEE — You must report to Social Security if:**

- The person for whom you receive SSI checks has any of the changes listed above. (You may be held liable if you do not report changes that could affect the SSI recipient's payment amount, and he/she is overpaid.)
- You will no longer be able or no longer wish to act as that person's representative payee.

APPLICATION FOR ENROLLMENT IN MEDICARE
THE MEDICAL INSURANCE PROGRAM

(TID) **SMI**

1. SOCIAL SECURITY CLAIM NUMBER

(CAN) ☐ ☐ ☐ — ☐ ☐ — ☐ ☐ ☐ ☐

2. FOR AGENCY USE ONLY

(BIC) ☐ ☐ ☐

3. DO YOU WISH TO ENROLL FOR MEDICAL INSURANCE UNDER MEDICARE?

(DEC) YES ☐

4. CLAIMANT'S NAME

(CLN)

Last name	First name	Middle initial

5. PRINT SOCIAL SECURITY NUMBER HOLDER'S NAME IF DIFFERENT FROM YOURS

6. MAILING ADDRESS (NUMBER AND STREET, P.O. BOX, OR ROUTE)

IF THIS IS A CHANGE OF ADDRESS, CHECK HERE ☐

7. CITY, STATE, AND ZIP CODE

8. TELEPHONE NUMBER

9. WRITTEN SIGNATURE (DO NOT PRINT)

SIGN HERE ➡ _____

10. DATE SIGNED

(DOF) _ _ / _ _ / _ _
MONTH   DAY   YEAR

IF THIS APPLICATION HAS BEEN SIGNED BY MARK (X), A WITNESS WHO KNOWS THE APPLICANT MUST SUPPLY THE INFORMATION REQUESTED BELOW

11. SIGNATURE OF WITNESS

12. DATE SIGNED

13. ADDRESS OF WITNESS

14. REMARKS

(TOA) 1

TO: (Circle one)

(1) NEPSC	(2) MATPSC	(3) SEPSC	(4) GLPSC	(5) WNPSC	(6) MAMPSC	(7) ODO	(8) DIO

FORM HCFA-40B (1-90)

PRIVACY ACT NOTICE

The Social Security Administration (SSA) is authorized to collect the information on this form under sections 1836, 1840, and 1872 of the Social Security Act, as amended (42 U.S.C. 1395o, 1395s, and 1395ii). The information on this form is needed to enable SSA and the Health Care Financing Administration (HCFA) to determine if you are entitled to supplementary medical insurance benefits. While completing this form is voluntary, failure to provide all or part of this information will result in your not being enrolled for medical insurance under Medicare. You should be aware that the information you furnish can be released by way of "routine uses" published in the Federal Register. Because they are too numerous to list here, SSA can furnish you with additional information upon request. You should also be aware that the information you provide on this form may be verified by way of a computer match (Pub. Law 100-503).

SPECIAL MESSAGE FOR INDIVIDUAL APPLYING
FOR MEDICAL INSURANCE UNDER MEDICARE

This form is your application for the medical insurance part of Medicare. It can be used either during your initial enrollment period, during any general enrollment period, or during a special enrollment period to which you **may** be entitled if you are covered under an employer's group health plan.

Your initial enrollment period lasts for 7 months. It begins 3 months before the month you reach age 65 (or 3 months before the 25th month you have received social security disability benefits) and it ends 3 months after you reach age 65 (or 3 months after the 25th month you received social security disability benefits). To have medical insurance start in the month you are 65 (or the 25th month of disability insurance benefits), you must sign up in the first 3 months of your initial enrollment period. If you sign up in any of the remaining 4 months, your medical insurance will start later.

If you do not file during your initial enrollment period, you can file any time after that during a general enrollment period which is the first 3 months of every year. If you sign up in a general enrollment period, your medical insurance begins July 1 of that year. However, when you file in a general enrollment period, your premium may be subject to a penalty increase. For each 12-month period elapsing between the end of your initial enrollment period and the general enrollment period in which you file, your premium will be increased 10 percent.

If you are age 65 or older and employed, or the spouse of an employed person, and are covered under an employer group health plan, you may be eligible to enroll during any of the 7 months after employment is terminated or, if earlier, after your employer group health plan coverage ends for any reason. Also, if you are under age 65, entitled to Medicare based on disability, and are covered under an employer's group health plan based on your own current employment or the current employment of your spouse, or are covered under a large group health plan based on your own current employment or the current employment of any family member, you may be eligible to enroll during a special 7-month enrollment period which begins when the employer group health plan coverage ends or the employment ends, whichever occurs first. Your medical insurance coverage will begin sooner under this special enrollment provision than it will if you delay enrollment until the following general enrollment period. Also, you may be eligible under this special provision for a reduction in the premium surcharge or penalty that usually applies to people who delay their enrollment in medical insurance under Medicare. If you are covered under an employer's group health plan and think that you may be eligible for a special enrollment period, please discuss your enrollment eligibility with a representative at the Social Security office.

DEPARTMENT OF HEALTH AND HUMAN SERVICES
HEALTH CARE FINANCING ADMINISTRATION

Form Approved
OMB No. 0938-0251

(Do Not Write in this space)

APPLICATION FOR HOSPITAL INSURANCE

(This application form may also be used to
enroll in Supplementary Medical Insurance)

I apply for entitlement to Medicare's hospital insurance under part A of title XVIII of the Social Security Act, as presently amended, and for any cash benefits to which I may be entitled under title II of that Act.

1.
(a) Print your name ➡ (First name, middle initial, last name)

(b) Enter your name at birth if different from 1 (a) ➡

(c) Enter your sex (check one) ➡ ☐ Male ☐ Female

2. Enter your Social Security Number ➡ ___ / __ / ____

3.
(a) Enter your date of birth (Month, day, year) ➡

(b) Enter name of State or foreign country where you were born ➡

If you have already submitted a public or religious record of your birth made before you were age 5, go on to item 4)

(c) Was a public record of your birth made before you were age 5? ☐ Yes ☐ No ☐ Unknown

(d) Was a religious record of your birth made before you were age 5? ☐ Yes ☐ No ☐ Unknown

4.
(a) Have you (or has someone on your behalf) ever filed an application for social security benefits, a period of disability under social security, supplemental security income, or hospital or medical insurance under Medicare? ➡ ☐ Yes ☐ No
If "Yes" answer (b) and (c).) (If "No," go on to item 5.)

(b) Enter name of person on whose social security record you filed other application ➡

(c) Enter Social Security Number of person named in (b), (If unknown, so indicate) ➡ ___ / __ / ____

5.
(a) Were you in the active military or naval service (including Reserve or National Guard active duty or active duty for training) after September 7, 1939? ➡ ☐ Yes ☐ No
If "Yes" answer (b) and (c).) (If "No," go on to item 6.)

(b) Enter dates of service ➡ From: (Month, year) To: (Month, year)

(c) Have you ever been (or will you be) eligible for a monthly benefit from a military or civilian Federal agency? (Include Veterans Administration benefits only if you waived military retirement pay) ➡ ☐ Yes ☐ No

6. Did you work in the railroad industry any time on or after January 1, 1937? ➡ ☐ Yes ☐ No

Form HCFA-18 F5 (02-91) Page 1

166

7.	(a) Have you ever engaged in work that was covered under the social security system of a country other than the United States? ➞	☐ Yes	☐ No
	(b) If "Yes," list the country(ies). ➞		

8.	(a) How much were your total earnings last year ➞ *(If none, write "None")*	Earnings $
	(b) How much do you expect your total earnings to be this year? ➞ *(If none, write "None")*	Earnings $

9.	Are you a resident of the United States? ➞ *(To reside in a place means to make a home there.)*	☐ Yes	☐ No

10.	(a) *Are you a citizen of the United States?* ➞ *(If "Yes," go on to item 11.) (if "No" answer (b) and (c) below.)*	☐ Yes	☐ No
	(b) *Are you lawfully admitted for permanent residence in the United States?* ➞	☐ Yes	☐ No

(c) Enter below the information requested about your place of residence in the last 5 years:

ADDRESS AT WHICH YOU RESIDED IN THE LAST 5 YEARS (Begin with the most recent address. Show actual date residence began even if that is prior to the last 5 years)	DATE RESIDENCE BEGAN			DATE RESIDENCE ENDED		
	Month	Day	Year	Month	Day	Year

(If you need more space, use the "Remarks" space on the third page or another sheet of paper)

11. YOUR CURRENT MARRIAGE	Are you currently married? ➞ *(If "Yes," give the following information about your current marriage.) (If "No" go on to item 12.)*	☐ Yes	☐ No
	To whom married (Enter your wife's maiden name or your husband's name)	When (Month, day, year)	
	Spouse's date of birth (or age)	Spouse's Social Security Number *(If none or unknown, so indicate)* __ __ __ / __ __ / __ __ __ __	

12.	If you had a previous marriage and your spouse died, OR If you had a previous marriage which lasted 10 or more years, give the following information. *(If you had no previous marriage (s), enter "NONE.")*	
YOUR PREVIOUS MARRIAGE	To whom married *(Enter your wife's maiden name or your husband's name).*	When (Month, day, year)
	Spouse's date of birth (or age)	Spouse's Social Security Number *(If none of unknown, so indicate)* __ __ __ / __ __ / __ __ __ __
	If spouse deceased, give date of death ➞	

(Use "Remarks" space on page 3 for information about any other marriages.)

Form HCFA-18 F5 (02-91)

13.	Is or was your spouse a railroad worker, railroad retirement pensioner, or a railroad retirement annuitant? ⟶	☐ Yes	☐ No
14.	(a) Were you or your spouse a civilian employee of the Federal Government after June 1960? ⟶ (If "Yes," answer (b).) (If "No," omit (b), (c), and (d).)	☐ Yes	☐ No
	(b) Are you or your spouse now covered under a medical insurance plan provided by the Federal Employees Health Benefits Act of 1959? (If "Yes," omit (c) and (d).) (If "No," answer (c).)	☐ Yes	☐ No
	(c) Are you **and** your spouse barred from coverage under the above Act because your Federal employment, or your spouse's was not long enough? ⟶ If "Yes," omit (d) and explain in "Remarks" below.) (If "No," answer (d).)	☐ Yes	☐ No
	(d) Were either you or your spouse an employee of the Federal Government after February 15, 1965? ⟶	☐ Yes	☐ No

Remarks:

_____

_____

_____

_____

_____

_____

_____

15.	If you are found to be otherwise ineligible for hospital insurance under Medicare, do you wish to enroll for hospital insurance on a monthly premium basis (in addition to the monthly premium for supplementary medical insurance)? ⟶ (If "Yes," you MUST also sign up for medical insurance.)	☐ Yes	☐ No

INFORMATION ON MEDICAL INSURANCE UNDER MEDICARE

Medical insurance under Medicare helps pay your doctor bills. It also helps pay for a number of other medical items and services not covered under the hospital insurance part of Medicare.

If you sign up for medical insurance, you must pay a premium for each month you have this protection. If you get monthly social security, railroad retirement, or civil service benefits, your premium will be deducted from your benefit check, if you get none of these benefits, you will be notified how to pay your premium.

The Federal Government contributes to the cost of your insurance. The amount of your premium and the Government's payment are based on the cost of services covered by medical insurance. The Government also makes additional payments when necessary to meet the full cost of the program. (Currently, the Government pays about two-thirds of the cost of this program.) You will get advance notice if there is any change in your premium amount.

If you have questions or would like a leaflet on medical insurance, call any Social Security office.

> SEE OTHER SIDE TO SIGN UP FOR MEDICAL INSURANCE

Form HCFA-18 F5 (02-91)

If you become entitled to hospital insurance as a result of this application, you will be enrolled for medical insurance automatically unless you indicate below that you do not want this protection. If you decline to enroll now, you can get medical insurance protection later only if you sign up for it during specified enrollment periods. Your protection may then be delayed and you may have to pay a higher premium when you decide to sign up.

The date your medical insurance begins and the amount of the premium you must pay depend on the month you file this application with the Social Security Administration. Any social security office will be glad to explain the rules regarding enrollment to you.

16.	**DO YOU WISH TO ENROLL FOR SUPPLEMENTARY MEDICAL INSURANCE?** ⟶ *(If "Yes," answer question 17.)* *(Enrollees for premium hospital insurance must simultaneously enroll for medical insurance.)*	☐ Yes ☐ No ☐ Currently Enrolled
17.	Are you or your spouse receiving an annuity under the Federal Civil Service Retirement Act or other law administered by the Office of Personnel Management? ⟶ *(If "Yes," enter Civil Service annuity number here. Include the prefix "CSA" for annuitant, "CSF" for survivor.)*	☐ Yes ☐ No — Your No. — Spouse's No.
	If you entered your spouse's number, is he (she) enrolled for supplementary medical insurance under social security? ⟶	☐ Yes ☐ No

I know that anyone who makes or causes to be made a false statement or representation of material fact in an application or for use in determining a right to payment under the Social Security Act commits a crime punishable under Federal law by fine, imprisonment or both. I affirm that all information I have given in this document is true.

SIGNATURE OF APPLICANT	Date *(Month, day, year)*
Signature *(First name, middle initial, last name) (Write in Ink)* **SIGN HERE ▶**	Telephone Number(s) at which you may be contacted during the day

Mailing address *(Number and street, Apt. No., P.O. Box, or Rural Route)*

City and State	ZIP Code	Enter Name of County (if any) in which you now live

Witnesses are required ONLY if this application has been signed by mark (X) above. If signed by mark (X), two witnesses to the signing who know the applicant must sign below, giving their full addresses.

1. Signature of Witness	2. Signature of Witness
Address *(Number and street, City, State, and ZIP Code)*	Address *(Number and street, City, State, and ZIP Code)*

FORM APPROVED
OMB NO. 0938-0008

PATIENT'S REQUEST FOR MEDICAL PAYMENT

IMPORTANT—SEE OTHER SIDE FOR INSTRUCTIONS

PLEASE TYPE OR PRINT INFORMATION	MEDICAL INSURANCE BENEFITS SOCIAL SECURITY ACT

NOTICE: Anyone who misrepresents or falsifies essential information requested by this form may upon conviction be subject to fine and imprisonment under Federal Law. No Part B Medicare benefits may be paid unless this form is received as required by existing law and regulations (20 CFR 422.510).

1 Name of Beneficiary from Health Insurance Card
(Last)   (First)   (Middle)

SEND COMPLETED FORM TO:

2 Claim Number from Health Insurance Card

Patient's Sex
☐ Male
☐ Female

3 Patient's Mailing Address (City, State, Zip Code)
Check here if this is a new address ➤ ☐

_____
(Street or P.O. Box — Include Apartment Number)

_____
(City)   (State)   (Zip)

3b Telephone Number
(Include Area Code)

(___ ___ ___)

___ ___ ___ — ___ ___ — ___ ___ ___ ___

4 Describe the Illness or Injury for which Patient Received Treatment

4b Was condition related to:
A. Patient's employment
☐ Yes   ☐ No

B. Accident
☐ Auto   ☐ Other

4c Was patient being treated with chronic dialysis or kidney transplant?
☐ Yes   ☐ No

5
a. Are you employed and covered under an employee health plan?
☐ Yes   ☐ No

b. Is your spouse employed and are you covered under your spouse's employee health plan?
☐ Yes   ☐ No

c. If you have any medical coverage other than Medicare, such as private insurance, employment related insurance, State Agency (Medicaid), or the VA, complete:
Name and Address of other insurance, State Agency (Medicaid), or VA office

Policy or Medical Assistance No.

Policyholders Name:

NOTE: If you DO NOT want payment information on this claim released, put an (X) here ➤ ☐

6 I AUTHORIZE ANY HOLDER OF MEDICAL OR OTHER INFORMATION ABOUT ME TO RELEASE TO THE SOCIAL SECURITY ADMINISTRATION AND HEALTH CARE FINANCING ADMINISTRATION OR ITS INTERMEDIARIES OR CARRIERS ANY INFORMATION NEEDED FOR THIS OR A RELATED MEDICARE CLAIM. I PERMIT A COPY OF THIS AUTHORIZATION TO BE USED IN PLACE OF THE ORIGINAL, AND REQUEST PAYMENT OF MEDICAL INSURANCE BENEFITS TO ME.

Signature of Patient (If patient is unable to sign, see Block 6 on reverse)

6b Date signed

IMPORTANT
ATTACH ITEMIZED BILLS FROM YOUR DOCTOR(S) OR SUPPLIER(S) TO THE BACK OF THIS FORM

Form HCFA-1490S (2-87)   DEPARTMENT OF HEALTH AND HUMAN SERVICES—HEALTH CARE FINANCING ADMINISTRATION

HOW TO FILL OUT THIS MEDICARE FORM

Medicare will pay you directly when you complete this form and attach an itemized bill from your doctor or supplier. Your bill does not have to be paid before you submit this claim for payment, but you MUST attach an itemized bill in order for Medicare to process this claim.

FOLLOW THESE INSTRUCTIONS CAREFULLY:

A. Completion of this form.

Block 1. Print your name shown on your Medicare Card. (Last Name, First Name, Middle Name)

Block 2. Print your Health Insurance Claim Number including the letter at the end **exactly** as it is shown on your Medicare card. Check the appropriate box for the patient's sex.

Block 3. Furnish your mailing address and include your telephone number in Block 3b.

Block 4. Describe the illness or injury for which you received treatment. Check the appropriate box in Blocks 4b and 4c.

Block 5a. Complete this Block if you are age 65 or older and enrolled in a health insurance plan where you are currently working.

Block 5b. Complete this Block if you are age 65 or older and enrolled in a health insurance plan where your spouse is currently working.

Block 5c. Complete this Block if you have any medical coverage other than Medicare. Be sure to provide the Policy or Medical Assistance Number. You may check the box provided if you do not wish payment information from this claim released to your other insurer.

Block 6. Be sure to sign your name. If you cannot write your name, make an (X) mark. Then have a witness sign his or her name and address in Block 6 too.

 If you are completing this form for another Medicare patient you should write (By) and sign your name and address in Block 6. You also should show your relationship to the patient and briefly explain why the patient cannot sign.

Block 6b. Print the date you completed this form.

B. Each itemized bill MUST show all of the following information:

* Date of each service

* Place of each service   —Doctor's Office   —Independent Laboratory
  —Outpatient Hospital   —Nursing Home
  —Patient's Home   —Inpatient Hospital

* Description of each surgical or medical service or supply furnished.

* Charge for EACH service.

* Doctor's or supplier's name and address. Many times a bill will show the names of several doctors or suppliers. IT IS VERY IMPORTANT THE ONE WHO TREATED YOU BE IDENTIFIED. Simply circle his/her name on the bill.

* It is helpful if the diagnosis is shown on the physician's bill. If not, be sure you have completed Block 4 of this form.

* Mark out any services on the bill(s) you are attaching for which you have already filed a Medicare claim.

* If the patient is deceased please contact your Social Security office for instructions on how to file a claim.

* Attach an Explanation of Medicare Benefits notice from the other insurer if you are also requesting Medicare payment.

COLLECTION AND USE OF MEDICARE INFORMATION

We are authorized by the Health Care Financing Administration to ask you for information needed in the administration of the Medicare program. Authority to collect information is in section 205 (a), 1872 and 1875 of the Social Security Act, as amended.

The information we obtain to complete your Medicare claim is used to identify you and to determine your eligibility. It is also used to decide if the services and supplies you received are covered by Medicare and to insure that proper payment is made.

The information may also be given to other providers of services, carriers, intermediaries, medical review boards, and other organizations as necessary to administer the Medicare program. For example, it may be necessary to disclose information about the Medicare benefits you have used to a hospital or doctor.

With one exception, which is discussed below, there are no penalties under social security law for refusing to supply information. However, failure to furnish information regarding the medical services rendered or the amount charged would prevent payment of the claim. Failure to furnish any other information, such as name or claim number, would delay payment of the claim.

It is mandatory that you tell us if you are being treated for a work related injury so we can determine whether worker's compensation will pay for the treatment. Section 1877 (a) (3) of the Social Security Act provides criminal penalties for withholding this information.

Public reporting burden for this collection of information is estimated to average 16 minutes per response, including the time for reviewing instructions, searching existing data sources, gathering and maintaining the data needed, and completing and reviewing the collection of information. Send comments regarding this burden estimate or any other aspect of this collection of information, including suggestions for reducing this burden to HCFA, P.O. Box 26684, Baltimore, MD 21207; and to the Office of Information and Regulatory Affairs, Office of Management and Budget, Washington, D.C. 20503.

✰ U. S. GOVERNMENT PRINTING OFFICE : 1988-571-781

APPROVED OMB-0938-0008

CARRIER

PICA

HEALTH INSURANCE CLAIM FORM

PICA

1. MEDICARE	MEDICAID	CHAMPUS	CHAMPVA	GROUP HEALTH PLAN	FECA BLK LUNG	OTHER	1a. INSURED'S I.D. NUMBER	(FOR PROGRAM IN ITEM 1)
☐ (Medicare #)	☐ (Medicaid #)	☐ (Sponsor's SSN)	☐ (VA File #)	☐ (SSN or ID)	☐ (SSN)	☐ (ID)		

2. PATIENT'S NAME (Last Name, First Name, Middle Initial)	3. PATIENT'S BIRTH DATE MM DD YY	SEX M☐ F☐	4. INSURED'S NAME (Last Name, First Name, Middle Initial)

5. PATIENT'S ADDRESS (No., Street)	6. PATIENT RELATIONSHIP TO INSURED Self☐ Spouse☐ Child☐ Other☐	7. INSURED'S ADDRESS (No., Street)

CITY	STATE	8. PATIENT STATUS Single☐ Married☐ Other☐	CITY	STATE

ZIP CODE	TELEPHONE (Include Area Code) ( )	Employed☐ Full-Time Student☐ Part-Time Student☐	ZIP CODE	TELEPHONE (INCLUDE AREA CODE) ( )

9. OTHER INSURED'S NAME (Last Name, First Name, Middle Initial)	10. IS PATIENT'S CONDITION RELATED TO:	11. INSURED'S POLICY GROUP OR FECA NUMBER

a. OTHER INSURED'S POLICY OR GROUP NUMBER	a. EMPLOYMENT? (CURRENT OR PREVIOUS) ☐ YES ☐ NO	a. INSURED'S DATE OF BIRTH MM DD YY SEX M☐ F☐

b. OTHER INSURED'S DATE OF BIRTH MM DD YY SEX M☐ F☐	b. AUTO ACCIDENT? PLACE (State) ☐ YES ☐ NO	b. EMPLOYER'S NAME OR SCHOOL NAME

c. EMPLOYER'S NAME OR SCHOOL NAME	c. OTHER ACCIDENT? ☐ YES ☐ NO	c. INSURANCE PLAN NAME OR PROGRAM NAME

d. INSURANCE PLAN NAME OR PROGRAM NAME	10d. RESERVED FOR LOCAL USE	d. IS THERE ANOTHER HEALTH BENEFIT PLAN? ☐ YES ☐ NO If yes, return to and complete item 9 a-d.

READ BACK OF FORM BEFORE COMPLETING & SIGNING THIS FORM.

12. PATIENT'S OR AUTHORIZED PERSON'S SIGNATURE I authorize the release of any medical or other information necessary to process this claim. I also request payment of government benefits either to myself or to the party who accepts assignment below.	13. INSURED'S OR AUTHORIZED PERSON'S SIGNATURE I authorize payment of medical benefits to the undersigned physician or supplier for services described below.
SIGNED _____ DATE _____	SIGNED _____

14. DATE OF CURRENT: MM DD YY ILLNESS (First symptom) OR INJURY (Accident) OR PREGNANCY(LMP)	15. IF PATIENT HAS HAD SAME OR SIMILAR ILLNESS. GIVE FIRST DATE MM DD YY	16. DATES PATIENT UNABLE TO WORK IN CURRENT OCCUPATION MM DD YY MM DD YY FROM TO

17. NAME OF REFERRING PHYSICIAN OR OTHER SOURCE	17a. I.D. NUMBER OF REFERRING PHYSICIAN	18. HOSPITALIZATION DATES RELATED TO CURRENT SERVICES MM DD YY MM DD YY FROM TO

19. RESERVED FOR LOCAL USE	20. OUTSIDE LAB? ☐ YES ☐ NO $ CHARGES

21. DIAGNOSIS OR NATURE OF ILLNESS OR INJURY. (RELATE ITEMS 1,2,3 OR 4 TO ITEM 24E BY LINE)	22. MEDICAID RESUBMISSION CODE ORIGINAL REF. NO.
1. _____ 3. _____ 2. _____ 4. _____	23. PRIOR AUTHORIZATION NUMBER

24.	A DATE(S) OF SERVICE					B Place of Service	C Type of Service	D PROCEDURES, SERVICES, OR SUPPLIES (Explain Unusual Circumstances)		E DIAGNOSIS CODE	F $ CHARGES	G DAYS OR UNITS	H EPSDT Family Plan	I EMG	J COB	K RESERVED FOR LOCAL USE
	From MM DD YY			To MM DD YY				CPT/HCPCS	MODIFIER							
1																
2																
3																
4																
5																
6																

25. FEDERAL TAX I.D. NUMBER SSN☐ EIN☐	26. PATIENT'S ACCOUNT NO.	27. ACCEPT ASSIGNMENT? (For govt. claims, see back) ☐ YES ☐ NO	28. TOTAL CHARGE $	29. AMOUNT PAID $	30. BALANCE DUE $

31. SIGNATURE OF PHYSICIAN OR SUPPLIER INCLUDING DEGREES OR CREDENTIALS (I certify that the statements on the reverse apply to this bill and are made a part thereof.) SIGNED _____ DATE _____	32. NAME AND ADDRESS OF FACILITY WHERE SERVICES WERE RENDERED (If other than home or office)	33. PHYSICIAN'S, SUPPLIER'S BILLING NAME, ADDRESS, ZIP CODE & PHONE # PIN# _____ GRP# _____

(APPROVED BY AMA COUNCIL ON MEDICAL SERVICE 8/88)   **PLEASE PRINT OR TYPE**

FORM HCFA-1500   (12-90)
FORM OWCP-1500   FORM RRB-1500

172

Index

ORDER PAGE

If you would like to order additional copies of this book for yourself or for a friend, please return the order form below. The price is $11.95 plus $2.50 for shipping; a total of $14.45.
Send it with your check or money order to:

FRASER-VANCE PUBLISHING COMPANY
PO Box 3056
Peterborough, NH 03458-3056

You can also order by telephone and pay by VISA or Mastercard. The number is 800-234-8791.
If ordering more than three copies, please contact our trade distributor at this number or write to
Williamson Publishing Company, PO Box 185, Charlotte, VT 05445-0185

Please send_____ copy/ies of THE COMPLETE & EASY GUIDE TO SOCIAL SECURITY & MEDICARE 1995 to the address on the label below. I enclose $14.45 for each copy.

> FRASER-VANCE PUBLISHING COMPANY
> PO Box 3056
> Peterborough, NH 03458-3056
>
> SPECIAL FOURTH CLASS BOOKRATE

The 1996 edition of this book will be available in January 1996